ECONOMICS
OF INDUSTRIAL
ORGANIZATION

A. Beacham, O.B.E., M.A., Ph.D.

ECONOMICS
OF INDUSTRIAL
ORGANIZATION

FIFTH EDITION BY
A. Beacham and N. J. Cunningham, B.A.

PITMAN PUBLISHING

Fifth edition 1970
First paperback edition 1970
Reprinted 1975

SIR ISAAC PITMAN AND SONS LTD
Pitman House, Parker Street, Kingsway, London, W.C.2
P.O. Box 46038, Banda Street, Nairobi, Kenya
PITMAN PUBLISHING PTY. LTD
Pitman House, Bouverie Street, Carlton, Victoria 3053, Australia
PITMAN PUBLISHING CORPORATION
6 East 43rd Street, New York, N.Y. 10017, U.S.A.
THE COPP CLARK PUBLISHING COMPANY
517 Wellington Street West, Toronto 135, Canada

Cased Edition ISBN: 0 273 31479 3
Paperback Edition ISBN: 0 273 31480 7

Printed in Great Britain by
Ebenezer Baylis and Son Ltd
The Trinity Press, Worcester, and London
G5—(B. 850/1024)

Preface to Fifth Edition

The preparation of this edition has presented a number of difficulties. To keep it abreast of events it has had to be produced quickly but even so there will have been fresh developments between the completion of the manuscript and final publication. Also it has not been easy to make it reflect the general advance in our understanding of industrial matters and the greater sophistication of government intervention without risk of making it too difficult for those first-year undergraduates and professional students for whom the book was first written.

In the event the book has been extensively re-written and much enlarged. Its scope is not very different but one new chapter on state intervention has been introduced and the description of the present structure of industry has been brought forward to Chapter 2 so that it immediately follows the discussion of the forms of enterprise and the classification problem in Chapter 1. The level of discussion has been raised in some parts of the book but for the most part it should not be beyond the intellectual reach of first-year students whilst serving, we hope, as a useful introduction for more advanced students.

This revised edition would not have been possible without the collaboration of Mr. N. J. Cunningham. Mr. Cunningham completed his share of the work before joining the Ministry of Technology, so that nothing in the book should be interpreted as reflecting an official view of industrial matters.

A. BEACHAM, N. J. CUNNINGHAM
November 1969

Preface to First Edition

Introductory textbooks of economics are often deficient in their handling of problems of industrial organization. There are obvious reasons for this. The main concern of such books is with the fundamentals of economic theory and in particular with the theory of value. If these matters are to be adequately dealt with and the books are not to become unwieldy, the organization of production must be very briefly dismissed. This book is mainly designed as a supplementary text to fill out the general economics textbook treatment of industrial organization. It attempts to set out the minimum background of theory and facts with which students should be familiar as a prelude to more advanced study and is intended primarily for students taking a first year university course in economics or other professional courses of equivalent standard. It may also be of some use, as an introduction, to more advanced students who frequently find specialization in this field difficult owing to lack of adequate background. An effort has been made to give the book a sufficiently practical bias to make it attractive to that vast army of students who take courses in economic subjects with the intention of achieving a better understanding of the world of affairs rather than of becoming expert economists. From this point of view it is hoped that it may meet the needs of engineers and others embarking on commercial or industrial administration courses or preparing for the examinations of the professional management societies.

As is usually the case, the greatest difficulty has been to decide what to include and what to omit. To make the book too long would be to defeat its purpose and so it was decided to omit those topics bearing mainly on the internal organization and management of the firm which are generally discussed under the heading of industrial administration, e.g. costing, labour management, wage systems, scientific management, and so on. Also, for the most part, the discussion has been confined to problems of manufacturing and extractive industry and not extended to cover agriculture, retail and wholesale trade, etc.

At various points the argument has been linked up with elementary value theory. This has involved some slight repetition which it is hoped the reader will find helpful rather than tedious. It has been found convenient to assemble most of the descriptive material in a final chapter, but some factual illustrations have necessarily been interspersed throughout the earlier chapters. A little overlapping has resulted, but this, on the whole, seemed preferable to any alternative arrangement. A warning should be sounded here. Important changes in the organization of several industries are probable whilst this book is in the press. So far as possible the reader has been warned where such changes appear to be imminent.

In putting forward this modest addition to the list of current textbooks, the author is not without hope that it will do something to stimulate the interest of students in an aspect of economic studies which so far has been comparatively neglected in this country.

A. BEACHAM

Contents

Contents

Chapter 1

The Industry and the Firm

1.1 Introduction

Industrial organization is concerned with the adjustment of the firm to its environment in real-life situations. The matters with which we shall be concerned will include how and why firms grow, how they are financed, the extent to which they may be able to control their own market situations, the effect of structure on performance, the forces which govern location of firms, and how firms are affected by various forms of government intervention.

Industrial organization has been called a form of applied price theory.[1] Price theory or the theory of value (micro-economics) attempts to elucidate the principles governing the allocation of scarce productive factors between alternative uses. In a free-market economy this allocation is achieved through a system of prices and markets and economists try to discover under what conditions our scarce resources are best allocated. The theory of price therefore has a good deal to say about the behaviour of firms which make decisions on the supply side of markets, e.g. what outputs will be offered at various prices.

Economic theory, however, can only offer limited guidance about what happens or is likely to happen in the real world. It assumes for the most part that firms will seek to maximize their profits. But whilst this is probably the motive which most persistently and consistently affects the decision-making of firms we know that in many real-life situations firms will not try to maximize their profits except perhaps in a very long-run sense.[2] The theorist reduces the variety and complexity of market situations to a few standard and highly simplified models and for the most part he assumes that the equilibrium output of the firm will be produced with the least expenditure of resources or, to put it another way, at the lowest possible cost. These are considerable over-simplifications of the industrial world which we shall be exploring.

But our purposes will be the same as those of the theorist. We will want to know whether firms reach their most efficient size, whether their planned outputs are produced as cheaply as possible, and whether too much of some kinds of goods are produced and too little of others. Theory will provide us with certain tenuous links between industrial structure, conduct, and performance. We are provided with some clues about what to expect but few industrial economists would consider that even the most detailed knowledge of market structure (e.g. relative size characteristics of firms, the position of potential sellers, relationships of buyers to sellers and of sellers to buyers) permits us to infer very much about how firms will react to changes in their environment and how their standard of performance will be affected.

Our knowledge of industry has enormously advanced since 1945, very largely because of increased Government intervention in the economy and heavier endowment of economic research. But this has only increased our awareness of the complexity of the real world. The problem of classifying this mass of material in a meaningful way and the difficulty of making it yield valid generalizations are more than ever with us. For this reason students often find industrial organization a difficult and unsatisfactory subject. We are less than ever inclined to offer firm opinions, for example, about whether monopoly (or some particular form of it) is good or bad, or about what factors are most likely to promote a high rate of technical innovation.

But let us start our exploration. In this first chapter we will mainly be concerned with some problems of definition and classification and will then go on to consider various forms of business enterprise.

1.2 Some preliminary notions

In economics we think of the 'firm' as being the primary unit within which productive resources are organized for the purpose of producing wealth. One writer[3] has called it the 'administrative planning unit, the activities of which are inter-related and are co-ordinated by policies framed in the light of the effect on the enterprise as a whole'. Edwards & Townsend[4] refer to the firm as 'any collection of business resources the planned use of which is unified . . . or more briefly it is an area of unified business planning'.

In all these definitions the emphasis is on the combination and deployment of productive factors by a single or unified will. In most theoretical text-books this 'will' is regarded as being embodied in the person of the entrepreneur. The 'industry' is conceived of as a group of firms producing identical products. Products of these firms are to be considered identical, not only in respect of their physical make-up, but also in respect of the attitude of consumers towards them. To the extent to which products are differentiated the perfection of competition is impaired and the theoretical notion of an industry is invalidated.

Within the limits of these definitions it is impossible in real life to identify the firm, the industry or the entrepreneur with any precision. The basic working unit is the establishment, that is, the whole of the premises under the same ownership or management, at a particular address, and occupying a particular site. Even this is not as simple as it sounds. Large establishments sometimes produce a wide variety of products and the various product divisions may be under separate management for most purposes. But such cases are comparatively rare.[5]

The firm, in a legal sense, is a person or group of persons or body corporate trading under a particular name. It may comprise one or more establishments, it has a legal personality, can hold property, sue and be sued, and, in the case of a joint stock company, accepts obligations to maintain a registered office, file accounts etc.

But the economic firm frequently embraces a much wider sphere of operations. A number of firms, each having separate legal identities, may in fact be subject to unified control. If one joint-stock company (the parent) owns more than fifty per cent of the voting share capital of another, the former can control the latter (the subsidiary) in much the same way as if both companies constituted a single undertaking. Indeed there may be *de facto* control if much less than fifty per cent of the voting share capital is held. Some 'firms' are jointly and equally owned and controlled by two other firms which are otherwise quite independent firms. It can also happen that a number of firms may be subject to unified control in some aspects of their business policy and not in others, as when a number of firms are parties to a cartel agreement by which the separate outputs they produce and the prices at which they sell those outputs are controlled by some authority external to each firm. Such an agreement might leave each firm free to determine the techniques and organization by which these outputs are produced.

The same sort of difficulty sometimes operates in reverse. Where a firm operates under a single name and has quite distinct legal identity we cannot assume that all the resources which it (legally) controls are subject to fully unified control. It may own a number of establishments, manufacturing quite different products, which are each autonomous for all practical purposes. In other cases the separate establishments are autonomous in certain respects (e.g. production matters) but are subject to the centralized control of the firm in others (e.g. capital development).[6]

The result is that we cannot easily identify in practice units which correspond closely to the economic concept of the firm. Great care is needed when statistics relating to firms are used to support an economic argument. The word *firm* is most generally used in the sense of legal firms though it sometimes refers to establishments. In research and government publications an effort is sometimes made to identify 'economic firms' by grouping together parent firms and subsidiary firms in which the parent holds more than fifty per cent of the voting share capital. These approximations to economic firms are called enterprises, units, or undertakings to distinguish them from firms in the legal sense (see p. 10).

The concept of industry gives rise to even greater difficulties. Basically the concept indicates a grouping of firms having some community of interest, i.e. it describes an area within which forms are sensitive to changes in the business transactions of other firms in the group. This community of interest or 'sensitivity' can arise from use of the same raw materials or of similar types of labour or technologies as well as the selling of identical products to consumers. (G. J. Stigler[7] has defined industry as comprising 'all products or enterprises with large long-run cross elasticities of either supply or demand'. But how do you measure these cross elasticities and how large is large?) Because economists have generally focused their attention on the product-pricing policies of firms they have preferred to identify industries with the existence of close substitutability of demand for the products of the constituent firms. (This still leaves us with the problem of deciding how close a degree of substitutability will define an industry. For example, do we conceive of cotton as an industry or do we think in terms of some wider grouping such as textiles? Since all consumer goods compete for the patronage of consumers they are all to some extent substitutes. At the same time, the products of most firms are to some degree different from the products of others.) If we are interested, for example, in concentration and monopoly power this is obviously the sort of industry classification we need. But other classifications are more appropriate for enquiries into the existence of monopsonistic power or rates of innovation.

Classification by different criteria will not necessarily produce the same results. Soap and margarine will be classified together if common raw materials or similar technologies are the determining factors, but not if the criterion is substitutability of the product. Tin cans and glass bottles are close substitutes but have very different technical characteristics.

Nevertheless, we find in practice that there is a good deal of overlapping between alternative methods of classification and we could hope to work out some compromise. If divisions are fine enough (or better still if we keep a full and up-to-date register of establishments) it should not be difficult to regroup firms for the purpose of any particular exercise. For some purposes we may wish to sort out groups of firms which are very capital-intensive, or mobile, or factory based.

Difficulties also arise because firms (and more rarely, establishments) produce a variety of products not all of which would be close substitutes for each other. The range of products produced by a firm is much more likely to be conditioned by technical considerations (identical raw materials, common technical processes) than by market considerations. Some firms produce a wide range of products which have no very obvious technical or market linkages.

In principle it is desirable that each multi-product firm should be allocated to one 'industry' or another since each firm is a decision-making unit. Industries, as we have seen, will be defined in terms of products which are reckoned to have something in common—from the economist's point of view it is preferred that they be close substitutes. It may happen, however, that the X industry produces some Y and Z because the constituent firms also produce Y and Z. If the production of goods other than X is high, the degree of specialization is said to be low. Equally, it may happen that a considerable amount of X is produced by the Y industry because firms allocated to Y (in which they are mainly interested) also produce some X. The degree of exclusiveness of the X industry is also low. Where the degrees of specialization and exclusiveness are low we need to be very careful in the interpretation of the published statistics. Obviously, the degrees of specialization and exclusiveness will be higher where the classification of industries is wider. The degree of specialization (proportions of gross output consisting of its principal products) and of exclusiveness (proportion of total output of the principal product produced by the industry) were more than ninety per cent for nearly two thirds of the 147 trades classified in the 1951 Census of Production. Input-output analysis based on 1963 Census of Production data should yield more up-to-date information on this. (See *Statistical News*, p. 8, HMSO, November 1968).

How are these difficulties sorted out in practice.[8] It is most important that there should be uniformity of classification of firms into industries by different Government departments and this is secured by use of a Standard Industrial Classification (SIC). The classification covers the production of all goods and services though the term industry is often used in common speech to cover only manufacturing industries. The Department of Employment and Productivity publishes information on employment, unemployment, earnings and hours of work on the basis of returns by establishments which are classified under the different SIC industrial groups. The Board of Trade publishes a Census of Production giving, for each group, details of numbers of establishments, employment, gross and net output and investment on the basis of establishment returns which are allocated to groups as defined by the SIC. (The Census of Production excludes agriculture, transport and communications and the service industries. Since 1951 a Census of Distribution has covered retail, wholesale and catering trades.) The decennial Census of Population also gives details of the industrial distribution of the population according to the SIC categories.

The SIC (as amended in 1968)[9] provides for twenty-seven orders (major industrial groups) which in turn are divided into 181 minimum list headings (or trades). Each Order and Minimum List Heading is defined in terms of its principal products. The Orders are—

I. Agriculture, Forestry, Fishing.
II. Mining and Quarrying.
III. Food, Drink and Tobacco.
IV. Coal and Petroleum Products.
V. Chemicals and Allied Industries.
VI. Metal Manufacture.
VII. Mechanical Engineering.
VIII. Instrument Engineering.
IX. Electrical Engineering.
X. Shipbuilding and Marine Engineering.
XI. Vehicles.
XII. Metal Goods not elsewhere specified.
XIII. Textiles.
XIV. Leather, Leather Goods and Fur.
XV. Clothing and Footwear.
XVI. Bricks, Pottery, Glass, Cement, etc.
XVII. Timber, Furniture, etc.
XVIII. Paper, Printing and Publishing.
XIX. Other Manufacturing Industries.
XX. Construction.
XXI. Gas, Electricity and Water.
XXII. Transport and Communication.
XXIII. Distributive Trades.
XXIV. Insurance, Banking, Finance and Business Services.
XXV. Professional and Scientific Services.
XXVI. Miscellaneous Services.
XXVII. Public Administration and Defence.

The logical sequence of the Orders is readily apparent. Orders I and II are extractive or primary industries and it seems proper to start with the oldest of all industries. Orders III to XIX comprise manufacturing or secondary industry. Orders XX to XXII span the gap between manufacturing and service (or tertiary) industries which are covered by orders XXIII to XXVII. The latter proceed from those handling physical goods, through banking and insurance to the personal service trades.

It should be very carefully noted that it is establishments and not firms which are allocated to SIC Orders and trades. The Board of Trade and the Ministry of Labour would not necessarily allocate the same establishment to the same trade. The former allocate a firm with reference to the value of the principal product; the latter will allocate a firm by reference to the principal product on the production of which most employees are engaged. This has the advantage of raising the degrees of specialization and exclusiveness of the groups since establishments are less likely than firms to produce a wide range of products and the allocation of an establishment is less likely to be in doubt. Since the range of products is likely to be dominated by technical rather than market considerations, the definition of trades by principal products will reflect technical similarities more than market substitutability. Occasionally, however, administrative considerations will produce an allocation of almost completely unrelated products (e.g. linoleum and leather-cloth) to the same group.

These difficulties reduce the value of official statistics to economists interested in some aspects of market behaviour. Nothing much can be inferred about the market power of a few firms producing the bulk of the principal products defining a particular trade. (The size of firms allocated to a trade is determined by the number and size of the establishments which are allocated to that trade. This is not necessarily a firm's real size because it may own establishments allocated to other trades.) The products may not be close substitutes, there may be competition from establishments and firms which also produce these products but which are allocated to other trades and the firms may have interests much wider than would be indicated by those of its establishments allocated to the trade in question. (This example is given only by way of illustration. Considerations other than number of sellers will determine the strength of a monopoly position. See Chapter 6.) Nothing much can be inferred about the growth prospects of firms allocated to trades which are rapidly growing if the trade is defined in terms of principal products as different as refrigerators and mining machinery (Minimum List Heading 339).

At the same time these difficulties should not be exaggerated. Some aspects of the behaviour of firms are best analysed in terms of classifications based on the technical characteristics of firms. Also, the extent to which non-competing products are found in the same group, though not precisely measurable, is probably not great enough to seriously invalidate the study of market behaviour of firms in terms of the SIC.

The identification of the entrepreneur is equally troublesome but perhaps less important from our present point of view. In theory, the entrepreneur is often regarded both as risk-taker and decision-maker. In the case of the small one-man business no difficulty arises. The owner who contributes the capital is most often the manager of the business as well. The income he derives from it is best regarded as partly earnings of management (i.e. what he would have to pay in salary to a manager if he chose to employ one) and partly profits (the reward for successful risk-taking). In the more usual case of the joint-stock company, risk-taking and decision-making are more or less divorced. The risks are borne by the ordinary shareholders but broad issues of policy are decided and carried out by the Board of Directors. The latter, however, are not normally called upon to exercise active day-to-day administrative control, which may be vested in the Chairman of the Board, a Managing Director, or perhaps a salaried General Manager. This chief executive officer and his immediately subordinate heads of sections (production manager, sales manager, etc.) will have a considerable area of independent decision in the running of the business. But too much should not be made of these distinctions. The ordinary shareholders may be regarded as having ultimate control of the business through their power to appoint the Board of Directors, although it may be doubted whether this control counts for very much, at least so long as things are going fairly well. On the other hand, the chief executive officer is often a shareholder and so has some profit interest in the business quite apart from his salary as a manager.

In the present context it is perhaps best to identify the function of the entrepreneur with decision-making. In most businesses it is possible to identify some person who is ultimately responsible for the day-to-day conduct of the firm's affairs and who has the biggest voice in deciding broad issues of policy. In large businesses there is a great deal of decentralization of managerial functions,[10] but even so there is nearly always some person or small body of persons whose function it is to co-ordinate important business decisions and to exercise final authority. It is nevertheless important to remember that practice varies a great deal between different industries and sizes of firms, that power to decide may shift from the chief executive officer to the Board of Directors when especially important issues have to be decided, and that in times of crisis the body of ordinary shareholders may suddenly assert itself. So once again we can see how difficult it is to apply the simple concepts of theory to industrial practice. We must therefore be on our guard when applying the results of theory to the complex and rapidly changing industrial world. To give but one illustration, it seems doubtful whether the professional managers of industry, with a very limited profit interest in their business, are going to be motivated solely by a desire to maximize the short-run profits of the firm. They are more likely to be interested in growth. This, admittedly, will be partly conditioned by the amount of profits which can be retained in the business. But the desire to build an industrial empire denotes a much more complex motivation than profit maximization.

1.3 Forms of enterprise

It will be convenient at this stage to say something further about the different types of firm. The simplest unit of business organization is the one-man business. This is particularly common in agriculture, the retail trades, and the professions, but many one-man businesses are still to be found in manufacturing and extractive industries. Such firms are generally small and work principally on capital supplied by the owner-manager.

The partnership is frequently a consequence of the growth of a one-man business, when one or more other persons put additional capital into it, and receive in return a proportion of the profits. The great disadvantage of this form of business, from the point of view of the partners taken into it, is that they become fully liable for its losses up to the limit of their resources. The fact that a number of people share in the net profits of the business is usually taken as evidence that a partnership exists and that the persons so sharing are partners with unlimited liability. Such liability may only be escaped if the persons contributing the additional capital and sharing in profits take no active part in the business, and have it clearly stated in the agreement with the owner of the business when the loan is made that no partnership rights exist.

Under the Limited Partnerships Act 1907 a business may constitute itself as a limited partnership by registering the fact with the Registrar of Companies and giving details of the nature of the business, the names of the partners, and the sums contributed by each limited partner. The limited partners in such a business are then liable for the firm's debts only to the extent of the amount of capital which they contribute individually. The limited partnership has not, however, become a popular form of business enterprise in this country.

The most common type of firm is the registered joint-stock company. This description covers all companies registered under, and subject to, the provisions of the Companies Acts. Such companies may be of various kinds. They may be unlimited companies, in which the liability of each member for the debts of the firm is unlimited, or they may be companies limited by guarantee in which each member is liable (in addition to his share capital, if any) for an amount which he undertakes to contribute to the assets of the firm in the event of its being wound up. Unlimited companies and companies limited by guarantee may or may not have a share capital.

Either of these two forms of the registered company is comparatively rare. The most common form is the company limited by shares in which the liability of members is limited to the amount unpaid on any shares held by them. The limited company may be either public or private. The private company may have as few as two members, whereas the public company must have at least seven. The private company is subject to certain restrictions in that the right to transfer its shares is restricted, the number of its members (exclusive of employees) is limited to fifty, and the company is unable to invite the public to subscribe to its shares.

The advantages of the private company under certain circumstances are obvious. The small one-man business may turn itself into a private company and get the advantage of limited liability by simply taking in one shareholder (in addition to the proprietor) who may hold only one share. Also, when a small business wishes to expand and requires additional capital, the private company form is often preferred to the limited partnership. The former proprietor of the business may easily retain complete control, the business retaining all its former flexibility and a good deal of freedom from unwelcome publicity, that is, so long as the business remains small (see p. 22). But when, and if, the business expands considerably in size, the advantages of the public company become more apparent. Additional capital is more easily forthcoming when an application to the public for subscriptions to its shares may be made and when those shares may be freely bought and sold. Comparatively few people wish to purchase shares which cannot be easily and quickly disposed of if occasion warrants. For this reason most large firms become public companies at a certain stage in their growth, although they may originally have been one-man firms or private companies.

The importance of the joint-stock company (particularly in its public limited form) to the growth of large-scale organization in modern industrialized communities can hardly be exaggerated. It greatly facilitates the bringing together of the necessary large aggregates of capital by drawing on the inumerable sources of small savings distributed throughout the community. Persons of modest means can acquire shares in, and the right to participate in the profits of, the largest company, and in most cases such shares are easily realizable through the machinery of the Stock Exchange. (Also, as will become apparent later, the financial structure of joint-stock companies is extremely flexible, and offers the public opportunities of investment on variable terms, and at varying degrees of risk.) The latter not only makes possible the avoidance of permanent commitments but, by organized trading in securities, reduces the risk of loss. The joint-stock company has the advantage of perpetual life and can afford to take a longer view than the one-man business. Also, it is less dependent than the latter on a continued supply of 'family brains' since it can hire the services of able executives who may be unable to set up in business on their own account through lack of capital.

The joint-stock company is not without its disadvantages. It facilitates growth, not only by its power of attractive capital, but also by the ease with which numbers of firms may be brought under common control. It may grow beyond its economic limit, growth being stimulated by pursuit of economic power rather than a desire for profits. A stage may be reached where the undertaking is beyond the effective control of the entrepreneur and where enterprise is stifled by bureaucratic procedures and 'red tape'. Ownership of the share capital may be so widely dispersed that the shareholders are unable to exercise effective control over the management. Management may become irresponsible and the interests of the shareholders may suffer. We shall have more to say on this subject at a later stage.

The method of floating a limited company may be briefly indicated. The new company files its Memorandum and Articles of Association, together with a statement of its nominal capital and particulars of its directors, with the Registrar of Companies. The Memorandum gives details of the name of the company, the situation of its registered offices, the objects of the company, the liability of its members, and the amount and nature of its share capital. The Articles regulate the internal affairs of the company, e.g. meetings and voting powers of the shareholders, the appointment and the powers of directors, etc.

The public company must also file a list of persons consenting to act as directors, the written consent of directors to act, and their agreement to take and pay for the shares which qualify them to act. After examination of these documents, the Registrar will issue a Certificate of Incorporation, and the new company acquires a legal existence. The private company may then start business operations, but the public company is precluded from doing so until it has made a declaration that each director has taken up and paid for his qualifying shares. Also, before it is able to exercise its borrowing powers and appeal for public subscriptions to its shares, it must file its Prospectus or a statement in lieu thereof. The Prospectus, which is issued with an approach to the public for subscriptions to shares, contains all relevant information relating to the company, including its assets, or the assets which it proposes to acquire, past earnings, future prospects, etc.

1.4 Capital structure of companies

The total nominal value of the shares which a company is authorized by its Memorandum to issue is known as its authorized capital, and the nominal (or par) value of the shares actually issued as its issued capital. Shares need not be fully paid up at once. For example the purchaser of a £1 ordinary share may be asked to pay £0·125 on application for each share, £0·25 on the allotment of the share to the purchaser and £0·125 three months later. The other £0·50 may be left as a reserve of uncalled capital to be paid at some unspecified future date when it is needed by the company. Occasionally, a certain proportion of the uncalled capital, known as reserve capital, can only be called up in the event of the company being wound up. Shares may be issued at a premium (i.e. a price above their nominal value) or at a discount.

It should be noted that the authorized capital gives little idea of the magnitude of a company's operations or of the real value of its capital assets. Neither does the issued capital, since a large part of it may not have been called up. Nor, again, do we get a much more accurate idea of the size of the company from the total value of its paid-up capital, since it may have been financing

13

capital development out of past profits or acquiring stocks of raw materials with the proceeds of bank loans. It follows that the dividend declared on an ordinary share may give a very false impression of the profitability of the investment to the holder, and of the profitability and efficiency of the company. The holder of the share may have purchased the share at a price far in excess of its nominal value, either because it was issued at a premium, or because it was purchased from a former holder subsequent to its issue by the company. A dividend of ten per cent on a £1 ordinary share represents a return of only five per cent if the holder had to pay £2 for it. It represents a much higher return if the holder obtained it on issue for £0·25 (£0·75 unpaid), although in this case the contingent liability to pay a further £0·75 per share when called for has to be reckoned with. As regards the efficiency and profitability of a company, a dividend of only one per cent may be declared on its £1 ordinary shares, although it is a profitable and well-managed concern, because it has paid more than their real value for the capital assets which it has acquired with the proceeds of its share issue. On the other hand a declared dividend of one hundred per cent on a £1 ordinary share does not necessarily indicate either that the company is highly efficient or that it is profiteering at the expense of the consumer. It may have financed itself extensively out of undistributed profits in the past so that the real value of its capital assets far exceeds the nominal value of its issued capital. It may, in fact, be earning less than ten per cent on its real capital assets, but may, nevertheless, as a result of past abstentions by shareholders, be able to declare a dividend of one hundred per cent on its ordinary share capital.

A share must have a par value but this may be as low as 1p. The argument for no-par-value shares is that the par value is of little significance after issue of the share. As the preceding discussion shows, argument based on nominal values of shares and dividends declared as a percentage on these values can be very misleading.

The authorized capital of a company may be divided into many different types of share. Preference shares permit the holders to share in profits before other shareholders, but after debenture holders. They generally bear a fixed rate of interest but occasionally they are made 'participating', i.e. they may participate in profits (over and above the fixed rate of return) with ordinary shares up to a certain maximum after the ordinary shares have received a certain minimum rate of return. In addition, preference shares may be cumulative or non-cumulative. Cumulative preference shareholders have the right to claim any arrears of their fixed rate of return (due in respect of a previous year or years when profits were insufficient to meet their claims) before the ordinary shareholders share in the profits. Non-cumulative preference shareholders have no rights to such arrears of dividends. In some cases first and second (or A and B) preference shares may be issued, the first preference shareholders being entitled to their fixed return before the second preference shareholders receive anything. Preference shares may be redeemable but only out of profits or the proceeds of a new issue of shares. Generally speaking, company dividends must be paid out of profits only.

Ordinary shares rank for dividend without limit after all prior claims on profits have been met. They are sometimes referred to as equities and holders of them substantially bear the risks of the enterprise. These risks arise mainly from the provision of fixed specialized equipment and the long-term capital provided by the holders of the equity is generally regarded as financing these particularly 'risky' requirements of industry. The return on ordinary shares naturally fluctuates much more than the return on other types of shares and depends on the magnitude of net profits, the proportion of net profits which the directors decide to distribute (a certain proportion will probably be allocated to reserve), and the extent of the prior claims of debenture and preference shareholders. Sometimes a class of preferred ordinary shares has a right to a certain dividend return before the ordinary shareholders can participate in profits.

Deferred and founders' shares constitute a category of deferred ordinary shares. It is generally stipulated that they share equally in profits with ordinary shares after the latter have received a certain rate per cent. Such shares are often issued, fully or partly paid up, to reimburse the promoters of the company or the sellers of the business which the new company is being formed to acquire. (In order to protect investors, details of such transactions must be given in the prospectus. In addition, any commissions payable for taking up shares, amounts payable to the promoters of the company, and the preliminary expenses of the flotation must be revealed.) It rarely happens that a limited company is formed other than to acquire and carry on a business which is already a going concern—perhaps a one-man business or partnership. Occasionally, it happens that a new limited company is formed to acquire the assets and carry on the business of two or more other companies.

A company may, by the issue of debentures, obtain capital additional to that received by the sale of its shares. A debenture is not a share; it is merely a document acknowledging the company's indebtedness to the holder for a certain sum. It is a fixed interest-bearing security, and may or may not be redeemable at some specified future date. A mortgage debenture is secured by a mortgage on the assets of the company. In this case the holder has a prior claim on the proceeds of the realization of the firm's assets in the event of its being wound up. Where different categories of mortgage debentures exist, the first mortgage debenture holders have their claims satisfied before the second mortgage debenture holders, and so on. The holder of a simple debenture (unsecured by mortgage) is in the same position as any other creditor of the firm in the event of its failure; that is to say, he can claim equally with ordinary trade creditors for a share in the proceeds of realization after the claims of mortgage debenture holders have been fully met.

The debenture holder is in no sense a shareholder in the concern. He is a creditor of the company—a person who has loaned money to it at a certain agreed rate of interest. Whilst his interest may in fact be paid out of profits and his claims have a first call on any profits that are made, his claims must be met whether profits are made or not. The interest due to debenture holders is the first charge on the earnings of a concern. Apart from the general riskiness of lending money to any person or corporate body, the debenture holder does not share in the risks of the enterprise, and is comparatively uninterested in whether it makes big profits or not.

Debentures may be issued singly and spasmodically, or a large issue of debentures may be made at the same time. In the first case, a debenture may be issued as a security for a bank loan. In the second case, a large issue may be made for subscription by the public. Where a number of debentures has been issued it is usual for the company to execute a trust deed in favour of certain trustees for the debenture holders. This deed, in effect, transfers the assets on which the debentures have been secured to the trustees, whilst specifying that the assets are to remain in the possession of the company so long as the claims of the debenture holders are met. The trustees can then safeguard the debenture holder by selling the assets or forcing the appointment of a receiver if there is any default on debenture claims. Also, the trust deed secures the debenture holders against the possibility of a further prior charge being made on the assets to their disadvantage.

1.5 Ownership and control

Ownership of a company is vested in the general body of shareholders, but they are much too unwieldy a body to exercise the functions of management. Management is vested in the Board of Directors, each director being normally paid a fee for his services. The number of directors varies, and usually each director must have a minimum shareholding qualification which is laid down in the articles of association, permission to deal in the shares on the London Stock Exchange being refused if this is not the case. The Board of Directors is responsible for the general conduct of the firm and for all statements set out in the prospectus of the company, but the majority will not be actively engaged in the day-to-day conduct of the firm's affairs. This is generally delegated to various executive officers, the chief of whom will probably be designated General Manager. The General Manager may be comparatively free from detailed supervision and control, but it is more usual for one or more active directors (the Chairman of the Board or the Managing Director or both) to give the greater part of their time to the conduct of the business. In the latter case the executive officers are directly responsible in a very real sense to the active directors who are in effective control of the policy of the firm. A public limited company must hold an annual general meeting at which the directors submit to the shareholders an audited balance sheet, and at which the Chairman of the Board of Directors usually makes a general statement on the affairs of the company. At this meeting a new Board of Directors is appointed by the votes of the shareholders or, as usually happens, the existing board is reappointed. The voting powers of shareholders are laid down in the articles of association, and may vary considerably from one company to another. Preference shareholders may not have the right to vote unless their fixed interest claims have not been met. Some classes of ordinary shares may carry much heavier voting powers (in proportion to their nominal value) than other categories of ordinary shares. In this way control of the company may be vested in a restricted group of shareholders who possess a very limited share in the ownership of the firm. Voting procedure varies so very much from one company to another that adequate generalization is almost impossible.

There is nothing to prevent the issue of ordinary shares without voting rights though it is comparatively rare in this country. The arguments for and against non-voting shares are vigorously debated. On the one hand it is considered that the owners of the capital who bear the major risks of the enterprise should have ultimate control. Non-voting shares may be unattractive to investors and make the raising of capital more difficult and expensive. They facilitate the control of companies by small groups of voting shareholders who may use their power to the disadvantage of non-voting shareholders. On the other hand, it is argued that many shareholders invest only to share in profits. They are neither fitted for, nor do they desire to have the ultimate voice in, management of the assets. Moreover, shareholdings are often so small and widely dispersed that the ordinary shareholders have very little power unless they are organized, and what power they have is rarely exercised by attendance and voting at shareholders meetings or by giving proxies. Management may be more far-sighted and more efficient if the contingent threat of overthrow by the mass of ordinary shareholders is removed.

'Take-over bids' have been on the increase in recent years. The term is usually applied to a formal offer by the directors of Company A for the voting shares of Company B, the offer being conditional upon acceptance by a specified majority of the voting shareholders of B. The offer may be in cash, shares in A, debenture stock in A, or in some combination of these.

In this sense take-overs are the usual means whereby a company grows by acquisition and merger (see Chapter 3). This is a normal feature of a healthy dynamic economy and the joint-stock company form of enterprise is not to be condemned because it facilitates a process whereby efficient, growing, firms take over the working assets of firms which for one reason or another may be having a difficult time. (Take-overs have been called a civilized alternative to bankruptcy. But a recent investigation of take-overs found in twenty-four out of forty-six cases examined the rate of return on capital of the acquired company was at least ten per cent above that of the purchasing company.)[11] Strong management groups often find that this is the most practicable and economical method of expanding their business. The knowledge that they may be taken over and displaced is an incentive to effort on the part of directors and management to improve their efficiency.

But take-overs may be inspired by other reasons. In a period of general inflation the market value of a company's shares may be much less than the real value of its capital assets which will include freehold land and building as well as machinery, raw materials, and goods in process. The take-over may be motivated by a desire to get control 'on the cheap', by offering something above the market value of the shares, and with the intention of selling off some of its assets for re-development. But even this form of speculative activity can be defended since as a result the assets are now being put to what the market has indicated as a better use.

Even so the frenzied speculative activities which accompany some take-over booms is difficult to defend. Directors of sound well-managed concerns may be deflected from their policies by the fear that they are making themselves more vulnerable to a take-over bid which may be made over their heads direct to the general body of shareholders. Also, rumours of impending take-overs can spark off a rush for shares on the stock exchange, since take-over bids are normally made at prices above the ruling market rate. A take-over may be inspired by a desire to create an active market for shares, rather than by the economic merits of merging the two companies. There is also an element of fashion involved. A feeling can develop on the part of tycoons anxious to preserve their reputations that they must find something to take over.

Some take-over bids are not successful and some acquisitions which do take place can hardly be described as being the result of 'take-over bids' (see p. 129). Furthermore, a high proportion of the assets taken over in completed acquisitions are accounted for by a few large mergers. In 1968, out of 598 acquisitions by 'large' companies (i.e. quoted on the Stock Exchange with net assets exceeding £0·5 million, or annual income exceeding £50,000 in 1964) seven accounted for about half of the total consideration paid by the acquiring companies to the shareholders of the acquired companies. For these and other reasons,

19

published figures of bids and actual acquisitions require careful interpretation.[12] But there is no doubt about the substantial increase in recent years in terms of the total assets taken over. This has probably resulted in a considerable increase in concentration of control, especially in manufacturing industry. A fixed population of 1,312 manufacturing companies in 1961 had been reduced by mergers to 908 by 1968, and in that year they controlled eighty per cent of the total assets of all UK manufacturing companies. About forty per cent of the total assets in manufacturing were controlled by the twenty-eight largest of these companies.[13]

This gives some idea of the magnitude of the take-over boom. Public attention tends to focus on the take-over bids in which very large companies are involved, or which are contested by the directors of the company which is the subject of the bid or by third parties. In fact the vast majority of acquisitions hardly justify the use of the term 'take-over', i.e. they are deals amicably worked out by the boards of the companies and recommended to shareholders. Very few acquisitions are the subject of 'bids' and fewer still are contested, though there appears to be a greater tendency for the larger acquisitions to be contested. But it is interesting to note that nearly all acquisitions of shares are made at prices above the market price prevailing prior to the bid. This suggests either that the market is not well equipped to assess the future profit-earning prospects of quoted companies or that the profit projections on which take-over bids are based are over-optimistic.

Obviously the ease with which joint-stock companies can be absorbed by others is open to abuse and a complicated code of conduct was agreed in 1968 by the City interests most concerned with the mechanics of take-overs.[14] Briefly it provides that offers should firstly be made to the Board of Directors, then immediately communicated to shareholders with the fullest possible information, especially about estimated profit forecasts; that if shares are acquired on the open market above the price offered then this higher price must be offered to shareholders; and that no attempt should be made to resist take-overs by the issue of further authorized capital.

Many important and difficult questions arise when it is decided to float a limited company. It is desirable to keep the authorized capital as small as possible in order to reduce registration fees. At the same time it is essential that the authorized capital should be large enough to provide for future expansion. The amount of capital issued should, from some points of view, be limited to the immediate needs of the company, but it needs to be remembered that a succession of relatively small issues of capital made over a period of years is very much more costly than one substantial issue. Whether or not the capital should be fully called at once depends very much upon the nature of the business. Banks, for example, may prefer to keep a substantial reserve of uncalled capital available to meet unforeseen contingencies. The question of the proportions in which capital is to be raised by the issue of various types of stocks and shares is also very difficult to decide. Let us take, for example, a highly profitable one-man business, which is to be refloated as a public limited company, which needs a good deal of capital for expansion, and which is very confidently expected to be highly profitable. A large proportion of the capital will probably be raised by the issue of debentures and preference shares. A comparatively small proportion of ordinary shares can then be expected to earn very high dividends. Such a company is said to be 'highly geared'. This is all the more likely to happen if the proprietor of the business (or the promoters of the company who have secured an option to buy the business and are floating the company to this end) wishes not only to reserve as high a proportion of the profits to himself as possible, but also wishes to retain permanent control of the company. A majority of the restricted number of the ordinary (voting) shares will probably be allocated to him in payment for the assets of his business which he is, in effect, selling to the company.

The prospective purchaser of ordinary shares will be most interested in the profit-making possibilities of the company, but the 'gearing' of the company will also be an important consideration to him. Other things being equal, he will be less inclined to purchase the greater the volume of fixed interest-bearing commitments which have to be met before the ordinary shares rank for dividend. Under certain circumstances, therefore, the promoters of the company will be careful not to gear the company too high for fear of lessening the attractiveness of the issue to the potential investor. Gearing may be measured by net fixed-interest distribution as a percentage of net income. On this basis an analysis of quoted companies in 1951 showed gearing to be low (under ten per cent) in sixty per cent of the companies, and high (above twenty per cent) in less than twenty per cent of the companies.[15]

Reference has already been made to the fact that companies are subject to the provisions of the Companies Acts. At present the legal position of companies is governed by the Act of 1948 (which consolidated companies legislation up to that time) as amended by the Companies Act of 1967.

Economists are not much interested in the detail of companies legislation. Its general purpose is to protect investors against fraud, to provide them with as much information as possible about the company in which they have invested or propose to invest, and to facilitate the control of the owners (ordinary shareholders) over management without placing unreasonable restrictions on the enterprise and initiative of management.

Company law has been progressively tightened during the past forty years and its purposes are subtly changing as it is adapted to changes in the economic and institutional environment. The Act of 1947 strengthened the control of shareholders over management by provisions for extending the period of notice for general meetings, the removal of directors by ordinary resolution before the expiry of their period of office, and voting for directors individually instead of *en bloc*. Investors were further protected by the provision of more information on the financial results of companies, by making directors responsible for material omissions from the prospectus, and by making them show good grounds for relying on the reports of technical experts.

The Act of 1967 was mainly concerned with forcing companies to make more disclosures of their affairs—directors emoluments (if exceeding £7,500), turnover (if exceeding £50,000 per annum), the average number of employees and the annual labour cost (if the number of employees exceeded one hundred). The Act also provided for the disclosure of the ownership of substantial holdings of voting shares in quoted companies in order to curb the practice of concealing the identity of large shareholders by registering them in the name of some nominee company.

The other principal effects of the Act were to give the Board of Trade more effective powers to investigate the affairs of companies and to take away from private companies the exemption they had formerly enjoyed of not being obliged to file accounts and directors' report, although some private companies (e.g. companies having corporate or nominee shareholders, and subsidiaries of public companies) had lost this privilege in 1947. This exposes most private companies to considerable publicity about their affairs for the first time, though the effect is mitigated, as we have seen in the previous paragraph, by exempting companies from some of the disclosure provisions if they are below a certain size. The only way in which a private company can escape the obligation to file accounts and reports is to re-register as a company with unlimited liability.

Further companies legislation has been promised by both of the main political parties to deal with the whole philosophy of the joint stock company. It is also expected to further strengthen the provisions to prevent fraud and to permit the issue of no par value shares. Presumably the duties of companies towards their employees and their customers will come under review. This will represent a considerable extension of the scope of company law though the Act of 1967 has already foreshadowed some changes. Some of the disclosure provisions (political and charitable contributions, emoluments of employees over £10,000 per annum) are hardly necessary to an evaluation of the economic prospects of the company. On the other hand, it can be argued that if the ordinary shareholders are to control management they have a right to know what is being done with their money.

1.6 Other forms of enterprise

The above summary treatment of the one-man business, the partnership, and the registered company does not cover all the possible types of firms. Certain joint-stock enterprises are registered under special Acts (Building Societies Acts, Friendly Societies Acts, and the Industrial and Provident Societies Acts) and are not, therefore, companies in the sense that they are subject to the provisions of the Companies Acts. Any society carrying on business may be registered under these Acts and is subject to special privileges and restrictions. Registered Societies are free (as such) from liability to income tax and the liability of members is limited. Their rules must be registered with, and approved by, the Chief Registrar of Friendly Societies, their accounts must be audited by a public auditor, single shareholdings are restricted to £500, and an annual return must be made to the Registrar whose function it is to see that each society is working within its rules and that the Act under which the society is registered is being complied with. Many of the societies registered under these Acts (thrift associations, trade unions, trust funds, etc.) are not 'firms' in the ordinary sense of the word. The great majority of the remainder are engaged in wholesale and retail trading (e.g. Co-operative Retail Societies and the Co-operative Wholesale Societies) and the finance of house purchase (Building Societies). On the whole, undertakings registered under these Acts are not significant for a study of industrial organization, though the Co-operative Wholesale Societies are engaged in a wide variety of manufacturing activities, and many small firms engaged in textile and clothing production, boot and shoe manufacture, printing, etc., are also registered in this way.

The most important of other types of firms are the large corporations established by statute to administer the assets of industries which have been nationalized (i.e. taken into public ownership) since 1945. The most important are coal, gas, electricity, railways, civil aviation, steel, and central banking (the Bank of England). (The nationalized industries will be considered separately in Chapter 7.) In a slightly different category are certain pre-war public corporations (e.g. the Forestry Commission, the Port of London Authority, and the BBC). These are of little significance in a study of this kind. Neither are the very few companies incorporated under Royal Charter like the Hudson's Bay Company or the East India Company.

It is very difficult to give any accurate indication of the relative importance of these different forms of enterprise. Public corporations employ rather less than eight per cent of the total working population in employment, companies about sixty per cent, one-man businesses and partnerships about eighteen per cent, and central and local government about fifteen per cent. Within the company sector a few thousand quoted non-financial companies account for about half of company income.

If we think of industry as comprising Orders II to XVIII (inclusive) of the Standard Industrial Classification there can be no doubt of the predominance of the large quoted public companies and the public corporations. The latter almost completely dominate Orders II and XVIII (mining and public utilities), whilst quoted public companies probably account for about half of the employment provided by Orders III-XVII (manufacturing industry and construction). But now we are beginning to trespass on the subject of the next chapter.

1 Caves, R. E., *American Industry: Structure, Conduct, Performance*, p. 2 (Englewood Cliffs, N.J., and London, Prentice-Hall, 1964). Curiously enough, very few texts on industrial organization say very much about how firms fix their prices.

2 Needham, *Economic Analysis and Industrial Structure*, pp. 2–12 (New York, Holt, Rhinehart and Winston, 1969).

3 Penrose, E. F., *Growth of Firms*, p. 16 (Oxford, Blackwell, 1969).

4 Edwards and Townsend, *Business Enterprise*, p. 64 (London, Macmillan, 1958).

5 Where, at a particular address, there are two or more departments engaged in different activities for which separate records are kept, each department is treated as a separate establishment. In 1968 the definition of establishment was expanded and a new concept of 'local unit' was introduced. But we are not much concerned here with such fine points of classification. See *Statistical News*, p. 20 (London, HMSO, November 1968).

6 See Edwards and Townsend, *op. cit.*, pp. 64–9, where some examples are given. A survey of large companies published by the Institute of Economic Affairs in 1959 showed that 134 large companies had 2,686 subsidiaries. Their internal arrangements varied from a broadly federal structure to highly centralized control, but even when the subsidiaries were allowed a great deal of autonomy the parent company retained control of general policy and finance.

7 Stigler, G. J., *Introduction to Business Concentration and Policy*, p. 4 (Princeton, University Press, 1955).

8 For fuller accounts see Evely and Little, *Concentration in British Industry*, pp. 25–35 (Cambridge, University Press, 1960); Conklin and Goldstein, *Business Concentration and Price Policy (a symposium)*, pp. 15–56 (Princeton, University Press, 1955); and Needham, *op. cit.*, Chapter 2.

9 For details see *Standard Industrial Classification* (London, HMSO, 1968).

10 'A factory manager in ICI may take decisions of far greater complexity, determine the use of far larger resources, and discharge far weightier responsibilities than the top executives of many smaller firms.' Edwards and Townsend, *op. cit.*, p. 67.

11 Rose and Newbould, 'The 1967 Take-over Boom,' *Moorgate and Wall Street Review* (Autumn 1967).

12 See Annex 4 of Board of Trade paper *Mergers* (London, HMSO, 1969) where some figures for recent years are quoted.

13 *Ibid.*, paras. 6–9.

14 *Ibid.*, Annex 6. About two-thirds of the consideration paid by large acquiring companies in the period 1964–68 was in 'paper', i.e. shares or loan stock.

15 Tew and Henderson (ed.), *Studies in Company Finance* (Cambridge, University Press, 1959).

Chapter 2

The Structure of British Industry

2.1 Introduction

The main purpose of this chapter is to describe the present structure and regional distribution of British industry and recent changes in it. By structure we mean the relative importance of different industries, their inter-relationships, the size structure of firms which are classified to particular industries, and so on. The chapter will inevitably be mainly factual and descriptive but some idea of the magnitude involved is necessary to the serious student of industrial organization.

The picture that follows can only be a very simple and superficial sketch of the anatomy of industry which, in its detail, is quite bewildering in its complexity. Also it is necessary to remind ourselves of some of the difficulties of identification, measurement and classification which make the interpretation of statistics extremely difficult. We have already noted the distinction between establishments, firms, and undertakings (firms under common control), often referred to as units or enterprises. The problem of industrial classification has also been discussed and although whenever possible the Standard Industrial Classification (SIC) will be used it is sometimes difficult to achieve complete comparability of figures over a period during which the SIC has been revised, therefore, most of the figures in this chapter are based on the 1958 SIC revision. Finally we need to remember that there are various ways in which the size of firms and industries can be measured—for example, by employment, output, or balance sheet valuation of assets—and that there is no reason to suppose that, in general, one way is superior to any other. It may well be, of course, that in particular contexts one measure of size would seem to be more appropriate than others. For example, we normally think of monopoly in terms of control over the output of an industry and therefore it would seem that in concentration studies (see p. 43) the size of firms should be measured in terms of output. Unfortunately, the structural picture is often much affected by the measure of size adopted. But in practice it may well be that we do not have much choice. The relative importance of firms and industries is most frequently measured in terms of employment because up-to-date figures are available—not to mention the fact that 'heads' are more easily counted than output.

2.2 The public and private sectors

If we take the economy as a whole the public sector may be taken to include not only the nationalized industries but also Civil Service establishments, armed forces, local authorities, river, dock and harbour boards, hospitals, etc. On this basis about one quarter of the working population is in the public sector and three-quarters in the private sector.

In a text-book on industrial organization, however, we are more interested in the relative importance of the public sector in industry—which may be defined as manufacturing industry (that is, Orders III to XVI of the 1958 version of the SIC) or production industries which includes not only manufacturing industry but also mining and quarrying, construction, and gas, electricity and water (that is, Orders II to XVIII of the 1958 SIC). Production industries are the industries covered by the Census of Production and the Index of Industrial Production.

If we exclude the public corporations in transport and the Post Office, the remaining corporations are within production industries and in 1967 employed about 865,000, i.e. less than eight per cent of total employment in these industries. This does not include the British Steel Corporation. The inclusion of steel probably raises the figure to ten per cent. Until Steel was re-nationalized in 1967 no significant part of manufacturing industry was in the public sector. It should be noted, however, that most of the nationalized industries in the production sector are very heavily capitalized. Some rough figuring suggests that gross capital stock of these corporations was a little under forty per cent of the total stock of the production sector. Gross fixed capital formation in 1967 by nationalized industries in the production sector was probably more than forty per cent of capital formation in the sector as a whole. It follows, that in terms of output the contribution of public corporations to the production sector was much higher than would be indicated by the employment figures. A rough estimate suggests that it might be about fifteen per cent.

It is not therefore a simple matter to sum up the relative importance of public and private enterprise. Much depends on whether we think in terms of the entire economy or merely of some part of it, and on how we measure relative importance. Table 2·1 probably gives a fairly accurate summary of the position in the economy as a whole.

Table 2. 1 *The Public and Private Sectors in 1968*

	Share of total working population (per cent) (25·3 millions)	Share of gross national product (per cent)
Private Sector		
Companies	} 76	56 }
Sole traders, partnerships, etc.		17 } 73
Public Sector		
Public corporations including post office	8 }	11 }
Central and local govt. including armed forces	16 } 24	16 } 27

Source: *National Income & Expenditure,* Table 13 (London, HMSO, 1969).

2.3 The basic structure

We now turn to consider the distribution of the industrial population. The most comprehensive source of information derives from the Census of Population. Table 2.2 gives the distribution of the employed population by SIC order for various census years between 1931 and 1966. The totals exaggerate the rise in the labour force since 1931 because the unemployed are excluded and there were two million more unemployed in 1931 than in 1966. But it would seem to be a pretty futile exercise in the circumstances of 1931 to allocate the unemployed to particular

Table 2. 2 *Industrial Analysis of the Employed Population, Great Britain 1931–1966 (in thousands)*

Order	1931	% of 1931 total	1951	1961	1966	% of 1966 total	Change in % share 1931–66	Absolute change 1931–1966
I Agriculture, forestry and fishing	1,196	6·3	1,100	855	762	3·2	−3·1	−434
II Mining and quarrying	1,077	5·7	845	722	561	2·3	−3·4	−516
III Food, drink and tobacco	652	3·4	755	704	743	3·1	−0·3	−91
IV Chemical and allied trades	225	1·2	444	499	493	2·0	+0·8	268
V Metal manufacture	352	1·9	580	626	588	2·4	+0·5	+236
VI Engineering and electrical goods	973 }	5·1 }	1,925	2,031 }	2,185	9·0 }	+4·6	+1,390
VII Shipbuilding and marine engineering				237	178	0·7		
VIII Vehicles	414	2·2	964	838	809	3·3	+1·1	+395
IX Metal goods not elsewhere specified	316	1·7	479	525	562	2·3	+0·6	+246
X Textiles	1,116	5·9	1,000	790	721	3·0	−2·9	+395
XI Leather, leather goods and fur	80	0·4	75	60	58	0·2	−0·2	−22
XII Clothing and footwear	827	4·4	696	546	515	2·1	−2·3	−312
XIII Bricks, pottery, glass, cement, etc.	242	1·3	326	321	329	1·4	+0·1	+87
XIV Timber, furniture	284	1·5	304	304	299	1·2	−0·3	+15
XV Paper, printing and publishing	436	2·3	510	605	617	2·6	+0·3	+181
XVI Other manufacturing industries	159	0·8	258	295	327	1·4	+0·6	+168
XVII Construction	999	5·3	1,364	1,600	1,880	7·8	+2·5	+881
XVIII Gas, electricity and water	226	1·2	369	377	411	1·7	+0·5	+185
XIX Transport and communication	1,531	8·1	1,716	1,673	1,608	6·7	−1·4	+77
XX Distributive trades	2,729	14·4	2,683	3,189	3,245	13·4	+1·0	+516
XXI Insurance, banking and finance	322	1·7	333	572	656	2·7	+1·0	+334
XXII Professional and scientific services	975	5·2	1,013	2,120	2,499	10·3	+5·1	+1,524
XXIII Miscellaneous services	2,746	14·5	2,645	2,317	2,648	11·0	−3·5	−98
XXIV Public administration and defence	1,032	5·5	1,079	1,426	1,407	5·8	+0·3	+375
Total	18,908	100·0	22,134	24,041	24,168	99·6		

Source: For 1931–1951 *Annual Abstract of Statistics*, No. 89, 1952. For 1961 and 1966, *Census of Population*. The 1931 and 1951 figures have been roughly adjusted to the 1958 revised Standard Industrial Classification which was used for the Census in 1961 and 1966.

Note: The unemployed have been excluded. Unemployed exceed 2·5 million in 1931 but were less than 400,000 in 1951, 1961 and 1966. The 1931 figures related to persons fourteen years of age and over in 1931 and to persons fifteen years and over in subsequent years.

industries. It needs also to be noted that the classification is industrial and not occupational, i.e. a typist employed by the National Coal Board is allocated to Order II and a typist employed by an engineering firm is allocated to Order VI. Finally we have to remember that over a period of nearly forty years the product content of particular orders may change substantially though it continues to be called by the same name.

The working population is that part of the population above the school-leaving age which is available for work. The employed population is that part of the working population which is actually employed. The Census of Population analysis summarized in Table 2.2 includes about 1·7 employers and self-employed persons and these are distributed over the various industries in which they work.

The working population will vary as a proportion of the total population. That proportion of the population which is at present of working age will reflect past birth and death rates. If there is a rise in the proportion of children under the age of fifteen, if there is a tendency for more of those over fifteen to continue full-time education, and if there is an increased proportion of over sixty-fives in retirement, the working population will shrink as a proportion of total population. On the other hand, this proportion may rise as more married women take employment. The proportion of females aged fifteen to sixty-four in employment has risen from about thirty-six per cent before World War I to about forty-eight per cent in 1968.

The working population is expected to increase only by about three per cent up to 1981, i.e. 0·25 per cent per annum. The average number of hours worked per week, which fell from 46·3 in 1939 to 43·2 in 1968, will probably continue to fall. Under these circumstances the growth of some industries (in terms of manpower) will depend in large measure on the decline of others and on the willingness of workers to move and retrain.

Table 2.2 shows the sort of movement which has taken place between 1931 and 1966. The percentage of the employed population in extractive industry (Orders I and II) has fallen from 12 to 5·5 and the share of manufacturing industry plus construction and public utilities has increased to much the same extent—from 38 to 44. The share of what may be loosely termed the tertiary industries (Orders XIX to XXIV) has changed only slightly from 49 per cent to 49·9 per cent.

Within these very broad groups some quite spectacular changes have taken place. Engineering and electrical goods has increased its share of the total employed population (from five to nine per cent), and construction has improved its position from just over five to nearly eight per cent. (The use of changes in percentage shares conceals some important changes. For example, both chemicals and vehicles doubled their labour force 1931–66.) The sharpest decline in manufacturing industry was registered by textiles, leather, and clothing. Within the service industries, professional and scientific services have doubled their share of the employed population to over ten per cent whilst miscellaneous services have declined from 14·5 per cent to eleven per cent. Many of these changes can of course be pinpointed in further detail. The decline in textiles and miscellaneous services is very largely accounted for by reduced employment in cotton and in private domestic service respectively. The decline in mining and quarrying is almost entirely a reflection of the reduced employment in coal mining.

Table 2.3 shows the distribution of the employed population for 1961 and 1968. These are derived from the mid-year analysis produced each year by the Department of Employment and Productivity (DEP). They have the advantage of being more up-to-date but also have the serious disadvantage that the distribution between industrial orders is confined to employees. Where the self-employed are an important component of the labour force, as in agriculture and distribution, total employment is seriously under-rated in the DEP figures. Apart from this, the totals are not closely comparable with the Census of Population figures in Table 2.2 because of differences and changes in classification. Table 2.3 suggests that most of the trends previously discussed are continuing and even accelerating. One exception is that the expansion of the distributive trades has been reversed, probably as a result of the introduction of new methods of retailing. The expansion of the construction industry has also been slowed down but it may be doubted if this has much long-run significance.

Too much weight should not be attached to all this since the relative importance of different industries is not necessarily indicated by their manpower requirements. An industry which is being increasingly mechanized may be employing less labour whilst making an increasing contribution to the national output. The Census of Production gives figures of net output for each industry

Table 2. 3 *Distribution of Total Working Population Great Britain at Mid-June* (in thousands)

	1961	1968
Total working population	24,773	25,239
H.M. Forces	474	407
Registered wholly unemployed	255	506
Total in civil employment	24,044	24,326
Employers and self-employed	1,672	1,681
Total employees in employment	22,372	22,645
of whom in		
Agriculture, forestry, fishing	591	413
Mining and quarrying	733	486
Food, drink and tobacco	803	807
Chemical and allied industries	530	497
Metal manufacture	633	580
Engineering and electrical goods	2,121	2,281
Shipbuilding and marine engineering	243	188
Vehicles	891	803
Metal goods n.e.s.	558	566
Textiles	836	690
Leather, leathergoods and fur	63	56
Clothing and footwear	569	492
Bricks, pottery, glass and cement	344	351
Timber, furniture, etc.	287	321
Paper, printing and publishing	613	635
Other manufacturing industries	305	348
Construction	1,478	1,506
Gas, electricity and water	380	413
Transport and communication	1,702	1,584
Distributive trades	2,801	2,774
Financial, professional and scientific services	2,609	3,355
Miscellaneous services including catering	1,978	2,100
National and local government service	1,303	1,402

Sources: *Annual Abstract of Statistics,* 1968, Table 129.
   Employment and Productivity Gazette, p. 228, Table 3 (March 1969).
Note: Because of changes in methods of estimation the figures for 1961 and 1968 are not *strictly* comparable.

order and minimum list heading but the last complete set of figures available relate to 1958 and are now seriously out-of-date. Some notion of recent changes in physical output can be derived from the index of production. Table 2.4 compares employment and output changes for the more important industrial groups 1961–67.

One interesting feature of this table is that industries declining very sharply in terms of employment have declined much less in terms of output, i.e. output per head (productivity) has increased. In fact, both mining and textiles have shown increases in productivity substantially in excess of the national average. This probably reflects increased concentration on the lower-cost mines and establishments, and increased capital per worker as the industry contracts. But other industries which are not declining

Table 2. 4 *Output and Employment 1960–1968 (selected industries)*

Industry	% change in employment	% change in physical output	% change in output per head
Mining and quarrying	−35	−14	+35
Metal manufacture	− 6	+ 3	+10
Engineering and electrical	+10	+39	+26
Vehicles	−11	+12	+25
Textiles	−18	+17	+42
Gas, electricity and water	+11	+48	+ 4
All index of production industries	−2	+24	+27

Source: *Employment and Productivity Gazette,* Table 134 (June 1969).

substantially in terms of employment may also register significant gains in output, e.g. Chemical and Allied which is not included in Table 2.4. Employment has been falling slowly since 1960 but output had risen by over forty per cent between 1960 and 1968. This result appears to have been achieved by a large increase in the capital stock.

Differences in capital per head is an important reason why the relative importance of industries by employment may differ from changes measured in terms of output, though it only rarely happens that an industrial order which is declining in relative importance by employment is increasing in relative importance in terms of output. As we shall see in a later chapter capital is not

Table 2. 5 *Replacement Cost of Fixed Assets in Manufacturing 1955*

Order (SIC 1948)	Employment (thousands)	% of total	Total fixed assets (£ million)	% of total	Fixed assets per person employed £
III Non-metalliferous mining	322	3·9	441	2·9	1,370
IV Chemical and allied trades	415	5·0	1,796	11·8	4,330
V Metal manufacture	560	6·8	1,564	10·3	2,790
VI Engineering, shipbuilding and electrical goods	2,013	24·4	2,574	17·0	1,280
VII Vehicles	895	10·8	1,430	9·4	1,600
VIII, IX Other metal goods and precision instruments	608	7·4	699	4·5	1,100
X Textiles	940	11·4	2,616	17·2	2,790
XI, XII Leather and clothing	641	7·8	499	3·3	700
XIII Food, drink and tobacco	830	10·0	1,792	11·8	2,160
XIV Wood and cork products	276	3·3	248	1·6	900
XV Paper and printing	519	6·3	1,147	7·6	2,210
XVI Other manufacturing	241	2·9	374	2·5	1,550
Total	8,260	100·0	15,180	100·0	Av. 1,830

Note: Vehicles in the 1948 SIC included garage services.

easily measured and such measures as exist do not adequately reflect differences in age and quality of capital equipment. Redfern[1] and Barna[2] have produced estimates of the value of fixed capital employed in different industries. Redfern's figures are derived from annual figures of fixed capital formation and are based upon estimates of the average life of different types of asset and of price changes over time. These are now regularly up-dated and published in the annual *National Income and Expenditure Blue Book* published by HMSO. Barna has used the valuation of fixed assets for insurance purposes to estimate the replacement costs of fixed assets in the different orders of manufacturing industry in 1955. Both sets of estimates are subject to numerous qualifications and reservations and it would be unwise to place too much reliance on them although they probably register accurately enough the relative values of fixed capital in different industries. Although they are now somewhat out-of-date Barna's figures, which are the most suitable for our present purpose, are still of considerable interest and are reproduced in Table 2.5.

For five of these industrial orders (chemicals, metal manufacture, textiles, food, etc. and paper) their relative importance is much more marked in terms of capital than in terms of employment. These industries, with much higher than average fixed assets per head, also reveal in the periodic Censuses of Production higher than average net output per head (although textiles are an exception probably, because the high capital per head figure is partly a reflection of serious excess capacity occasioned by the rapid decline of the cotton industry). These are typically the industries which improve their ranking when industries are placed in order of proportional importance by output instead of employment.

2.4 Inter-industry connections

In recent years there has been a great improvement in statistics tracing the flow of transactions between industries. Each industry purchases goods from other industries. It also buys inputs of labour, capital, and risk bearing. These purchases can be regarded as the total inputs of each industry which, if we add indirect taxes, represent the gross market value of the output. They are set out in the columns of Table 2.6. Column 6 for example, shows that engineering and allied industries purchased £3,174 million of goods and services from other industries and

Table 2. 6 *Summary Input-Output Flow Table for 1963 (£ million)*

Purchases by → Sales by ↓

Sales by	Agric. Forestry and Fishing 1	Mining and quarrying 2	Food, drink and tobacco 3	Chemical and Allied 4	Metal Manufacture 5	Engineering and Allied 6	Textiles and Clothing 7	Other Manufacturing 8
1 Agric. Forestry and Fishing	—	5	571	167	26	29	28	9
2 Mining and quarrying	1	—	17	35	—	—	16	95
3 Food, drink and tobacco	315	—	—	—	—	—	2	3
4 Chemical and allied	111	18	135	26	106	259	33	164
5 Metal manufacture	—	48	5	85	76	1143	2	15
6 Engineering and allied	36	44	67	14	2	—	25	100
7 Textiles and clothing	4	8	13	92	15	86	—	104
8 Other manufacturing	61	49	91	11	8	438	16	—
9 Construction	30	18	13	65	60	33	7	14
10 Gas, electricity and water	16	28	42	398	255	133	35	83
11 Services and Public administration	250	96	440	497	308	816	159	492
12 Imports	157	6	605	2	62	213	463	441
13 Sales by final buyers for one another	—	—	3	—	—	24	3	3
14 Total goods and services	981	321	2002	1520	918	3174	789	1523
15 Expenditure Taxes	−270	19	1353	46	36	98	28	69
16 Income from employment	353	592	545	412	501	2759	769	1165
17 Gross Profits	605	151	464	322	268	953	292	407
18 Total input	1669	1073	4364	2300	1723	6984	1878	3164

| | Construction 9 | Gas, Electricity and Water 10 | Services and Public Administration 11 | Final Buyers | | | | Total output |
				Persons 12	Public Authorities 13	Capital[1] Formation 14	Exports 15	16
1	—	—	—	965	16	33	42	1669
2	47	345	44	209	26	−2	52	1073
3	—	—	101	3584	43	55	226	4364
4	132	54	213	329	136	−9	491	2300
5	124	29	28	—	1	13	289	1723
6	182	70	683	867	817	1890	2042	6984
7	8	—	87	1076	25	13	438	1878
8	417	25	832	692	75	53	308	3164
9	—	8	117	400	303	2173	15	3150
10	9	—	236	680	81	131	4	1603
11	247	161	—	8156	489	451	1667	17077
12	150	18	781	1689	163	293	176	5960
13	2	—	35	31	−145	−87	67	—
14	1318	710	3157	18678	5030	5007	5817	50945
15	53	68	435	1371	52	114	—	3472
16	1364	371	9299	—	—	—	—	18120
17	415	454	4186	—	—	—	—	8517
18	3150	1603	17077	20049	5082	5121	5817	81054

Source: Derived from *Economic Trends*, pages XXVI & XXVII (1966). To reduce and simplify the table some groups have been aggregated and totals will not necessarily add.

[1] Includes stocks and fixed capital formation.

from foreigners (imports). The most substantial item was purchases amounting to £1,143 million from the metal manufacturing industry. If we add purchases of factor inputs (wages and gross profits) and indirect taxes the gross value of engineering output comes out at £6,984 million.

When similar columns have been filled in for all industries we have a matrix showing the purchases of each industry from all others by columns and sales of each industry to all others by rows. If the table is to show the sales of all products then the rows have to be extended since some output will not be sold to other industries but to final buyers or exported. (We are not here concerned with national income accounting aspects of Table 2.6. Gross domestic product at factor cost is the sum of rows 16 and 17 (£26·6 million). Alternatively it is the value of final output (the sum of columns 12 to 15) minus imports (row 12) and indirect taxes (row 15).) The main source of information for the compilation of these input-output tables is the Census of Production which requires returns of purchases and sales from firms in production industries (manufacturing, mining, construction and public utilities). Table 2.6 is a slightly reduced version of a small fifteen industry input-output table produced partly on the basis of the Census of Production 1963 and partly by up-dating an earlier table produced for 1954. A more elaborate table with twenty-eight industry groups has been published[3] with the additional refinement that imports purchased by each industry are distributed over the various industry groups to which they would be classified if produced at home. Thus imports by food, drink and tobacco are shown as products mainly classifiable to food, agriculture or chemicals.

Obviously the information derived from these tables becomes more valuable as the industry groups become more finely divided. They are invaluable for planning purposes since we are enabled to estimate the effects of an expansion of output by one industry on the output of other industries (e.g. an increase in the output of *A* will result in increased purchases from (output of) *B* which, in its turn, will react on the output of other industries— and so on) and on the balance of payments. Also they enable some estimate to be made of the effects of price increases by one industry as they ripple through the economy. There are some obvious limitations on their use. Estimates of effects of output expansion will almost invariably assume that the input-output relations (technical coefficients) will remain the same. That is to say, if the table shows that the production of each ton of steel requires the purchase and use of one hundredweight of coal, then it will be assumed that this relation will continue to hold if an additional million tons of steel are produced. In fact, output expansion may permit the introduction of new techniques which will change the technical coefficients. Another limitation is that industry groups are not likely to be sufficiently narrowly defined to equate with reasonably homogeneous commodities.

Input-output statistics are now being rapidly improved in this country.[4] Even the comparatively simple statistics being produced at present are of considerable interest to students of industrial organization. The nature and extent of the dependence of one industry upon others and differences in labour-cost components will suggest a great deal about possibilities and limitations on its growth. The close linkage of engineering to metals helps to explain the tendency of these industries to locate close to each other. The limited links of textiles and clothing with other industries and its heavy dependence on imports and exports may throw some light on the swiftness of its decline in an economy which has been fully employed almost continuously since the end of World War II. (Expansion of other industries being less likely to boost output in textiles and clothing whilst draining the latter of surplus labour.) In the future it may be possible to discover whether differences in, and changes in, technical coefficients can be related to differences and changes in the size of establishments and firms.

2.5 Size of establishments and firms

Statistics illustrating the size of establishments are published in the Census of Production reports, but recent figures are not available from this source. Table 2.7 gives comparable information respecting the size of plants for all factory trades (Orders III to XVI) in 1935 and 1954 taken from these reports, and for 1961 as published by the Department of Employment and Productivity.[5] The size of a plant is measured here by the number of employees.

It will be observed that the great majority of establishments are very small (i.e. employing less than ten persons) but they employ only a small and diminishing proportion of the total man-power employed—less than four per cent in 1954. At the other extreme

Table 2. 7

Size in workers employed	1935		1954		1961	
	No. of plants	No. of workers (000's)	No. of plants	No. of workers (000's)	No. of plants	No. of workers (000's)
1–10	132,338	536	61,319	299	n.a.	n.a.
11–24	16,490	279	16,832	275	12,571	222
25–49	12,542	437	14,726	518⎱	27,478	1,420
50–99	8,582	602	10,826	760⎰		
100–199	5,754	805	7,162	1,001⎱	12,213	2,552
200–499	3,996	1,210	5,076	1,553⎰		
500–999	1,047	716	1,534	1,048	1,693	1,163
1,000+	533	1,106	1,054	2,476	1,206	2,821
Total	181,282	5,694	118,529	7,930	—	—
Total (over 11 workers employed)	48,944	5,158	57,210	7,631	55,161	8,178

large establishments employing over 1,000 in 1954 comprised less than one per cent of the total number of establishments but employed over thirty per cent of the total manpower in 1954.

The table shows quite clearly that the size of establishments is tending to increase. The crude average of employees per establishment employing more than ten rose from 106 in 1935, to 133 in 1954, and to 148 in 1961. Plants employing more than 1,000 employees employed nineteen per cent of all workers in 1931 and thirty-five per cent of all workers in 1961. In the latter year very large plants employing more than 2,000 workers accounted for over twenty per cent of the labour force.

The average size of plants in 1961 was highest in vehicles (340), metal manufacture (280), chemical (190), and engineering (185). The reasons for this are probably mainly technical. Except for engineering none of these industries have been growing in terms of employment in recent years although they have all increased their proportionate share of the labour force since 1931. In terms of physical output only chemicals and engineering have grown at above average rates since 1958. The statement that large plants are typical of growth industries must therefore be regarded with some reserve. Neither is it true to say that the industries with below-average size of plants (e.g. clothing (80), paper, etc. (110), bricks, etc. (120)) are slow growing. Paper and bricks, etc., on their performance in recent years must be classified as growth industries on any criterion.

Inspection of the size distribution of plants for different industries does not reveal much evidence of a 'typical' size of plant. Using the size classification used for the 1961 data in Table 2.7, only in textiles (plants employing 100–499) and in metals and vehicles (plants employing more than 1,000) did any particular size of plant employ more than fifty per cent of the labour force. For most industries employees were surprisingly evenly spread across size categories in excess of ninety-nine employees. Across manufacturing industry as a whole, as we have already noted, thirty-five per cent of aggregate employment is provided by establishments employing more than 1,000. But over thirty per cent is provided by firms employing 100–499 employees. Thus there is certainly no typical size of plant in manufacturing industry and very little evidence of it in particular industries. But if the size of plant is dominated by technical considerations we should not expect to find any evidence of typical size of plants in industrial orders which are very widely defined. If an industry is defined in terms of one fairly homogeneous commodity (e.g. cement) there is much less variability of size of plants.

We return, however, to the point that measurement of size by employees is open criticism. It is no more a valid indicator of size than net assets and for most purposes less valid than output. A pre-war enquiry[6] suggested that in terms of employees the prevailing size of plant in US manufacturing industries was about the same as in their British counterparts. But since American productivity in manufacturing at this time was about two-and-a-half times that of Britain it is clear that in terms of output US plants were, on average, much larger. More recent enquiries[7] suggest that the average size of the largest twenty plants in a number of US manufacturing industries was about twenty per cent higher in terms of employment than in the corresponding industries in Great Britain. But capital per head in manufacturing is believed to be about double that of the UK.[8]

This suggests that a different picture of relative size of plants between countries may emerge depending on the size criterion used. It does not follow that similar differences will emerge in a study of the size of plants within the same industry in a particular country. One would not expect it to happen except when there are marked differences in capital used per head between different plants. This may occur where an industry is composed of mechanized units producing large outputs of standardized products and firms employed in producing specialities by less capital intensive methods.

Not much interest attaches to a size analysis of firms, i.e. corporate bodies comprising one or more establishments trading under a particular name. (The average number of plants per unit in 1951 was only 1·3 but varied a great deal between large and small units.)

We are more interested in those decision-taking entities which we described in the previous chapter as enterprises, units or undertakings. The relative size of enterprises in the economy as a whole or in manufacturing industry generally is of some significance. If relatively few enterprises control the economy, decision taking is concentrated in few hands and the possibilities of abuse of power and of serious mistakes of economic judgment would appear to be increased. Procedures may become more bureaucratic, industrial relations made more difficult through inadequate communication, and control of the enterprise by its owners (the ordinary shareholders) becomes more difficult. The risks should not be exaggerated however. Although most very large firms have a long history, some do not retain leading positions in the size league table for very long.

No up-to-date figures of the size of enterprises are available. In 1958, 1,052 enterprises (with 100 or more employees) controlled forty-nine per cent of total employment in the Census of Production industries and produced about fifty-five per cent of total net output. This concentration is more marked in terms of capital. In 1968 about 908 companies controlled eighty per cent of the total net assets of UK manufacturing, of which the twenty-eight largest controlled about forty per cent of total net assets.[9]

Also, in this connection we must not forget the presence of the large public corporations which control the nationalized industries and the fact that many 'firms' are *de facto* under joint control although they do not come within the terms of the definition of enterprise.

Economists are generally more interested in the control of particular industries by a few enterprises because of the possibilities of market control and abuse of monopoly power which this conjures up. For this purpose enterprises which span several industries are measured for size in respect only of those of its establishments which are classified to the particular industry and to this extent the enterprises which are alleged to dominate particular industries are rather fictitious. We now turn to a brief review of the extent and significance of industrial concentration in this sense.

2.6 Concentration of control of industry

Pioneer work for Great Britain was made in this field by Leak and Maizels.[10] A central feature of this work was the provision of concentration ratios for about 300 Census of Production trades and sub-trades (generally defined as the specialist producers of a product or group of products) based on the results of the 1935 Census. Concentration was measured by the concentration ratio defined as the percentage share of each Census trade controlled by the three largest business enterprises (units, i.e. firm plus subsidiaries) in the trade. This share was measured in terms of net output or employment though there is no reason why it should not be measured in terms of other size characteristics (e.g. net assets) if the information is available. The ratio is most generally measured in terms of employment because the information is more easily available and unless otherwise stated concentration ratios quoted here will be expressed in terms of employment. One complication is that the concentration ratio will vary according to the size criterion used. They are generally highest when measured in terms of asset values, rather lower when measured in terms of net output and lowest when measured in terms of employment. Cases of wide divergence are rare but can occur. In 1951 mineral oil refining had an unemployment concentration ratio of 85 but this was only 35 in terms of net output.

The Leak and Maizels report is still worth reading but since it is now very much out-of-date it will be more convenient to summarize the results of a follow-up enquiry by Evely and Little[11] which was based on data derived from the 1951 Census of Production and covered 220 trades with an aggregate employment in 1951 of nearly 6·4 million or sixty-three per cent of the total employment in Census of Production trades.

The concentration ratios show a very wide spread. At one extreme there are sub-trades like valves and cathode-ray tubes which show a concentration ratio of eighty-five per cent and sugar and glucose with eighty-four per cent; at the other extreme are trades such as the repairing of motor vehicles and cycles with four per cent and woven cotton cloth with five per cent. Of the 220 trades fifty had a high concentration ratio (sixty-seven per cent and over), sixty-nine had a medium concentration ratio (thirty-four to sixty-six per cent), and 101 had a low concentration ratio of thirty-three per cent and under. The high concentration trades accounted for ten per cent, the medium for twenty-four per cent and the low for sixty-six per cent of the total employment in these trades.

This suggests that only a small sector of British industry was markedly monopolistic whilst much the greater part was strongly competitive. For reasons explained later a more sophisticated appreciation is possible if we take into account not only the concentration ratio but also the total number of firms in the trade and their size ratio, i.e. the average size of the three largest firms divided by the average size of the rest of the unit. A trade is said to have many units if it has more than thirty and few if it has thirty or less; it is considered to have a large size ratio if this is sixteen or over and a small size ratio if it is less than this.

Table 2.8 shows the distribution of trades according to degrees of concentration, number of units, and size ratio. It modifies the impression given by consideration of concentration ratios alone. A substantial degree of monopoly is most likely in those twenty trades (with 3·3 per cent of total employment) which have a high concentration ratio, large size ratio, and a small number of enterprises. A little less certainly one may say that monopoly is also likely in the thirteen trades (with four per cent of total employment) with high concentration-ratio, large size ratios, and many units. Conditions seem most likely to approach those of perfect competition in the sixty trades (with 20·8 per cent of total employment) with low concentration, small size ratios and many units and perhaps also in the twenty-nine (with 6·4 per cent of total employment) with medium concentration, small size ratio and many units. In all the other categories, accounting for ninety-seven trades and 67·5 per cent of total employment some degree of oligopolistic behaviour seems most likely to exist because the number of units is small or because a large size ratio indicates the likelihood of dominance or leadership by a few large firms. The suggestion that oligopolistic competition of one form or another is the most prevalent type in British industry confirms the

Table 2. 8 *Distribution of Trades According to Degree of Concentration, Number and Size Ratio of Units, 1951*

Concentration Category	Large Size Ratio of Units (16 and over)				Small Size Ratio of Units (15 and under)				Total	
	Few Units (30 and under)		Many Units (31 and over)		Few Units (30 and under)		Many Units (31 and over)			
	No. of trades	% of total employment	No. of trades	% of total employment	No. of trades	% of total employment	No. of trades	% of total employment	No. of trades	% of total employment
High (67% and over)	20	3·3	13	4·0	17	3·4	—	—	50	10·7
Medium (34–66%)	—	—	25	17·5	15	2·0	29	6·4	69	25·9
Low (33% and under)	—	—	40	42·6	—	—	60	20·8	100	63·4
Total	20	3·3	78	64·1	32	5·4	89	27·2	219	100·0

Source: Evely and Little, *op. cit*, p. 67.

impression of most observers, but the seemingly high comparative importance of fairly competitive trades (from a structural point of view) is rather surprising.

An attempt was made by Evely and Little to arrange the large number of trades into industrial groups (based on, but not identical with, the SIC orders) to obtain some indication of group or order concentration. This was derived by weighting the employment concentration ratio for each trade in a group by the numbers employed in that trade. The results are given in Table 2.9. They need to be interpreted with some caution but they probably represent accurately enough the relative degrees of concentration between major groups of industries. Chemicals, electrical engineering, and vehicles appear to be the most highly concentrated whilst at the other end of the scale are building, contracting and civil engineering, clothing and footwear, and woollen and worsted.

This suggests that growth is associated with concentration. *A priori* reasoning gives little clear guidance. It is arguable that growth creates opportunities for the more efficient firms to get bigger and to come to dominate a trade. On the other hand, market expansion will create opportunities for newcomers which will tend to reduce concentration. Stagnation and decline of industries will probably produce some consolidation but there is no reason to suppose that a reduction in the number of units will or will not exceed the rate of reduction in output and employment. The evidence had been differently assessed by different writers. Shepherd[12] has observed that most of the increase in concentration between 1951–58 was due to increased concentration in certain expanding industries and that growth and increased concentration were directly related. George[13] on the other hand finds that forty-two out of sixty-three industries conform to the hypothesis that growth is inversely related to increased concentration and concludes that raising the rate of growth of the economy tends to offset any long-run trend towards increased concentration.

There is no clear indication that concentration increased between 1931 and 1951, but it does seem reasonably certain that it increased between 1951 and 1958. In a comparison of 139 industries in 1951 and 120 in 1958, Shepherd quotes the figures produced in Table 2.10 showing the percentage of total employment and net output produced by industries in various

Table 2. 9 *Concentration of Employment by Trade Groups, 1951*

Trade Group	Total group employment (000s)	Number of sample trades in group	Total employment of sample trades (000s)	Aggregated employment of three largest units in each trade (000s)	Group degree of concentration
Chemical and allied trades	376·7	16	335·8	170·2	51
Electrical engineering and electrical goods	614·3	8	341·1	164·1	48
Vehicles	767·5	8	443·9	181·9	41
Iron and steel and non-ferrous metals	548·8	15	511·6	199·7	39
Drink and tobacco	177·1	7	172·0	62·4	36
Mining and quarrying, mining products	374·4	21	312·2	108·5	35
Shipbuilding and non-electrical engineering	1,115·3	20	754·6	235·7	31
Food	495·4	18	453·5	136·4	30
Other metal industries	539·6	27	402·5	116·8	29
Other textiles	510·2	18	360·2	98·8	27
Paper and printing	466·1	10	421·6	87·8	21
Cotton	290·9	3	246·0	51·6	21
Other manufacturing and service trades	689·0	23	539·2	105·2	60
Woollen and worsted	192·4	6	164·3	29·8	18
Clothing and footwear	559·7	17	476·9	65·7	14
Building, contracting and civil engineering	1,006·1	3	433·3	53·8	12
Total	8,735·5	220	6,368·7	1,868·4	

Source: Evely and Little, *op. cit*, p. 62.

Table 2. 10 *Concentration 1951–1958*

Concentration ratio	% of employment given by industries with concentration ratios shown		% of net output given by industries with concentration ratios shown	
	1951	1958	1951	1958
80–100	1·6	5·8	2·0	6·7
70–100	4·4	12·4	5·6	14·2
60–100	5·2	14·6	6·5	16·8
50–100	10·8	18·9	12·7	21·7

concentration categories. Later figures are not available but it seems probable that the take-over boom of the nineteen-sixties produced another sharp increase in concentration.

It is, however, necessary to utter a few words of warning about regarding this as evidence of increased monopoly power and behaviour. As we shall see in Chapter 5 one (but not the only) aspect of monopoly is a scarcity of sellers of a single product or closely substitutable group of products (though this is not, of course, a certain predictor of monopoly behaviour). But, as we have seen in Chapter 1, the products which define a trade or industry are more likely to be linked by technological considerations than by substitutability in use. Also, in the process of classifying establishments to trades, a 100 per cent degree of exclusiveness and specialization is almost impossible to achieve. It follows that if the largest three firms control (say) ninety per cent of net output of a trade (concentration ratio of ninety) they do not necessarily have a high degree of monopoly power in respect of some single differentiated commodity. On these grounds Evely and Little excluded some trades from their sample.

The firms in question are measured for size only in respect of the establishments classified to the trade. But large firms which span several trades may exercise considerable market power. A large vertically-integrated firm, for example, may restrict competition in a trade by virtue of its control of the raw materials. Moreover the degree of monopoly may be as much affected by the size ratio and number of firms as by the proportion of output or employment controlled by the three largest firms. If the other firms are a large number of small firms the extent of competition is likely to be less than if the remaining firms are few and nearly as big as 'the big three'.

There are a host of other objections to regarding high concentration ratios as unequivocal evidence of monopoly. Clearly the concentration ratio is raised as trades are more narrowly defined so that it is fairly easy to present a picture of high concentration. Also, if transport costs are heavy in relation to the price of the product, some firms may be in a strong local monopoly position in spite of concentration ratios being low for the trade as a whole. Finally, concentration ratios take no account of firms which are *de facto* under unified control but where the parent does not own a majority of the equity, or of associations of independent firms jointly controlling some aspect of the marketing of the product (cartels).

2.7 The location of industry

There are obvious limits to the extent to which firms and the occupied population of a country will locate themselves in a particular region. Agriculture, coal-mining and tourism are likely to be as widely dispersed as good agricultural land, easily worked seams of good quality coal, and areas of outstanding natural beauty. Some dispersal of the working population is therefore inevitable. This is reinforced by service industries and public utilities which have, more or less, to produce goods and services at or near the point of consumption. But for the general run of manufacturing industry there is no reason why it should not be heavily concentrated in a particular place and many sound economic reasons why it should. (This geographical concentration must be carefully distinguished from the concentration of control referred to in the previous section.) Where there is a heavy concentration of a particular industry or inter-connected group of industries external economies of one kind or another develop so that, if markets are favourable, it achieves a state of self-generating growth. As more manufacturing industry is attracted to a particular place, service industries are attracted and public utilities, educational and cultural services expand. It becomes more attractive as a market for consumer goods and more manufacturing industries move into the area. A point is reached however where increased congestion and rising land values puts some curb on further growth and the state may have to intervene to actively promote a wider dispersal of industry.

These issues are further explored in Chapters 4 and 8. Here we are concerned mainly with the facts. But the preceding paragraph explains in very general terms why economic activity is not evenly spread across the country—why there are pronounced tendencies for heavily industrialized areas to develop but which are rarely strong enough to completely de-populate any part of the country. It also explains why discussion of location problems is dominated by analysis of the factors which determine the location of manufacturing industry—or more precisely, industries which usually supply markets wider than the region itself.

Great changes have taken place in the distribution of the population during the past fifty years. Between 1911 and 1958 there was a decline in the percentages of the population resident in Scotland ($-1\cdot4$), Wales ($-0\cdot7$), North-West England ($-1\cdot3$), Northern England ($-0\cdot4$) and the East and West Ridings ($-0\cdot6$), but an increase in the percentage shares of the Midlands ($+1\cdot2$), Eastern England ($+1\cdot9$), Southern England ($+1\cdot2$) and South-Western England ($+0\cdot1$). There has therefore been an extensive shift of population from the Western and Northern parts of Great Britain to the Southern and Eastern parts of the country. The proportional importance of London and the South-East declined slightly ($-0\cdot3$) over this period but this is probably explained by enforced dispersal of industry during World War II, government policy to restrict the further growth of the London area and improvements in transport which enables people to live further away from their work.

The decline in proportional importance of the Northern and Western parts of the country has been largely due to the decline in the coal, cotton, and shipbuilding industries on which our industrial predominance in the nineteenth century largely depended. The South-East benefited from the expansion of foot-loose light industries attracted by the large London market, and the Midlands from the rapid expansion of engineering, metals and vehicles which were extensively located there. Table 2.11 shows recent changes in, and the present distribution of, the population.

There are two features of note in this table. In the first place it reveals the extent to which the population is now concentrated in the Midlands and South-East regions which now contain nearly fifty per cent of the total population of Great Britain. Secondly, in spite of the government's efforts to control movement to the

Table 2. 11 *Resident Home Population in New Standard Regions** (thousands)

Region	1961	1967	Percentage change
North	3,249	3,330	+2·5
Yorks. and Humberside	4,596	4,783	+4·1
North-West	6,547	6,756	+3·2
East Midlands	3,139	3,296	+5·1
West Midlands	4,763	5,067	+6·4
East Anglia	1,490	1,412	+8·1
South-East	16,351	17,186	+5·1
South-West	3,436	3,652	+6·3
Wales	2,635	2,710	+2·9
Scotland	5,184	5,187	negligible
Great Britain	51,390	53,576	+4·2

* Abstract of Regional Statistics (HMSO) No. 4, 1968, Table 5. The new standard regions do not coincide with the old standard regions in the preceding paragraph. Definition of the regions will be found in Appendix I of the source cited.

South and Midlands (see Chapter 7) all these regions have increased their population by more than the national average. Although no region has suffered an absolute decline in population it is clear that the 'peripheral areas' are still relatively slow-growing in terms of population—this being particularly true of Scotland. It does not follow of course that Government policies have been ineffective. Without government intervention the movement to the south would almost certainly have been far greater.

If we study the movement of the working population a similar pattern emerges. The real causes of this movement are rather obscure. But one factor has undoubtedly been the concentration of more rapidly growing industries in the Midlands and the South. Table 2.12 illustrates the extent to which each area specializes in particular industries. The percentage of the total employed population of each area which was engaged in each industry in 1959 has been calculated and this can be compared with the percentage of the employed population of Great Britain as a whole engaged in that industry. In order to simplify the table only mining, agriculture and manufacturing industry have been covered and the percentages have only been reproduced where the regional figure for an industry exceeds the Great Britain figure. It must be emphasized that the table shows the extent to which

51

Table 2. 12 *Regional Specialization in Particular Industries, 1959*

Short description of industry	London & S.E.	E. & S.	S.W.	Mids.	N. Mids.	E. & W. Ridings	N.W.	N.	Scot-land	Wales	Great Britain
Agriculture		6·9	5·9		4·7				4·8		3·0
Mining					8·7	7·9		13·0	4·7	13·0	3·8
Non-metalliferous mining products				4·0	1·7	1·7					1·5
Chemicals							4·4	4·5		2·7	2·4
Metal manufacture				6·3	3·8	5·0		4·4			2·7
Engineering and electrical goods	10·0	9·3		11·2			9·5			8·8	8·8
Vehicles		6·3	6·7	10·1	4·1						4·0
Other metal goods				9·1		3·5					2·3
Shipbuilding		1·6	1·8				1·5	4·9	3·4		1·3
Textiles					7·5	11·0	10·3		4·9		3·9
Clothing	2·6				5·9	3·3	3·4				2·4
Food, drink, tobacco			4·8			3·7	4·4		4·5		3·6
Wood	1·5	1·8									1·3
Paper	4·1	2·9	2·7				2·7				2·6

Figures show percentages of total employed population of each area devoted to each industry in May 1959.

Source: *Ministry of Labour Gazette* (May 1960). This Table is based on the Standard Industrial Classification as revised in 1958.

regions specialize in particular industries and not the extent to which the industries are highly localized.

The degree of specialization is shown by the excess of the regional over the national percentages for each industry and not by the number of industries for which such differences are shown. London and the South-East for example shows 'specialization' in only four industry groups and in neither case is the degree of specialization very marked. London's expansion is largely explained by the growth of non-manufacturing sectors and by the fact that the area is not specialized in any line of industry which has been declining.

The specialization of Wales and the North in the declining mining industry and of Yorkshire and the North-West in the declining textile industry is at once apparent. So is the specialization of the Midlands in engineering, vehicles, and metal manufacture which until comparatively recent years have been rapidly expanding industry groups in terms of employment, for details see Section 2.2. But clearly this is only a partial explanation of shifting industrial location. The Midlands have benefited as much from the absence of specialization in declining industries as from the presence of specialization in expanding industries. Scotland's dismal experience is probably explained as much by the absence of expanding industries as by heavy concentration of declining industries.

Table 2.13 shows for 1959 the extent to which industries are localized in particular regions. It shows the percentage of the total employed in each industry which is employed in each region. Every region will have some workers in each industrial group but in order to bring out the salient features of industrial localization only percentages above ten have been recorded. This table is also confined to mining, agriculture and manufacturing industry. It is important to remember that the figures are percentages—a high degree of localization is not very significant for overall location of industry if the total employment in the industry is small. The fact that thirty per cent of the leather and fur industry (total employment about 60,000) is located in the London area does not explain much about the size and growth of the region.

The industrial predominance of the South-East and North-West is well illustrated by the Table. Both regions employ more than ten per cent of the total employment in nearly all the industries listed—the big difference bieng the heavy localization

Table 2. 13 *Localization of Industries, 1959*

Short description of industry	London & S.E.	E. & S.	S.W.	Mids.	N. Mids.	E. & W. Ridings	N.W.	N.	Scotland	Wales	Great Britain
Agriculture	11	24	11		11				16		100
Mining					16	17	14	20	12	15	100
Non-metalliferous mining products	17			26							100
Chemicals	22						25	11		14	100
Metal manufacture				13	16		14				100
Engineering and electrical goods	29	11		14			12				100
Vehicles	16	17		25			10				100
Other metal goods	18			38		13	15				100
Shipbuilding		14						23	26		100
Textiles					13	24	36		12		100
Leather	30						17				100
Clothing	26	10			16	11	18				100
Food, drink, tobacco	23						16		12		100
Wood	32	14					11				100
Paper	40	12					14				100
Other manufacturing	31			13			20				100

Figures show percentage of total employed in each industry, employed in each region.
Source: *Ministry of Labour Gazette* (May 1960). This Table is based on the Standard Industrial Classification as revised in 1958.

of textiles in the North-West and the comparative absence of mining, textiles and shipbuilding in the South-East. There are few exceptions to the rule that industries declining in terms of employment are most heavily localized in the Western and Northern regions and expanding industries like engineering, metal goods and paper are most heavily localized in the Midlands and the South. It is not a simple matter to measure the degree of localization since this can be affected by relative size of regions (e.g. about twenty-two per cent of the population is in the (old) London and South-East region) and the classification of industries. Of the industry groups listed in Table 2.13 only four can be said to be highly localized in the sense that fifty per cent or more of its employment is provided by only two regions—textiles, metal goods, paper, and miscellaneous manufacturing. Professor Sargant Florence has devised a co-efficient of localization based on the deviations of the distribution of workers in the various trades and in various areas, from the distribution over the whole of the industry and over the whole country.[14] He applied this to 1935 Census trades and found that the most highly localized industries were jute, tinplate, lace, linen, and cotton weaving. A post-war enquiry by Nicholson[15] using 1948 data has generally confirmed these results—most of the trades with location co-efficients of more than 0·6 being in textiles, tinplate, cutlery, china, needles, jewellery, and steel sheets.

The shifts of population between regions as various industries have built up or reduced their labour force has obviously had its effect on the general economic performance of regions. Unemployment and net outward migration has been higher in the regions to the west and north of the country—the so-called peripheral areas. Because there is no excess demand for labour the level of earnings tends to be lower in those areas which in turn affects the prosperity of service trades (the level of earnings is also affected by the regional mix of industry since wage rates are higher in some industries than others). Because there is on balance an outward movement of population the amount of new construction is reduced. The average age of the social capital (e.g. schools, housing, roads, etc.) begins to rise and the area begins to look run-down and unattractive. It would appear that regional growth breeds growth and regional decline breeds decline. Table 2.14 sets out some comparisons of regional performance between 1961 and 1968.

Table 2. 14 Some Regional Comparisons, 1961–68[1]

Region	Unemployment exc. school leavers. 1961–66 av.	Weekly household income 1961–6 av.	Male earnings 1964–7 av.[3]	Av. industry adjusted male hourly earnings April 1967[4]	Employee activity rates Male	Employee activity rates Female	5 year inter-regional net migration per 100 population 1966[5]	Growth rate of population of working age including migrational 1961–6 difference from G.B. = 2·7
North	185	84	93	99	96²	85²	−1·6	−0·5
Yorks & Humberside	75²	95	94	96	104	100	−0·4	−0·5
North-West	120	95	97	99	103	107	−0·3	−1·0
East Midlands	65²	98	95 }	} 102	99	96	+1·5	+1·4
West Midlands	65	109	102 }		106	109	−0·4	+2·1
East Anglia	90	93	91 }	} 102	102	106	{ +3·5	+3·5
South-East	65	112	108 }		102	106	{ −0·1	+0·5
South-West	100	92	92	96	85	87	3·1	1·0
Wales	165	90	96	98	90	74	0·0	0·8
Scotland	205	94	92	98	100	88	1·7	3·9
Great Britain	100	100	100	100	100	100	—	zero

[1] Derived from *The Task Ahead* Table 9·1 (London, HMSO, 1969). Except for last two columns the figures are regional relatives G.B.=100.

[2] Not strictly comparable owing to boundary changes.

[3] Av. annual earnings of men of working age who worked for a full year.

[4] Av. male hourly earnings adjusted for regional differences in proportion to workers in industries by Minimum List Headings.

[5] Excludes those under five years of age.

It is this variation of economic performance which has persuaded Governments of the necessity to intervene with the object of increasing the level of activity in the peripheral areas. Clearly there can be some waste of economic resources if regional disparities of earnings, unemployment, growth of population, etc., become too pronounced. We shall be reviewing problems and policies in this field in Chapter 8.

2.8 Ownership and control of industry

Ownership and control of industry are obviously related. By ownership of industry we understand ownership of the real capital assets involved in productive processes and for legal purposes this is vested (except in the case of the one-man business) in the corporate body concerned, whether it be a limited company, public corporation or co-operative society. If, however, we require to know the ownership of industry in personal terms, then in the most important case of the limited company, we look to those who have contributed the risk capital—the ordinary shareholders and perhaps, in certain circumstances, preference shareholders as well. They take the risks and reap the benefits or suffer the losses involved in operating the business, and, in theory at any rate, they exercise control of the business. Knowledge of ownership is mainly desired because of the light which it may throw on control. If ownership is highly concentrated, then control is also likely to be concentrated with all the risks and dangers we have previously seen to be entailed in this. (It does not, however, necessarily follow that, if ownership is widely dispersed, control will not be concentrated.) This is not the only reason for the interest taken in investigating the personal ownership of industry. High concentration of ownership in a few hands will, for example, result in an extremely uneven distribution of property incomes. But we are not much concerned with this aspect of the matter here.

We have previously estimated that about twenty-five per cent of the economy is in the public sector, i.e. the capital assets are communally owned and politically controlled. Approximately seventeen per cent is in the hands of self employed persons, sole traders, and partnerships where, generally speaking, the owner of the capital is in effective control of its use. We may reckon therefore that for something like forty per cent of the economy ownership of capital is likely to be widely diffused and theoretically coterminous with control. But it must be emphasized that these figures are very tentative. Our earlier estimates of the public and private sectors were based on either employment or product. The division of capital assets between the sectors is likely to be very different.

We must now consider the private sector of the economy. Here there are formidable obstacles to any investigation of the ownership of industry in personal terms. There were in 1961 just over 400,000 companies with share capital, but about 390,000 of these were private companies about which nothing much can be done, since there is no information available. Fortunately this is not as serious as it sounds because, although private companies are overwhelmingly preponderant in numbers, they are outweighed in aggregate importance by the public companies. Public companies quoted on the stock exchange with assets of over £0·5 million or income of £50,000 per annum or more were responsible for about seventy-five per cent of all gross trading profits in manufacturing construction and distribution in 1966. This suggests that the absence of information concerning ownership of private companies is not entirely crippling.

So far as public companies are concerned we can, in theory at least, discover the holders of ordinary shares by consulting the shareholders' lists. But a full census of the share registers of over 10,000 public companies is an almost impossible task, especially as the number of shareholders in some large public companies runs into hundreds of thousands. The task would be further complicated by the fact that to obtain the number of individual shareholders it would be necessary to eliminate the inevitable duplication of investors who have holdings in more than one company. Still more seriously, shareholdings are often registered in the names of nominees, thus concealing the identity of the beneficial owners, whilst the most important shareholders are often other companies which in their turn are partly owned by others. Any impressions conveyed by this section must, therefore, be regarded as extremely tentative.

In spite of the difficulties, several useful studies have been made in this field. One of these,[16] published in 1951, was based on an analysis of shareholdings in the thirty public companies whose equity shares figure in the Financial Times Ordinary Industrial Share Index. Their aggregate nominal capital was about £347 million and their total market value at the time of the inquiry about £875 million. On the basis of a one in twenty sample of the shareholdings in these companies, it was concluded there were about 1,113,000 holdings of the £347 million nominal capital. This suggested an average holding of £312 nominal (£788 as market prices), whilst eighty per cent of all holdings were less than £300 nominal and ninety per cent less than £500 nominal.

A more recent investigation[17] was based upon the slowly-growing practice by some companies of publishing details of their share ownership in their annual reports. This showed that for twenty-five companies whose nominal equity capital in 1958 was £480 million, there were 858,691 shareholders with an average nominal holding of £558. (This sample, unlike the one above, excluded preference shares.) These companies represented about nine per cent of the total issued equity capital of the 4,400 companies of all kinds quoted on the London Stock Exchange. This suggests that, if the sample was reasonably representative, the equity capital of the quoted companies was spread over about ten million holdings. But without knowing the number of holdings in separate companies by each person or institution we cannot estimate the number of individual holdings this represents.

In the face of the considerable attempts in recent years to stimulate ownership of stock-exchange securities, it seems likely that the tendency has been for the number of persons owning shares to increase. There are many, too, whose investments are indirect. No doubt it would be specious to argue that, since the insurance companies hold massive amounts of stock, this makes all their bonus policy-holders industrial investors. It can more reasonably be argued that in buying shares in investment- or unit-trusts, which have grown significantly in recent years, people are quite consciously making an indirect investment in industry. Not much is known about the relative size of personal and institutional holdings. One recent survey, based on a questionnaire which, on this topic, was answered by 120 of the largest public companies, suggests that individuals still hold the bulk of the equity in most firms. In thirty-nine of the firms, individuals held seventy per cent or more of the equity and in another fifty-two companies they held between fifty and seventy per cent. Insurance companies and pension funds together held between twenty and forty per cent in twenty-five firms, between ten and twenty per cent in another fifty-six firms and less than ten per cent in thirty-nine firms.[18] But confident conclusions are difficult to make, since both individual and institutional investors frequently conceal their identity behind nominees.

The average personal holding still appears to be comparatively modest. Averages, however, tell us little when the distribution of the data is uneven. In the Parkinson sample of companies there were altogether 2,726 holders of over £10,000 nominal. These were only one-quarter per cent of all holders, but they held twenty-six per cent of all the ordinary and preference capital. Over ten per cent of the voting capital in these thirty companies was concentrated in the eighteen largest holdings. It is not easy to see what this means in personal terms. The importance of large personal holdings is under-stated in so far as cross-holdings have not been aggregated, but over-stated in so far as about half of these large holdings were, in fact, held by institutions and not persons.

A fair conclusion seems to be that over a large part of the British economy (say, forty per cent) the means of production are communally owned or owned by the people who use them. The remainder is mainly owned by limited companies. Ownership of these companies is pretty widely dispersed throughout the community, probably substantially more than a million persons having some sort of stake in them.[19] (An interesting illustration of this dispersal arises from the discovery that out of 139 of the largest public companies in 1958, in sixty-eight, nearly one-half of the sample, the number of shareholders exceeded that of employees. This was partly because some of the firms were highly-capitalized property and shipping companies with relatively few employees, but nevertheless this surprising result is forceful evidence of the extent to which shareholding has spread.)[20] The great majority of personal holdings are small, but a comparatively small number of large holders, own, in the aggregate, a considerable part of the voting capital of companies. The statistical basis on which all this rests is extremely slender, however, and it would be unwise to place reliance on any actual figures.

The control of industry is even more difficult to investigate statistically. In the case of nationalized industries, our first reaction is to say that control is highly concentrated, but since the relevant Minister has important over-riding powers and the Minister has to have serious regard to public opinion, it could be argued that ultimate control lies in the hands of the community at large. This, however, hardly accords with the normal realities of the situation and if we extend the argument so far we have to take into account such control over private enterprise as is exercised by the State through the Companies Act or other special statutes.

We have previously seen that, in most of the private sector, control does not necessarily involve ownership of more than fifty per cent of the voting capital. *De facto* control may be exercised for a long time by a small minority of shareholders and, having been established and recorded by the investigator, may suddenly be upset by concerted action on the part of other shareholders. In fact, such control groups are almost impossible to identify without very detailed knowledge of the company concerned. All this concerns control of the individual company but we also need to know whether some measure of unified control over a number of companies is being exercised through interlocking directorates or even by powerful trade associations.

Control is, then, an extremely vague concept. The factual evidence is, moreover, very slender but perhaps a few tentative conclusions can be drawn from it. Control by the general body of ordinary shareholders would usually seem to be impossible, since their numbers often run into thousands and occasionally into hundreds of thousands. The majority of the shareholders have little knowledge and less interest in the policy of the business and are rarely represented at annual general meetings. Probably the typical case today is that of fairly complete divorce of ownership and control. However, very occasional cases do occur, usually when a business has not been doing well, of the shareholders asserting their normally dormant authority, whilst the influence of the general body of shareholders can also be decisive in such crucial matters as take-over bids.

If control has typically slipped away from the shareholders as a whole, into whose hands has it fallen? Somebody must exercise control. It seems to be fairly common for a small number of large shareholders to own a sufficient proportion of votes to give a virtual majority. Investigation suggests that, in a sample of the most important British companies, the twenty largest shareholders (a number small enough for personal contacts) in the 1930s held a sufficiently large proportion of the votes to give them control in nearly one-half of the companies examined.[21] If these large holders do act together and do exercise their potential power, then it may be said that, in these cases, ownership and control are fairly closely aligned. This, especially where the large holders are individuals or family groups, is the closest parallel one finds today in large business to the capitalist entrepreneur who was generally supposed to be characteristic of British industry in the nineteenth century. Some of the large holders are, of course, institutions and some of these, like insurance companies, do not normally seem to intervene directly in the running of companies. On the other hand, the capital structure of some companies is definitely geared to maintain control by a small group. The practice of issuing capital in the form of non-voting or 'A' shares is aimed explicitly at divorcing ownership from control over management in order to retain effective control in the hands of a family or group. Out of a sample of 151 large companies in 1958, thirteen were found to have a large part of their capital in non-voting shares, so that in these cases the picture of a wide spread of ownership and control amongst a considerable number of small shareholders is partly illusory.[22]

In so far as directors, as a whole, exercise leadership and control over companies, it is not easy to assess the relationship between ownership and control. The extent to which a very small percentage of voting capital confers a director's qualification and the substantial pluralism which obtains amongst directors suggest that the degree of concentration of personal power in British industry may be higher than analysis of shareholdings in individual companies would appear to indicate. But it is not certain that this accurately describes the position of directors. One study of 1,404 directors in 148 large companies revealed that seventy per cent of them were full-time directors and sixty-five per cent of them had worked in their companies for five years or more before appointment to the Board. Only in thirteen companies did the Board members hold more than twenty-five per cent of the equity and between five per cent and twenty-five per cent was so held in another twenty-two cases.[23] This picture of directors as being typically full-time, rising from within the firm, and without any substantial shareholding, does not necessarily contradict the picture given above of the possibility of control by a few large shareholders. It often happens that only one or a few Board members will control the proceedings, while large shareholders do not necessarily have to be on the Board to exert their influence. In any event, the diversity of practice and structure amongst companies is wide enough to allow both patterns to appear prominent and still leave enough room to lend some basis for assertions that, over much of industry, it is the salaried managers who are the real controllers.

In most companies the fact that control is exercised by some small but not easily identifiable group, may not be of much significance outside the company itself. In the much smaller group of giant companies, such control confers power in a wider sense. In many industrial groups, the three biggest companies loom large in relation to the rest of the group (see Section 2.5)[24] and they frequently have numerous subsidiaries.[25] But the possibly sinister connotations of all this may be vitiated by a number of considerations. It is not really known who exercises control in these concerns, nor even which concerns should be included amongst the giants, since different criteria give different rankings; by any criteria the actual composition of, say, the 500 largest companies seems to change fairly rapidly as a result of different growth-rates of firms, different amalgamation experience, and so on,[26] whilst the organization of these firms frequently allows for substantial degrees of autonomy within the structure itself.[27]

1 Redfern, P., 'Net Investment in Fixed Assets in the UK. 1938–53,' *Journal of the Royal Statistical Society*, Vol. 118, Part II (1955).

2 Barna, T., 'The Replacement Cost of Fixed Assets in British Manufacturing Industry in 1955,' *Journal of the Royal Statistical Society*, Vol. 120, Part I (1957).

3 *Economic Trends* (August 1968).

4 'Developments in input-output statistics,' *Statistical News*, No. 3 (London, HMSO, November 1968).

5 *Abstract of Statistics*, Table 139 (1968).

6 Florence, P. S., *Logic of British and American Industry*, p. 22 *et seq.* (London, Routledge, 1953).

7 For example Bain, J. S., reported in Caves (ed.), *Britain's Economic Prospects*, p. 288 (London, Allen and Unwin, 1968).

8 Barna, T., 'Investment in Industry,' *The Banker* (April 1967).

9 *Board of Trade Mergers*, Annex 4, paras. 6–9 (HMSO, 1969).

10 Leak and Maizels, 'The Structure of British Industry,' *Journal of the Royal Statistical Society*, Vol. 108, parts 1–2 (1945).

11 Evely, R. and Little, I. M. D., *Concentration in British Industry* (London, NIESR, 1945).

12 Shepherd, M. G., 'Changes in British Industrial Concentration, 1951–58,' *Oxford Economic Papers* (March 1966).

13 George, K. D., 'Changes in British Industrial Concentration, 1951–58,' *Journal of Industrial Economics* (April 1967).

14 Florence, P. S., *Investment, Location and Size of Plant* (Cambridge, University Press, 1948).

15 Nicholson, R. J., 'The Regional Location of Industry,' *Economic Journal* (September 1956).

16 Parkinson, H., *Ownership of Industry* (London, Eyre and Spottiswoode, 1951).

17 *The Times* (8 and 9 January 1959).

18 Harris, R. and Solly, M., *A Survey of Large Companies*, p. 21 and Table XVIIIb (London, Institute of Economic Affairs, 1959).

19 Rix, M. S., *Stock Market Economics*, p. 82 (London, Pitman, 1954), thinks a figure of 2 million or over is more likely, but this includes personal investors in all forms of stocks and shares, including Government and Municipal stock.

20 Harris and Solly, *op. cit.*

21 Florence, P. S., *The Logic of British and American Industry*, pp. 186–203 (London, Routledge, 1953).

22 Harris and Solly, *op. cit.*, p. 21.

23 Harris and Solly, *op. cit.*, p. 21 and Table XVI. A recent analysis, *Times Business News* (8 and 9 September 1969), shows that in the largest 100 UK companies (by asset values) the Boards of Directors control 7·5 per cent of the equity voting power and the Chairmen about 2·5 per cent.

24 See also NIESR, *Company Income and Finance 1949–53*, Appendix B (1956).

25 Harris and Solly, *op. cit.*, Table XIV.

26 *Ibid.*, pp. 5–15.

27 For examples, see Edwards and Townsend, *op. cit.*, Part II.

CHAPTER 3

The Finance of Industry

We now have to consider how industry raises the money with which to exploit its productive opportunities. In this connection it is natural to think first of the banks, which exist mainly for the purpose of receiving money on deposit and lending it out to sound borrowers.

3.1 The role of the banks and other financial institutions

Banks are not important direct sources of industrial finance in this country (see p. 81). They are extremely conscious of their obligations to their depositors and, since the bulk of bank deposits are liable to instant withdrawal or withdrawal at short notice, are loath to take the risks which industrial financing frequently entails. These risks are of two kinds: the risk of total default, and the risk that although the borrower may prove to be sound, he may not be able to repay the loan at the convenience of the bank. The risk of total loss of the money loaned is normally greatest when the bank is asked to advance money to assist in the establishment of a completely new enterprise. Although the bank manager may be satisfied that the person asking for a loan is an honest man, he may have little or no evidence of his business ability and will probably lack the technical knowledge to judge the prospects of the new concern. Unless the loan required is small and well secured, it is unlikely that the bank will consider advancing money for this purpose.

The banker is on firmer ground in considering an application for a loan from a profitable and going concern. Here the greater risk is that of illiquidity, and the banker will normally be prepared

65

to make an advance provided it is required for working-capital purposes and can be regarded as self-liquidating. Thus, for example, the banks will be prepared in approved cases to provide finance by way of loan or overdrafts for the purchase of raw materials which, when worked-up and marketed, will provide funds for repayment of the loan in a relatively short space of time. But the banks will not normally provide medium- and long-term capital for industry, for the purchase of machinery, for buildings and the like. Here the risks of illiquidity are too great and the risk of default can rarely be completely discounted. The banks maintain, with some justification, not only that such risks are incompatible with their duty to their depositors but also that the provision of medium- and long-term capital is the business of the proprietor (in the case of a joint-stock company, the ordinary shareholders) of the firm, who draws the profits. The banks, apart from all question of risk, will be reluctant to take up ordinary shares in a company since this may involve them in functions of industrial management for which they are in no way fitted.

It would be unwise to conclude from this that the banks never provide medium- and long-term capital for industry. Overdrafts may be renewed so regularly and systematically that long-term capital is in fact being provided. One reason for such renewal may be an awareness that, if repayment is pressed for, the borrower may be forced into liquidation. In this case the bank (ranking after mortgage debenture holders and equally with other trade creditors) may get little or nothing in settlement of its claims. This sort of thing happened on a fairly considerable scale during the nineteen-thirties. The banks could not remain indifferent to the manner in which firms, heavily indebted to them, carried on their affairs. They became very active in promoting financial reconstructions, amalgamations, and even cartels in the hope that substantial losses of bank money could be averted. An outcome of many such reconstructions was that more money was loaned by the banks and ordinary shares were often taken in settlement of outstanding claims.

It must be remembered that this was a period of exceptional depression and that the banks could hardly have avoided the position in which they found themselves. Nevertheless, they were much criticized for the influence they acquired in industrial management and for the ways in which they used this influence. There can be little doubt, however, that the banks were not only concerned to protect their own interests but also to avoid the social consequences of large-scale business failures. In many cases they disposed of large holdings of shares as soon as they thought it prudent to do so.

Things have been very different since 1945. Full employment has been maintained and business has been generally prosperous. The banks have been in a very liquid position and most desirous of increasing their advances. Although they retain a strong preference for short-term lending of self-liquidating types, they are likely gradually to modify their theoretical confinement to short-term lending.[1] There are signs of this already in personal loans' schemes and in the extent to which the banks have acquired interests in finance houses and industrial banks. The latter specialize in hire-purchase business and draw their funds mainly from the public and commercial concerns on deposit, and partly from bank loans. But hire-purchase credit for the purchase of industrial capital is relatively small, although growing, and of more importance to small companies than to large.

More significant from our point of view are the specialized institutions set up, with bank participation, to invest rather than lend money by taking up securities in a business. This is probably the only satisfactory way in which the banks can finance the long-term capital requirements of industry. A number of such institutions (mainly intended to assist small business) were established during the nineteen-thirties. Perhaps the most important was Charterhouse Industrial Development Company which was founded in 1934 by Charterhouse Investment Trust (an issuing house) with the participation of an insurance company and two joint-stock banks. It was intended to provide money in amounts up to £100,000 for small business, and the Company had to be satisfied that the firm raising the capital had a good profit record, was competently managed, and needed the money for new development rather than for working capital. Money has generally been advanced in the form of payment for participating preference shares in the firm assisted.

Two new financial institutions were established in 1945 in a further effort to improve the provision of capital for industry. The larger of the two—Finance Corporation for Industry—had its capital of £25 million subscribed by a number of insurance and investment companies and the Bank of England. It has borrowing powers of up to £100 million, the money being mainly provided

67

by the deposit banks. Finance is normally provided by means of long- or short-period fixed-interest loans secured by a mortgage on the assets of the borrower, but the FCI is not debarred from participitating in the equity of the business which it finances. The Corporation was most deeply concerned with the steel industry while it was not nationalized. This industry met the conditions of needing large sums in circumstances (particularly impending nationalization) which made normal sources difficult, but more recently there has been a tendency for industries with special problems to have special bodies created for them (e.g. the Shipbuilding Industry Board) and this has made the Corporation almost redundant.

The smaller institution—Industrial and Commercial Finance Corporation—was established to provide medium- and long-term capital for industry, in amounts up to £200,000. Its capital of £15 million (part paid-up) was provided by the Bank of England and the joint-stock banks. The Corporation had borrowing powers up to £30 million, solely by advances from the member banks. It was allowed to advance capital either on fixed-interest terms or by participation in the equity of the concern which was being financed.

Both institutions have enjoyed modest success. FCI has made possible large-scale development projects which, by reason of their scale or the time necessary to bring them to fruition, might not have appealed to any of the established agencies for capital provision. It has generally taken an option of being repaid in cash or in preference and ordinary shares. ICFC has invested quite substantially in preference and ordinary shares and the bulk of its holdings are in unquoted securities. The Corporation has done a great deal to meet the long-term capital requirements of small business (see pp. 82–8, where this problem is considered further) but has not fulfilled all that had been expected of it. It has been criticized for overcaution, particularly since less than one-fifth of the approaches to it actually result in a firm offer of finance. However, it is questionable whether more than a tiny proportion of the four-fifths had any prospects of commercial success. The Corporation's vetting process extends far beyond a simple 'creditworthiness' approach, and includes the product, the process, the management, and the future plans of the applicants. An application is unlikely to be rejected just because a company is 'overborrowed' or 'overtrading', since a balanced mixture of loan and equity capital can be injected into a company with good commercial or technical prospects, and specialist advice is available to make good specific deficiencies in the management. ICFC was never intended to *subsidize* small businesses (although the high fixed costs of investigation and negotiation make transactions at the lower end of its range almost inevitably unremunerative) and it was hoped that it would have great influence as evidence to the rest of the City that investment in small businesses could be profitable. There has since been a proliferation of private finance houses attracted by the possibility of very rapid growth rates in successful small companies and ICFC has certainly been an important influence in this.

In 1959 the banks paid up the unpaid part of the equity ($£7\frac{1}{2}$ million) and the Corporation was allowed to make debenture issues in the market in order to raise additional funds for investing in industry. In the same year the shareholding banks in ICFC agreed that the extent to which the Corporation could participate in any issue be raised from £200,000 to £300,000.

Thus it will be seen that the banks do contribute more than is generally believed to the long-term capital requirements of industry, although their participation is often somewhat indirect. Their role is to be sharply contrasted with that of other financial institutions such as insurance companies. The latter make substantial investments in industry through the new issue market and they have provided a substantial proportion of the finance for industrial and commercial buildings, particularly blocks of offices. By the arrangement known as 'sale and lease-back' an insurance company will buy an office building from a company and then lease it back for an annual payment which would be close to the market rate of interest on the capital. The company could then invest the money in more profitable uses, such as machinery. Companies may economize on capital by leasing much of their equipment, especially vehicles, aircraft, computers and machine tools. By leasing, the company 'borrows' the asset, rather than the money. The annual charge is usually higher than the equivalent interest rate, but the lessor carries the risks of breakdown and obsolescence and this is reflected in the charge. Many finance houses (including ICFC) now offer this service and some large manufacturing companies (e.g. computer manufacturers) have joined forces with merchant banks in order to lease rather than sell their products.

3.2 The new issue market

When a public registered company starts its life it most frequently raises the capital it requires by a public issue of shares, i.e. it offers its shares for subscription by the general public. The importance of the public issue as a means of raising new capital for industry, however, is frequently exaggerated (see page 80). As previously stated, most new public companies are formed for the purpose of taking over some existing business which is being converted into a public company, whilst others are formed by the merger of two or more public companies into a new public company. Much of the money raised by share issue may be used to pay in cash for the business which is being taken over or, more probably, many of the shares issued are not paid for in cash but offered to the former proprietors as payment for their business.

It is very rare for an entirely new business to be floated immediately as a public company because, having no previous trading record, it is impossible to form any sound opinion as to its prospects. The public will, therefore, be reluctant to subscribe to its shares, and even if persons could be found who would take them up, it would be impossible to create a market in them on the Stock Exchange until the degree of success of the new company became apparent.

In spite of what has been said above, some new capital for industry is raised in the open market by public issue. The purpose of transforming an existing business into a public company is generally to facilitate its further development, and the size of the issue will normally be gauged so as to provide the money for new development after the business taken over has been paid for and the expenses of the issue met. Also, within the limits of its authorized capital an existing public company may make a new issue of shares to finance further development, although the facilities of the new issue market are not available to private companies.

An issue of capital is generally handled on behalf of a company by an institution specializing in this business. This could be one of the old-established merchant banking houses which combine issuing with acceptance business and which, in the past, have generally been associated with the flotation of foreign loans in London. Alternatively, the issue could be handled by one of the finance houses like Charterhouse Investment Trust, which specializes in the financing of industrial development; or by some syndicate formed by the promoters of the company for the special purpose of handling the particular issue; or by a firm of stock-brokers. (Issuing houses have been responsible for sixty per cent by value of new issues since the war, the remainder being made by issuing brokers.)

Where the public are being invited to subscribe direct, a prospectus, drawn up and signed by the directors of the new company, is issued by the company's bank which undertakes to receive applications for shares and such money as is payable on each share on application. The firm which has agreed to sponsor the issue generally agrees to underwrite it, i.e. it agrees to take up such shares as are not taken up by the public. For this service, which often entails considerable risk, it receives a commission. By means of sub-underwriting contracts the issuing house may contract out of part of its risk, which is borne by the sub-underwriters. These are generally insurance companies or other large institutional investors but the issuing house makes itself responsible to their clients for raising the money. It may or may not take up part of the issue itself. The sponsorship of an issuing house is a guarantee that the money will be raised and some assurance to potential investors of the merits of the issue.

When the last date for the receipt of applications is past, they are opened and examined. If the issue is not fully subscribed, each applicant is allotted the shares for which he has applied. If the issue is over-subscribed some method of rationing the allocations is applied. A further payment on the shares is then made by persons to whom the shares have been allotted, this amounting to the balance of the purchase price of the shares if they are fully paid up.

The issue may be made directly by the company concerned or by an offer for sale by an issuing house. In the latter case the issue is sold outright to the issuing house which subsequently offers the shares to the public. Both these methods are relatively expensive, requiring a full prospectus and advertisement in leading news-papers. A company making an additional issue of shares for cash may raise the money more cheaply by offering them by circular to existing shareholders, although the price of the shares may be adjusted to make the offer a favourable one.

An alternative method of raising capital for industry through the new issue market is the private placing with or without quotation on the Stock Exchange. The company making the issue places the shares, through the broker or issuing house in charge of the issue, with various Stock Exchange firms or institutional investors such as insurance companies or pension funds. If permission to deal in the shares is asked for and granted, they become freely marketable securities with a Stock Exchange quotation. The Stock Exchange is particular about ensuring that an adequate market is created for each new issue and that the technique is not used just to 'make a price' for the shares in order to value the company for Estate Duty or merger negotiations. A placing will normally have to amount to at least thirty-five per cent of the firm's equity and twenty-five per cent of the new issue has to be made generally available through the market (the proportions are lower with fixed interest placings).

A placing may be contrasted with an introduction, which is simply a method of introducing a small quantity of *existing* shares into the market in order to obtain a quotation. There is no intention of raising new money for the company, although the introduction may be followed very quickly by a rights issue, and ensures that the new shares are quoted and marketable.

The advantages and disadvantages of these methods of making new issues of capital are not easily summarized and the decision on how best to proceed will depend on the circumstances of each case. The firms will have expert advice available through its accountants, lawyers, stockbroker and merchant bank, but a recent study has produced evidence that the quality of the advice available can vary very greatly[2] and bad advice can prove very expensive. The same study systematically analyses the costs of new issues, greatly extending the path-breaking studies of R. F. Henderson.[3] Henderson had shown that the expenses of new issues varied immensely with the size of the issue, owing to the large element of fixed costs involved in advertising, printing, prospectuses, payments to auditors and advisers, etc. Small issues are thus uneconomic. Professor Merrett and his colleagues have shown that the issuing expenses may be a minor part of the total costs, and that the difference between the price at which the shares are issued and the price which they attain in the market immediately afterwards can be much larger. The aim of a company in making an issue of ordinary shares is to gain as large a sum as possible in return for the proportion of the equity which it is selling. If a company sells half of its equity for a sum of £1 million, and then as soon as the shares are traded, a price is reached which values this half share at £1¼ million, the company has in effect 'lost' £250,000 on the deal.

The incidence of such costs appears to vary significantly between one method of issue and another. Companies are particularly likely to strike a bad bargain through placings or offers, and this can easily outweigh the relatively small economies in the expenses of new issues which these methods permit. The main difficulty is that the difference between the issue price and the subsequent market value is hypothetical before the event, whereas the small differences in expense can be calculated exactly and probably carry too much weight in financial decisions on this account. The apparent variations in the efficiency of Issuing Houses shows up particularly in the size of the subsequent premium over the issue price, and these are far larger than the systematic variations in the expenses arising out of differences in the size of the issue.

The New Issue Market thus has a bias against small issues, and *ipso facto* smaller companies. Perhaps more importantly, it also contains a large random element arising from variations in the judgment and the efficiency of a relatively small number of professional financial advisers. The broad impersonal forces of the market, which are in principle supposed to allocate capital funds between industries and companies become effective largely after the money has been allocated. The principle beneficiaries of underpriced issues are the 'stags', who subscribe for new issues in the hope that a premium will soon appear, but with no intention of holding the shares for a long period (stags do not always win of course, and their activities can be partly justified by the fact that they help to make a market for a new issue). Companies and their advisers have often taken a perverse pride in the 'success' of a new issue when it is vastly oversubscribed and immediately shoots to a large premium, apparently unaware that the larger the premium, the larger the loss to the company and, other things being equal, the bigger the mistake.

The method proposed to reduce the importance of this random element is that shares should be issued by tender, i.e. subscribers should nominate their price and the shares should be sold to the highest bidders. The method is administratively expensive and does not *guarantee* that the stags will be eliminated, but it does have the advantage of bringing in broader market forces at an earlier stage in the process. The tender method is developing very slowly, and it will obviously take time before it is fully accepted.

The really big issues are usually made by established quoted companies raising fresh capital from their shareholders through a 'rights' issue. With a rights issue, the shareholders are given the first option to subscribe for new shares as a right, and the size of their entitlement to the new shares will be proportional to their holding of the old. The price at which a rights issue is made is a secondary matter, since if the new issue is underpriced, the shareholder will gain as the buyer of the new shares exactly what he loses as the owner of the old. If any shareholder does not wish to take up his allotment of new shares, he may sell his 'rights' to somebody else, and an active market in rights will exist when several companies are making such issues around the same time. They are cheap, since it is not necessary to go through the full routine of a new issue and constitute the main means by which new money is introduced into industry through the market.

Up to about 1929 the issuing houses were mainly engaged in finding capital for overseas borrowers but the market is now much better adapted to the needs of British industry. Overseas issues are now comparatively unimportant and some of the younger issuing houses do no overseas business. Whether or not the market is sufficiently adapted to the needs of small business is another matter, although the number of small issues has been tending to increase. Between 1952 and 1956 an average of about forty issues of less than £250,000 were made each year and about one-third of these were £50,000 or less. These issues were mainly private placings at a cost of 2½–3 per cent on a placing of £100,000 but as pointed out previously this low cost may have been counterbalanced (particularly in the case of unquoted securities) by the low price (high yield) which has had to be offered.[4] The particular problems of financing small business will be considered in more detail in a later section of this chapter.

3.3 The Stock Exchange

The New Issue Market does not exist as a separate institution, but it is inseparably linked with the Stock Exchange. The Stock Exchange is a market for existing securities, and the group of firms making up the New Issue market adds to the stock of securities which are traded there. The stock of quoted shares and bonds is very large—in March 1968, the estimated value of company stock and shares quoted on the London Stock Exchange was £82,800 million, of which £38,000 million was accounted for by British firms operating in Britain. (March 1968 was very close to the peak of the 1967/68 boom, so that these values are somewhat inflated, but they represent the orders of magnitude involved.) New issues would not normally add more than two per cent to the total stock in any year.

If the Stock Exchange were simply a place where second-hand shares are bought and sold it would be of minor economic significance. However, it is generally accepted that it has great influence on the allocation of capital funds between industries. Although the actual trading is carried on by relatively few people (the jobbers) each of whom tends to specialize in a particular area of the market, they are responding to the instructions of thousands of individual and institutional shareholders. Countless pieces of information and gossip go into forming the pattern of demand for different shares, and it is argued that this generates a form of collective wisdom and objectivity in ranking one firm's prospects against another's and one industry's against another's. Where there are generally optimistic expectations concerning an industry's future it will be easier for firms in that industry to raise fresh capital through a new issue. Not only will shares be more readily marketable, but existing shareholders will be keener to add to their investment in the industry and better prices will be obtainable on any new issues.

The efficiency of the market, or at least of investment analysts advising stockbrokers and institutions such as pension funds and insurance companies, has been seriously questioned by recent studies[5] showing that there is a marked lack of consistency in the performance of companies over a period, and that the forecasting methods used by the analysts do not forecast very well. The concept of the 'collective wisdom' of the market lacks a theoretical foundation, although in the case of large companies at least, the market price is objective in being determined by anonymous forces of supply and demand. However, in spite of the difficulty in establishing exactly how it works, the market does succeed in putting the bulk of the new money into growing companies, and this after all is the main objective. An important factor in this result is that it is mainly growing companies which approach the market for funds. The situation in which the suppliers might survey *all* companies and decide which will get more capital and which will not, therefore does not arise in practice.

75

If the efficiency of the market in allocating new savings between industries is a matter of dispute, there can be no question that it contributes very greatly to increasing the aggregate supply of savings to industry as a whole. It does this by enabling the individual investor to liquidate his investment by selling it to somebody else. Without this facility all investment would be indefinitely long term and consequently very riskly. Industry would therefore find new money both scarce and expensive.

Another extremely important function of the market is to establish the average and relative prices of the different forms of capital. These prices have an important function in balancing the supply of, and demand for, different kinds of capital funds. They can also guide companies investing retained earnings as to the retention costs inflicted upon their shareholders in terms of the rate of return which they could have obtained by investing their funds in the shares of other companies. The tendency of the Stock Exchange to produce exaggerated responses to short term influences (for example, share values almost doubled between late autumn 1966 and summer 1968, and then fell by a third during the following winter and spring) reduces its value as a *sensitive* indicator of capital costs, but it provides useful and independent 'rule of thumb' guidance to industry.

3.4 Investment appraisal
The capital markets do not allocate funds to particular investment projects nor do they, in general, allocate funds to industries as such. Instead, funds are allocated to firms, which may span several industries, and spread the new funds in a wide range of investment projects. The initiative rests with the firm to approach the market, rather than vice-versa, and the terms on which the funds will be made available by the market will depend partly on the investors' assessment (Little's analyses[5] question the accuracy of such assessments, but not the principle of how efficient the company's management is in investing their money).

Company managements are thus the principal agents for allocating funds to particular purposes and the success of the company, the industry and ultimately the whole economy will be affected very greatly by their efficiency in this function. A company's investment policies will be largely determined by the management's knowledge, insight and feelings of optimism or pessimism about the future, but only recently have techniques been developed to permit a systematic approach to investment decisions.

The method is to compare the expected future returns from each project with the cost of the capital invested in it. (These of course are very difficult to estimate since we have no certain knowledge of future trends of tastes, incomes, technology, or other factors affecting particular markets.) This may be done by 'charging' each future year's expected revenue by the compounded cost of the capital in the form of a discount rate. There are two basic approaches, of which the simplest is the method of calculating the *present value* of the project. This may be illustrated by a numerical example. Suppose that an investment is expected to return £100, £200 and £300 in the first, second and third year respectively from now. If the cost of capital is estimated at ten per cent per annum, the Present Value is then

$$\frac{£100}{(1 + \frac{1}{10})} + \frac{£200}{(1 + \frac{1}{10})^2} + \frac{£300}{(1 + \frac{1}{10})^3} = £482 \text{ (approx.)}$$

This may be extended for any number of years up to n, at which the discount factor is $(1 + \frac{1}{10})^n$.

The present value of the expected returns can now be compared with the outlay of capital required to initiate the project. If it is greater, then the project is justified, because it will repay the original investment and compensate for the cost of the capital tied up in it. Thus, if the outlay is £481 or less, the investment is justified, if it is £482 or more, it is not.

The second method is to treat the rate of discount as an unknown, and calculate that rate which will produce a present value of returns exactly equal to the capital outlay. This calculated discount factor is then the *yield*, or internal rate of return, on the project. The rule would then be that if the yield exceeds the cost of capital, the investment is justified, if it does not, the project should be rejected. For example, suppose that for an outlay of £300, you will receive a return of £60, £144 and £260 over the following three years. It will be found that a discount rate of twenty per cent will reduce these future earnings to a present value of approximately £300, so that the project could be said to yield twenty per cent on the original investment. The calculation of the yield is mathematically complex, although short-cut methods of close approximation are available, but in the great majority of cases, the two methods of yield and present value will produce the same decisions concerning the viability or otherwise of the project.

These methods of investment appraisal are usually referred to as Discounted Cash Flow (or DCF) analysis. Practical applications are naturally far more complex than the simple examples shown here, and in particular risk and uncertainty about future returns present many problems, but nevertheless DCF techniques appear to be gaining rapid acceptance in industry. (This is part of a more general process, associated with the widespread use of computers, of applying mathematical techniques to the solution of industrial problems. This was formerly known as 'scientific management', but it has now acquired a new status as Operational Research.) This could have important implications for the future behaviour of industrial investment. In the first place, investment should be guided more accurately to the most profitable uses. Secondly, the level of investment should become more sensitive to external market influences, particularly the cost of capital. It can be seen from the above examples, that the higher the cost of capital, the less likely is any given project to prove acceptable. A higher rate of discount will produce a lower present value, while a higher cost of capital is also more likely to exceed the yield from a project. Finally, investment will prove more sensitive to official incentives and deterrents. This is because DCF calculations are based on *net* cash flows, after deducting taxes and adding allowances.[6] In short, this development could contribute significantly towards making the capital market operate in the way in which economists have argued that it should work.

3.5 Some facts and figures

We have already discussed two sources of finance for industry: the banks and the new issue market. There are two other major possibilities. The first is the ploughing-back of company profits into the business instead of distributing them to the shareholders. The second is the extension of trade credit by one firm to another. Whilst it is true that trade credit cancels out over firms taken as a whole (since what is owed to one is owed by another) a general willingness to increase credit facilities does reduce the need for working capital.

The main purpose of this section, however, is to discuss the relative importance of different sources of company finance. Our information on this is not complete but has been much improved in recent years. It mainly relates to the 3,000 public companies quoted on the Stock Exchange whose main activities were in manufacturing, building and distribution.[7] These companies account for about half the output of all companies and a quarter of the entire national output although they constitute less than 0·1 per cent of all business (including unincorporated businesses). These limitations need to be borne in mind in considering the following paragraphs but the figures quoted form a fairly reliable guide to the financing of the private sector of the economy. The financing of the nationalized industries will be considered in Chapter 7.

For purposes of comparison, we can take average figures for three periods. The first is 1949–53, which is the earliest period after the Companies Act 1948 (which resulted in consistent consolidated accounts and made comparisons with later periods possible), then 1958 to 1964 and finally 1965 to 1967, which shows the early effects of the introduction of Corporation Tax.

(1) Internal sources are the most important throughout, although tending to decline in relative importance. The percentage of company finance from depreciation and tax reserves and retained profits fell from sixty-four per cent to 61·5 per cent and finally to fifty-four per cent. Less than half of the internal funds represent net savings, the greater part being earmarked for replacement of obsolete or worn out assets or to meet imminent liabilities. However, depreciation funds do not *necessarily* have to be spent on purchasing the same kind of assets as those which are now worn out, and if the firm wishes to change its structure, it may use reserves accumulated on its old activities to develop its new interests. It is therefore difficult to make a precise distinction between gross and net saving in this context.

The amount of retained profits varies quite sharply from year to year. It appears that most firms attempt to maintain reasonably stable dividends, so that variations in the level of profits affect mostly the level of retentions. This is probably the main reason for the relatively low figures in the last period—company profitability (reflected in the ratio of profits to capital employed) had been falling in most industries through the later nineteen fifties and most of the sixties, whereas dividends rose fairly steadily.

One of the main purposes of Corporation Tax, introduced in 1965 at an initial rate of forty per cent (later raised to 42·5 per cent and then forty-five per cent) was to discourage dividend payments and hence encourage higher retentions. Prior to 1965 Companies paid Profits Tax (at a rate of fifteen per cent) and then Income Tax on their profits. Now the Company pays Corporation Tax on its profits, and the shareholder will then pay Income Tax on his dividends. Dividend income is thus subject to 'double' taxation, while retained profits are taxed once only. It should thus pay the shareholder in the long run to let his income accumulate inside the business, since this should add to its capital value, and capital gains are taxed at a rate lower than income. It is by no means apparent that this effect was produced in 1965–67, but it is impossible on the evidence to separate the effects of the tax changes from those of declining profitability.

It is almost certain that profitability has increased in 1968 and 1969, but even these years will not provide an adequate test of the efficiency of Corporation Tax in increasing profit retentions, since these years saw the imposition of the Incomes policy, which was much more effective in restraining dividend increases (to a normal maximum of 3·5 per cent per annum) than wages. It will clearly be a very long time before this question is satisfactorily answered.

(2) As internal funds have declined in importance, new issues have increased from fifteen per cent to twenty-two per cent and to 26·5 per cent of all sources. This reflects partly industry's ever-increasing demands for capital. (The total use of funds by quoted companies rose from £1,271 millions in 1958 to £3,199 millions in 1967) with increasing capital intensity, but it is also a reflection of the very substantial increase in the level of personal savings, which could only be tapped by industry through new issues. [8]

The composition of the new issues changed quite radically over the whole period. In 1949–53, they were equally divided between equity and fixed interest, in 1958–64, two-thirds were equity and one-third fixed interest, while in 1965–67, these ratios were reversed, with more than three-fifths fixed interest and less than two-fifths equity. The popularity of equity in the middle period is hard to explain. Interest rates were rising through this period, but were still relatively low after allowing for tax. [9] (British law distinguishes between interest, which is treated as a transfer of income, so that the recipient pays tax on it, while the payer is deemed to have reduced his income by the amount of interest, and hence escapes tax on it, and dividends, which are treated as a new income, i.e. as a payment for a service (presumably risk-taking).) British companies have shown a persistent tendency to employ lower 'gearing' (the ratio of debt to equity capital) than, for example, American companies, and this may perhaps be indicative of a generally more cautious approach to business. High gearing increases the fixed commitments of the business, and in a severe trade depression would increase the risk of insolvency but by way of compensation, it increases the profitability of the equity in prosperous times. Most British companies have remained well within the limits of prudence in this respect.

The sharp reversal in the third period was almost certainly a response to the new tax system. Interest payments became free of Corporation Tax and this made the relative cheapness of loan capital far more apparent than it was previously. At the same time, it hastened the final demise of the Preference Share, which has the disadvantages of a fixed commitment without the compensation of tax relief. Preference shares have been of decreasing importance throughout the post-war period, and now they will only be issued in very special circumstances.

(3) The balance is made up of a variety of sources, mostly short-term in nature, but with trade credit and bank advances the most important. The individual elements may fluctuate a great deal in the short run, but over the whole post-war period, they have, in total, kept close to about one-fifth of all the sources. Companies appear to be able to offset fluctuations in one short-term source by adjusting their intake of the others. Although attempts to prove that firms deliberately manipulate trade credit to offset bank credit squeezes have not shown this to be a consistent and powerful pattern of behaviour.[9] Increases in trade credit are probably a more important source of finance for the small and growing company than for the established large concern. It may be difficult to distinguish in some cases between trade credit and a trade investment, where a large firm may help to finance the working capital of a smaller firm supplying it with components, or to improve the facilities of the distributors marketing its products.

Bank credit has shown a steady increase in importance compared with trade credit, from about one-fifth of the value of trade credit in the middle fifties to about one-third by the middle sixties. However it is not possible to try to explain this trend without a very far reaching discussion of the British monetary system.

3.6 The financing of small business

One of the defects of the above figures was that they excluded not only public unquoted companies but also all private companies unless they happened to be subsidiaries of a large quoted public company. The bulk of these are small firms and financing them sets special and important problems.

They are special problems because small firms are denied access to some of the sources available to other companies; private companies, for example, cannot raise money through the new issue market. They are important problems because small firms are often young and seeking to grow, in some cases trying to develop some new product or technical process, and if the economy is to remain healthy and progressive it is important that their growth should not be stunted. This will happen if they are thrown back too much on their own resources because it follows almost inevitably from their size that they can hardly be making the big profits necessary to sustain rapid growth. Also, there is often a special degree of risk attaching to such ventures which makes it difficult to attract capital on the terms available to larger and older firms. Furthermore we have seen that a large proportion of the funds available to industry is derived from and reinvested within the firm. There is an element of circularity in this problem. The private business finds it most difficult to raise equity capital, and this forces them to rely on loan capital, particularly short-term borrowing through trade and bank credit. Short-term borrowing is risky because it can be withdrawn at short notice, and this increased risk makes it all the more difficult to raise equity capital, since this ultimately bears all the risk. The large firm thus has a built-in advantage over the small, and the larger and more prosperous it is, the greater the advantage. The prospects of vigorous newcomers toppling, or even shaking, the standing giants is remote in all but the very new industries.

Nevertheless, the small business is an indispensable part of even the most advanced industrial economies. Its main function is to fill in the gaps and interstices left by the larger firms, producing small runs, filling batch orders, and carrying out special processes, which the larger firm, with its more rigid structure and heavy overheads, would find prohibitively expensive to carry out itself.

(The motor vehicle industry is a good example, with many independent firms producing small items such as window trims and wing mirrors, which are assembled into the completed vehicle by the industry's great firms.) They may also be a means for introducing new ideas into industry[10] and they are being increasingly appreciated by large firms as a breeding ground for young managers with a width of experience and a level of responsibility which the more hierarchical large firms find difficult to generate for themselves. The vast majority of take-overs consist of large firms drawing in ready-made productive capacity, new ideas or new managers from the pool of private firms, so that it can be argued that the principal sufferers from any weakening of small business would be big business.

In 1931 the Macmillan Committee referred to the lack of provision for supplying long-term capital, in amounts too small for a public issue, to small and medium-sized firms. This was the famous 'Macmillan gap' and there is some argument as to whether the gap still exists.[11] A number of institutions emerged during the nineteen-thirties to deal with this problem but they did not do so very adequately. Charterhouse Industrial Development Company tended to concentrate on financing companies likely to grow sufficiently to make a public issue rather than on providing a market for unquoted securities. Credit for Industry Ltd. (a subsidiary of United Dominions Trust Ltd.) loaned rather than invested money to small companies with a good profit record, the loan being secured by mortgage debentures. The establishment of ICFC in 1945 (see pp. 68–9) was a further step forward. It did provide a market for unquoted securities but was in no position to take abnormal risks and it generally chose to support the well-managed business with reasonable growth prospects. ICFC has now assisted over 2,000 companies, and a substantial part of its business consists of making continuous further injections of capital into its existing customers, until a point is reached when the most successful can be floated as public companies. Once the initial hurdle has been overcome, ICFC becomes the ideal partner for the ambitious firm, with an endless supply of tactful good advice and a deep purse, but its customers possibly account for little more than five per cent of the total population of small firms which might qualify in terms of size (although not necessarily in terms of prospects).

Two of ICFC's associated companies fulfil special roles in this field. Technical Development Capital Ltd. (TDC) was launched in 1962 with a capital of a million pounds subscribed by ICFC and insurance companies to finance the *commercial* promotion of new ideas and inventions which had proved their technical feasibility (i.e. they had passed the prototype stage). It was (and still is) widely believed that there is a vast pool of inventions and bright ideas just requiring a bit of capital and some expert management in order to become profitable, but TDC has had to search hard to find them. Estate Duties Investment Trust Ltd. (EDITH)[12] on the other hand found a very strong demand for its services. One of the greatest problems of the private company is that its shares will often be very closely held, often within a single family. If the principal shareholder holds most of his personal wealth in the form of shares in the family company, his heirs may find great difficulty in finding the cash to meet Estate Duty after his death, and be forced to sell part of his shareholding, possibly on very adverse terms. EDITH negotiates to take a large shareholding in the company, on reasonable terms, before the death of the principal owner, thus relieving his heirs of this anxiety. The companies involved are usually well established and substantial by the standards of family companies, and EDITH has become a very successful enterprise in its own right, with its own Stock Exchange quotation and a rating as a 'growth' investment.

Why do small businesses find it difficult to attract capital? It is easy to find reasons but it should be borne in mind that they would not all apply to any particular category of small firms. The problem of the small business is not easily summarized because there are so many possible variations of it. One reason is the drying-up of private sources of capital on which small firms used to rely to a considerable extent. In the past, the local solicitor, accountant or successful tradesman would often back small firms at a critical stage of growth and family sources of funds could also be tapped. But more private money is now being channelled into the capital market through superannuation funds, insurance companies, and investment and unit trusts instead of being made directly available to small firms. Also, one consequence of modern financial journalism has been to make direct investment by private persons in quoted securities more possible and attractive.

Another factor to be reckoned with is the reluctance of many proprietors of small businesses to part with more than a small share in the equity of the business lest they should lose control. From the investor's point of view, the classical 'sleeping partner' role may not be very attractive—he is unlikely to be prepared to put up a substantial part of the capital without having some say in the management, unless he knows the entrepreneur very well and has exceptional confidence in him. The small entrepreneur is usually a man who values his independence very highly indeed —perhaps more highly than a large stake in a growing concern and a personal fortune. He is often badly informed in financial matters, being as often as not a technical expert in engineering or marketing rather than finance and possibly suspicious of financial experts and institutions. Thus, despite strenuous advertising by ICFC, probably more than four-fifths of small companies have never approached the Corporation for assistance. Professor Bates[13] demonstrates that a large majority of small businesses have made no use of outside finance from *any* source. There is a strong in-ference that if there is a Macmillan gap it exists as much in a deficiency in the demand from small businesses as in gaps in the supply side.

Better access to the new issue market would help to tap wider sources of funds for small businesses. Naturally enough, unquoted securities are not very attractive to the large institutional inves-tors because of their limited marketability and they prefer fixed interest securities (well backed by marketable assets such as land and buildings), to unquoted ordinary shares. In any case they find it administratively easier and cheaper to make larger single purchases of blocks of shares than any small firm can offer and even a modest investment in a small firm might involve them in tiresome management functions. If, as is most likely to be the case, the firm has not a well-established record of high profits, the shares can only be made attractive by being offered on very favourable terms and this in turn makes it an expensive way of raising capital.

On the whole it seems probable that the facilities of the new issue market are only available to the strongest of small firms which are in any case fairly well placed to find capital. Private companies have no access to the market and most small firms are private companies. There are sources available to them but it is a risky business and, unless the proprietor is well informed and fortunate, a worthwhile venture might easily fail for lack of capital.

Bank overdrafts are liable to be called for repayment at inconvenient moments, extended trade credit involves serious risks, hire-purchase contracts are a standing burden on the business and their own reserves are tenuous. Investment trusts, insurance companies, and issuing companies will only venture in this field very occasionally and ICFC has been fairly selective. There are other alternatives but they almost invariably involve offsetting disadvantages. For example, if a small firm is prepared to move into an area of high unemployment, special assistance may be forthcoming from the State (see Chapter 8).

The Finance Act 1965 made life rather more difficult for some family companies by exposing part of their profits to Surtax. The entrepreneur in a private company has always enjoyed favourable tax treatment. Many family companies earn substantial profits, and if these were all treated as the income of the family, or the individual, owning the company, they would be subject to tax at the highest marginal rates and very little would be left after tax. Since retained profits are the principal source of finance for their companies, this would at the very least prevent all further growth, and probably liquidate most of them very quickly. If such companies could demonstrate that the profits were actually being ploughed back into the business, they were relieved of surtax, so that the entrepreneur was allowed to accumulate personal wealth within the business, subject only to profits tax and income tax. Anybody earning the same income by way of salary would pay far heavier taxes. (Many private companies have been created simply as tax avoidance devices. A highly paid professional person or entertainer could form a company to sell his services, while he would draw a relatively small salary as an 'employee' of the company.) Successive governments over many years have thus chosen to ignore the equity aspects of high progressive taxation in order to assist the private company.

With Corporation Tax, the situation became more extreme. Closely held family companies ('close' companies) could opt to pay no dividends at all and therefore pay only Corporation Tax on the family income, with the owners supporting themselves on directors' salaries and the periodic sale of part of their capital. They are therefore now deemed to pay at least sixty per cent of their profits in the form of dividends (whether they do so or not), and this becomes subject to personal taxation. (The legislation is complicated, and it is possible to reduce this by proving that the money is genuinely required within the company.) This still leaves the family entrepreneur less heavily taxed in total than the equivalent salary-earner.

It is very difficult to know how serious the problem of small business finance now is. The Board of Trade has recently been producing aggregated figures of private company accounts and these confirm the general points made earlier in this section. Private companies are much more heavily dependent on internal funds than quoted public companies, especially the larger private companies (over £50,000 capital) which in 1962 drew nearly four-fifths of their funds from this source (against half for the quoted companies in that year). The small private companies drew less than three-fifths from internal sources, but this was probably because of their generally lower profitability and the fact that the personal income needs of the directors would make larger proportional calls on their profits. It was also clear that private companies were far more dependent on short-term funds. A comparative analysis of the balance sheets showed that whereas twenty-five per cent of the quoted companies liabilities were short term, the figures for large, medium and small private companies were thirty-five per cent, thirty-six per cent and 45·5 per cent respectively. The small companies were thus particularly vulnerable to business recessions and 'credit squeezes'.

The evidence offered to the Radcliffe Committee was rather conflicting. The Chairman of ICFC suggested that the difficulties of the small firm in the new issue market are increasing but it cannot be doubted that the market is now better adapted to the making of small issues than ever before. Whilst it reached no firm conclusion on the size or importance of any present-day 'gap' the Committee were clearly impressed by the fact that there is no recognized and readily accessible channel (corresponding to the new issue market for large firms) through which the small industrialist can raise long-term funds. The Committee proposed the establishment of an industrial guarantee corporation which could guarantee, for a small commission, an agreed proportion of loans made by existing financial institutions to borrowers wishing to finance novel processes or new types of product. This proposal aims to meet the abnormal risk factor involved in financing small business. It would still be left to existing institutions to investigate the merits of particular proposals put to them and to decide whether or not to lend. Nothing has yet come of this.

Something has already been done about the two other proposals of the Radcliffe Committee in this field. One was that term loans (i.e. loans for a specified period) should be offered to small businesses by the banks and two banks have already announced their willingness to make such loans. The other proposal was that ICFC should raise the limit of its participation in any issue and, as we have previously noted, this has been done. It remains to be seen what effect these recent changes will have in solving the problems of financing small business.

3.7 Inflation and company finance

Since 1945 there have been complaints of a shortage of capital and in particular of risk capital. It is always difficult to pin down what exactly is meant by this and how much substance there is in the complaint. Shortage of capital may be the result of rising demand or falling supply or some combination of both. As a proportion of gross national product, savings (and investment) have increased substantially since 1938. This, however, is quite compatible with a shortage of capital for industry because much post-war investment has taken 'unproductive' forms (housing, schools, etc.) whereas the demand for capital by industry has risen with the need to make good war-time arrears and maintain full employment. The evidence suggests that large companies in particular have not lacked the capital they needed and indeed that throughout the post-war period, companies in general have held more than adequate liquid reserves.[14] A general shortage of risk capital is also difficult to reconcile with the very high level of activity in the equity market. But it is probably true that many marginal borrowers find it difficult to raise risk capital and we have seen good reason to believe that many of these are small firms who find it difficult to tap the available supply of capital. If a capital problem exists it is more likely to be a problem of distribution rather than inadequate supply.

The difficulty of increasing the supply of capital for industry has been increased by the high level of company taxation on profits. In its first year, Corporation Tax (and the residue of Profits Tax) raised the sum of £1,118 millions and then Income Taxes further reduced the potential savings of the individual shareholders. This is partly compensated by the payment of investment grants and other forms of assistance from the government (investment grants in 1967 totalled £315 millions, although

the net cost of investment grants is of course much less than this since they reduce the depreciation chargeable against profits) but there is still a very large net deficit remaining.

Rising prices have accentuated these problems. Where the prices of raw materials and goods in process have been rising, businesses have often appeared to be making profits through stock appreciation. The profits, however, are largely illusory since the cost of stockholding has increased and more working capital is required for this purpose. If the profits are taxed, the company is in effect being deprived of part of the funds which should be available for this purpose.

The effects of rising prices are even more serious where the fixed capital assets of the business are concerned. If depreciation is charged on the original cost of the assets, then profits are artificially inflated in that current output is not being charged with the real extent to which capital is being worn out. Once again taxation on these inflated profits is in part a tax on the firm's capital.

But quite apart from taxation, firms are often hard put to maintain their capital intact in times of rising prices since depreciation allowances, even if charged each year on current replacement costs, may not yield enough over the life of the asset to replace it. We may not in fact be adding to our net stock of industrial fixed assets to anything like the extent which money figures would suggest.

Some of these problems arise because the value of fixed capital assets is always difficult to establish. Accounting and Inland Revenue practice is often based on original cost partly because that is at any rate a definite and ascertainable sum. When prices are generally rising it is certain that it would cost more to replace the asset but it is often difficult to say how much more, because it might not now be expedient or practicable to replace it with another physically identical asset. More efficient machines of different design might now be available and it is difficult to decide how much of the increased cost is due to improvement and how much to rising prices.

Quite apart from cost it is clear that the value of an asset when in use is closely related to its present and future earning power and this may vary appreciably from time to time. When a firm is taken over by a new company some estimate is made of the value of its assets which are paid for either in cash or in securities. In times of boom and rising prices a greater value is often set on the assets than is justified by subsequent experience. In this case the dividend yielded by the shares is very low in relation to yields elsewhere and the value of the shares falls below the par price. The firm is said to be over-capitalized. This may hinder the raising of new capital for the business since it will be difficult to attract subscriptions for new shares if the existing shares are selling well below par. Existing shareholders may therefore be asked to agree to a financial reconstruction which will involve writing down the par value of existing shares. This has the apparent effect of raising yields (expressed as a percentage) and puts the market value of shares above par. The real effect on the company is of course negligible but it does facilitate the raising of new money. Many such reconstructions took place during the inter-war years after the break in the post-1918 boom.

So long as rising prices and boom conditions persist, however, the risks of over-capitalization and the need for capital reconstructions are rather remote. The more likely condition is one of under-capitalization in one or other of two senses. The business may find itself, for reasons suggested previously, short of the necessary working capital to maintain the high level of activity which would be justified by market conditions and the productive capacity of its fixed equipment. Alternatively, it may be under-capitalized in the sense that the real value of its assets may be far in excess of the market value of its shares, because its assets appreciate as prices rise and possibly because it has been paying low dividends and ploughing much of the profit back into the business. We have seen previously how this may give rise to take-over bids and the proprietors may feel it desirable to avoid this form of under-capitalization by making bonus issues of new shares to existing shareholders.

Inflation has provided one major compensation to companies which have been prepared to take advantage of it. Industry is normally a borrower rather than a lender of money, and inflation benefits the borrower and penalizes the lender. If you borrow £100 today and repay it in one year's time, and if in the meantime price levels have risen by four per cent, the £100 you repay is worth only £96 in terms of the original purchasing power, and if repayment takes place in two years' time, in effect the borrower is repaying slightly less than £92. If the rate of interest has been four per cent, then the interest rate and the price movements cancel out and the borrower has had his loan interest-free. If the interest rate is less than four per cent, the lender is in fact paying the borrower to borrow his money! For much of the post-war period, the net interest rate payable by industry (after allowing for tax relief) has been less than the ruling rate of interest. In the light of this, the unwillingness of so many companies to borrow becomes all the more surprising.

Interest rates have recently risen very sharply, due partly to international influences, partly to internal credit restriction, but probably also to a growing awareness on the part of lenders that they have been giving their money away for many years. Even so, if a firm has to pay a nominal ten per cent on a new loan (compared with six per cent ten years ago, and as little as four per cent twenty years ago) it is unlikely to be costing more than three per cent in real terms after allowing for inflation and Corporation Tax relief. The argument that money is 'too dear' for industry thus holds little water in these circumstances.

We have now viewed very briefly the forms which an industrial concern may take and the facilities available for its finance. Both these topics will be found to bear intimately on more general questions of the organization of industry. The possibilities of firms developing to their most efficient size will depend in some measure on the form which it is open to firms to take and upon the possibilities of obtaining adequate finance. The control of modern industry and the possibilities of the exercise of monopoly power are closely bound up with the peculiarities of the structure of the most important form of industrial enterprise—the public limited company. Also, as we shall see later, the rights of different classes of debenture holders and shareholders are directly relevant to any discussion of combinations and amalgamations.

Many new influences have come to bear on the capital market. Many more companies are prepared to raise capital abroad if the terms are more favourable than the domestic market offers, and this, together with the increasing importance of international companies in the British economy, has tended increasingly to tie British industry to international rather than national market conditions. The European Common Market is eliminating barriers to the free movement of capital inside Europe, so that British entry will mean that British industry would eventually have access to, for example, German savings, but will have to compete with German firms for British (and German, French, Italian, etc.) savings.

Meanwhile, greater expertise in the use of capital is developing rapidly in both private and public industry and a much wider public is now well informed about the Stock Exchange (many daily and Sunday newspapers devote special pages or supplements to financial matters). The Companies Act 1967 obliged companies to divulge far more details of their activities than ever before (including figures of sales, broken down by the firm's main products). These developments should help to increase the efficiency of the market in allocating capital to its best uses, although such changes take a long time to show their effects.

1 *Report of the Committee on the Working of the Monetary System*, Cmd. 827, pp. 46–9 (London, HMSO, 1959), referred to as the Radcliffe Report.

2 Merrett, Howe and Newbould, *Equity Issues and the London Capital Market* (London, Longmans, 1967).

3 Henderson, R. F., *The New Issue Market and the Finance of Industry* (London, Bowes and Bowes, 1951).

4 *Radcliffe Report*, p. 81; Merritt, Howe and Newbould, *op. cit.*

5 Little, I. M. D., 'Higgledy Piggledy Growth,' *Bulletin of Oxford Institute of Economics and Statistics* (1962); and Raynor, A. C. and Little, I. M. D., *Higgledy Piggledy Growth Again* (Oxford, Blackwell, 1966).

6 This is one reason why NEDC has been keen to promote the widest possible use of DCF Technique. See Chapter 8 and *Investment Appraisal* (London, NEDC, 1965).

7 This inquiry into the finance of public quoted companies (1949–53) was sponsored by the National Institute for Economic and Social Research. The results were published in *Company Income and Finance* (NIESR) and *Studies in Company Finance* (ed. by Tew and Henderson). The work has been continued by the Board of Trade. Many of the figures quoted in this section have been drawn from those collected by G. D. Newbould, *Business Finance* (London, Harrap, 1970). We are grateful to Mr. Newbould for his help in this.

8 Gross saving in the 'personal sector' rose from £616 million in 1958 to £2,165 millions in 1966 while personal capital formation in the same years was £522 millions and £969 millions respectively, giving rise to a progressively larger 'surplus' of private saving. *National Income Blue Book*, Table 20 (London, HMSO, 1969).

9 Lipsey and Brechling, 'Trade Credit and Monetary Policy,' *Economic Journal* (December 1963).

10 Jewkes, J. and others, *The Sources of Invention* (revised edn.) (London, Macmillan, 1969).

11 See for example, Frost, R., 'The Macmillan Gap,' *Oxford Economic Papers* (June 1954); and Tew, B., 'I.C.F.C. Revisited,' *Economica* (1955).

12 Tew, B., 'EDITH,' *The Three Banks Review* (June 1955).

13 Bates, J., *The Financing of Small Business* (London, Sweet and Maxwell, 1964).

14 Rose, H., 'Company Liquidity under Strain,' *The Investment Analysis* (August 1962).

Chapter 4

Location of Industry

4.1 Introduction

The economists of the last century paid comparatively little attention to the problems of industrial location. Such issues were indeed largely irrelevant to their purposes. Their energies were directed primarily towards evolving a theory of the organization, for production, of a given aggregate of resources and the distribution of the resultant product under conditions of perfect competition. Within each market—about the possible limits of which little or nothing was said—transport costs were necessarily assumed to be non-existent. It is not surprising that economic theorists who were for the most part preoccupied with the economic problems of a timeless, frictionless and spaceless world should have very little to say on the subject of the location of industry. More recently the growth of the theory of imperfect competition, bringing with it a new interest in the problems of the individual firm, has led to a substantial change in emphasis. At the same time a more general impulse, prompting interest in the problems of industrial location, has stemmed from the pressure making for Government intervention to soften the impact of secular changes in the industrial structure.

None the less there is still no generally accepted theory of location in the sense of a formalization of the principles according to which new enterprises locate themselves.[1] Difficulty arises because the factors determining industrial location are extremely diverse and their relative importance tends to change considerably with the passage of time. Moreover, many of the factors involved cannot be expressed in quantitative terms. A firm cannot, for example, place any very precise monetary value on the possible advantages (in terms, say, of the effects of workers' morale upon productivity) of a relatively healthy site over one less congenially placed. Still further complications arise from the existence of sources of conflict within the firm itself. For example, the location needs of the firm as a buyer and user of raw material might be quite different from its needs as a producing unit or as a distributor and seller. For reasons such as these, attention in this field has usually been directed towards singling out a few factors which, both in their application and their importance, are of general significance. This approach facilitates concentration upon the wider principles involved and upon their relative strength in different sets of circumstances, but it must still be remembered that for any individual firm its own peculiar circumstances might result in some less general, and perhaps non-economic, issue over-riding these.

4.2 Extractive and local industries

These complications, however, are not universal. In certain industries, notably those which are local or extractive in character, the existing location pattern can be more simply explained. It is not difficult to see why, for example, the water-supply, timber and soft drinks industries, the bus, petrol station and local government services, the hotel, laundry and retail grocery trades, etc., have remained dispersed and local in character. They provide goods or services which must either be supplied direct to the consumer or are uneconomic to transport over long distances. Thus the so-called service industries must by their very nature be set up wherever the customers are to be found and although there are exceptions to this—the tourist industry, for example, exhibits the reverse trend of the customers seeking out the service locations—they tend to be the sort of exception which proves the rule. In other industries the economies of large-scale production (of bottled soft drinks, for example) will be insufficient, beyond a certain point, to cover the additional cost of supplying distant consumers. For all these industries, therefore, the dominating influence upon their location pattern is that of the distribution of the total population, although the precision with which the location pattern reflects the spread of population is modified by such considerations as the uneven distribution of income and personal expenditure.

The location limits of industries concerned with the extraction of raw materials such as coal, iron, and bauxite are fixed by the distribution of the material deposits. Obviously these industries can only be carried on in places where there are raw materials to be extracted. It does not follow, however, that the industries will be located wherever there are existing deposits. The working of any particular deposit depends upon such factors as its accessibility, its quality and the demand for it, i.e. upon the costs of working it relative to the price which it can command. The steam coals of South Wales, for example, were not extensively worked until, in the mid-nineteenth century, the coming of railways enabled them to be carried cheaply to the sea and, with the development of the steamship, the growth of a special demand for their steam-raising qualities enabled them to command a price premium sufficient to overcome the higher costs involved in working this type of coal. It is the operation of forces such as these which determines where the industry will be located at any particular time since, whenever deposits are widely dispersed, the industry is always liable to be on the move away from areas which have become uneconomic and towards those which, because of technical advances in extractive methods, transport improvements or the development of fresh markets, have become more productive.

The extractive industries are particularly important from one point of view. They must by their nature be dispersed and it is primarily their influence, together with that of industries which, for one reason or another, are tied to their raw materials or their markets, which acts as the main countervailing force to the steady trend towards industrial concentration. In this connection the influence of the major extractive industry, agriculture, is especially significant.

4.3 Major economic factors bearing on location

Any discussion of the economic factors of location must be largely based upon a consideration of costs. There are normally several locations from which it is possible for the firm to operate. If, however, the entrepreneur acts rationally (in the economic sense) and if he has the necessary knowledge, he will choose the location which offers the lowest cost per unit of output. Of the numerous factors which could play some part in determining which location this will be, transport costs form one of the most obviously impor-

tant. Transport costs are likely to be incurred at two main stages
in the activities of a firm: in the procurement and assembly of its
raw materials, and in the distribution of the finished product.
Producers thus have some incentive to choose a site near to their
raw material suppliers and also near to their market, but unless
these coincide there is likely to be some conflict between these
two sets of attractions. At first sight it might seem that the
solution pointed to would indicate some intervening point where
the total ton-miles of transport to and from the firm are
minimized. (This was substantially the Weber solution, but later
work has considerably modified it.) The structure of transport
rates, however, tends to mitigate against such a solution. There
are usually important economies for long hauls and lower rates
for materials which are bulky in relation to their value, so that
transport costs do not in fact vary directly with distance. Moreover, location at some intermediate point would involve a break
in carriage (which is expensive) besides sacrificing the gains, in
specialized services and knowledge, which can be derived from
close contact with either the material source or the markets. The
result of all these influences is a tendency to push the point of
minimum transport costs either towards the raw materials or
towards the market, rather than to some point in between.

Thus in so far as transport costs affect location decisions at all,
their major effect is to make industries either material-orientated
or market-orientated. The comparative strength of these different
pulls is largely determined by the nature and the relative quantities of the raw material and final product which have to be
transported. If the materials are bulky, heavy, and costly to
transport, whilst the finished product is relatively compact, light,
and cheap to transport, the effect of the transport cost factor on
location, although it might be offset by other considerations, is to
indicate a site near to the source of raw materials. This pull is,
moreover, greatly reinforced when the manufacturing process
involves a substantial loss of weight, through combustion or waste,
since this means that the total quantity which has to be transported will be much less if manufacture is carried out near the
raw materials.

The operation of these considerations is seen most clearly in
such processes as the reduction of ores and the curing or canning
of fish, processes which involve the removal of a large proportion
of waste. They are also important in industries which have heavy

fuel requirements where the attraction is towards the fuel source. Coal has exerted a powerful influence in this respect, since it is relatively costly to transport whilst its weight does not enter into the final product. Where more than one heavy and bulky raw material is used in a process, the greatest pulling power will be exerted by that material which loses most weight in manufacture, unless one of the other materials is used in much greater quantities. When the richest iron ores were to be found in the coalfields the manufacture of steel was naturally attracted there. But when the low-grade ores of eastern England came to be worked, the tendency was to locate new blast-furnaces there, since it would have been less economic to convey ore with a low iron content to the coalfield. Where they have become dependent upon imported ores, the tendency has been for the blast-furnaces to be moved towards the coast.

The recent development of very large bulk carriers has significantly affected the economics of location in the steel industry. The costs of transport per ton-mile diminish with increasing size, but increasing size reduces the number of harbours capable of handling such ships. In addition expensive bulk handling equipment must be installed in order to turn the ships around quickly, since otherwise the cost advantages would be lost. Large-scale steel plants are thus being drawn to a relatively few deep-water sites, which may not be influenced by the location of domestic sources of fuel or raw materials, e.g. Taranto in Southern Italy.[2] This new factor has come along before the previous trend to the East Midlands orefields in this country had worked its full effect, so that the geographical distribution of the steel industry falls far short of anything like an economic equilibrium—it represents a series of incomplete dynamic processes, some of which will now never be completed.

Industries are attracted towards their markets wherever the transport costs are higher for their finished products than for their materials. This may arise for a variety of reasons.[3] Some processes involve a weight gain; brewers and mineral water manufacturers use large quantities of water which make their final products bulkier than their materials. In other cases, transport costs per ton-mile are greater for products than for materials because the products are fragile or perishable or because the structure of transport costs makes it more expensive to move goods of high value in relation to weight. It frequently happens, too, particularly in the manufacture of consumer goods, that the manufacturer buys standardized materials in bulk and sells a range of differentiated products to meet relatively small orders involving a large number of individual consignments. In such cases, the transport costs of distribution are likely to be higher than those of procurement and exert a pull towards the market. This market pull is, however, often dissipated where the manufacturer is catering for a national market. Where the market is wide and fairly evenly dispersed, the manufacturer might establish a number of production centres in various parts of the country. On the other hand, if the processes permit considerable economies of scale, it may be preferable for him to establish one, or a few, large plants in which the lower production costs would outweigh the extra transport costs which this would entail.

An important exception to the tendency of transport costs to pull industries either towards their material sources or towards their markets is provided by transport junction centres. In processes where a number of materials are used and the final product seeks a variety of outlets, a major transport junction exerts a strong attraction because it facilitates both the assembly of materials and the distribution of products. A similar influence is operative at points where two different transport media converge. By locating at such centres, which for many producers will be intermediary points between raw materials and markets, the industrialist can often avoid costly trans-shipment of goods since he can, for example, bring his raw materials entirely by water carriage and use road or rail for distributing the finished product. Such considerations as these bestow special advantages on ports as centres of industrial activity.

The significance which attaches to the arguments outlined above depends, however, on the ratio of transport costs to total costs, and the extent to which transport costs vary at different possible locations. But one of the most important long-term trends in British industrial development has been the decline in the relative importance of transport costs. The combined impact of constant technical improvements in methods of transport together with the wider, finer, spread of the transport network has been to increase the flexibility and efficiency of transportation and thus reduce the limitations imposed by distance. This tendency has been further reinforced by changes in the industrial structure whereby the heavy industries, in which transport costs tend to be most significant, have become relatively less important. Moreover, the substitution of electricity or oil for coal as sources of heat and power has much weakened a further influence —the great weight loss in processes where large amounts of coal were used—which in the past made transport costs a strong and pervasive influence on location decisions. Indeed, nothing epitomizes all these trends more forcefully than the decline in the relative position of the British coal industry, since it was the pull of the coalfields upon other heavy industries which was the most potent single factor producing the characteristic location pattern of British industry in the last century. For some industries, transport costs remain a decisive determinant of location but, over an increasingly wide range of industry and, it may be noted, for many of the characteristic growth industries of this century, transport costs are a relatively minor consideration. Compared with countries such as Canada, U.S.A. and Australia, or even Italy and Spain, Britain is a small country. A journey of 300 miles in Great Britain may be considered long, but it could take place inside the borders of most American States. With the exception of the concentration of a fifth of the population in the London area, the remaining four-fifths tends to be distributed around the geographical centre. It is not surprising therefore that within Great Britain, transport costs tend to be a minor objective factor, although a *sense* of distance or isolation could still weigh heavily in the minds of entrepreneurs. According to Luttrell,[4] two-thirds of manufacturing industry could be located in any of the industrial areas of the country without vitally affecting its costs. Florence[5] found that in both Britain and the U.S.A. the twenty most highly localized industries were not on balance markedly drawn to markets or materials. The Toothill Committee[6] found that Scottish industry, while facing the longest journeys to southern markets and suppliers, nevertheless did not meet any insuperable obstacle in this. The additional transport costs compared with a central location could amount to two or three per cent of total costs in some cases, but this is within the spread of costs which would normally be found in industry even between reasonably efficient firms, and in any case there are compensating advantages in cheaper land and lower wages in more distant locations.

None the less the greater flexibility of transport and the smaller relative cost which it involves have not resulted in industry becoming more dispersed. This is partly because it is not only transport costs which vary at alternative locations; there can also be differences in processing costs. Fundamentally these arise because the factors of production are less than perfectly mobile. If all factors were completely mobile, their prices would be uniform throughout the economy so that they would have no effect on location decisions. This situation is most nearly approximated to in the case of capital which, in Britain, is generally highly mobile in the sense that its price (the rate of interest) shows little geographical variation. Even so, capital availability can sometimes exercise a large, and even decisive, influence on location. As was shown in Chapter 3 small firms have some difficulty in raising capital through the market and are more dependent upon local personal connections which may tie them to a particular area. In contrast to capital, land is almost completely immobile and rents consequently exhibit a considerable variation. None the less the level of rents rarely plays a decisive role in determining location. In a negative sense, the very high land values in urban centres are prohibitive for most forms of industrial activity, but usually there still remain a large number of possible sites where the rent variation is not significantly wide, especially as the rent element normally forms only a small proportion of total costs. Labour is considerably more mobile than land, but since wages frequently form a significant part of total processing costs, any regional variation in its price exerts a greater impact upon industrial location.

Labour is relatively immobile in the short run. Personal preferences, family and social ties, costs of moving—these and other factors deter movement and make for regional differences in real wage levels. It is, of course, the difference in real labour costs which is important. Lower wage rates will not on their own attract industry because they might be offset by lower efficiency and productivity. Where real costs of labour are lower there will, other things being equal, be a tendency for industry to be attracted towards the area. The strength of the attraction will, however, vary considerably from industry to industry depending upon the proportion of labour cost to total cost. Moreover, its influence may be offset if establishment in the area involves an increase in transport costs greater than the expected saving in labour costs, if it means foregoing substantial external economies which could be secured by setting up at the existing centres of the industry, or if the industry requires particular labour skills which are not in fact available in the low-cost region.

Too much should not be made of the locational pull of lower labour cost. In the long run, labour is sufficiently mobile to limit regional differences in real wage levels and the trend towards national agreements and minimum wages has further narrowed the field within which they operate, although in areas of labour shortage, firms may in fact have to pay rates much above those embodied in national agreements. Moreover, regional cost-of-living variations are not (except perhaps for the London region) sufficiently marked to have a great effect on labour costs. In recent years variations in labour supply seem to have been much more important. The high national level of employment since 1945 has concealed a significant degree of regional variation between those areas, like the Midlands and London, where there has generally been a shortage of labour, and others, like south-west Wales, Merseyside and parts of Scotland, where relatively easy labour conditions have persisted. For industries which are not 'tied' by transport costs to their raw materials or their markets, the existence of a labour supply must have been a source of attraction for industrialists. Studies of the clothing industry and of boot and shoe manufacturing, suggest that the shortage of labour at established centres can be a major consideration in the location of new plant.[7] The extent to which the pre-war clothing industry was concentrated in London, the north-west and Yorkshire has, for example, declined because of some movement towards Wales and the Northern region, which were able to supply labour. Much depends on the type and quality of labour which is being sought. In the case of the clothing industry, what was chiefly required was a pool of relatively cheap labour. The fact that this was unskilled was welcomed to some extent, because it facilitated the introduction of new production methods which might have aroused considerable opposition from the skilled workers in the older centres. In the case of the radio industry, however, greater obstacles have been encountered in setting up in new centres because of the difficulty in recruiting labour with the particular skills needed by the industry. This entails a greater expenditure on training schemes, although the problem has been partly countered by concentrating the more routine tasks in the development areas where, as one result, the industry employs a much higher proportion of female labour than it does in the older centres.[8]

The attractions of a labour pool may then, even at a time of general labour shortage, be greatly diminished if the labour available is not of the right type. Apart from the question of skills, if the unemployed labour of an area is, or is thought by entrepreneurs to be, aggressive, union-minded and strike-prone, industrialists will be nervous about basing their plans on its utilization. This was perhaps a significant factor in the failure of industry to move towards the regions of high unemployment in the inter-war years. (Another reason was that the other parts of the country were only relatively prosperous. There was no desperate shortage of labour outside the depressed areas to push industry towards them, whilst the labour surplus in the depressed areas was often not of the particular skills needed by the expanding industries. Industrialists were also generally reluctant to set up in a depressed area just because it was depressed.) Probably of more importance today is the extent to which many of the currently expanding industries demand a high proportion of skilled labour, which makes them reluctant to leave their existing centres.

The pull of the existing centres is, however, much more general than this. An industry may be attracted to a particular area by some natural advantage—power supply, raw material, climate, etc. But even where these initial advantages have been exhausted or have dwindled in significance, the concentration of an industry, or of a considerable section of it, in a relatively small area affords large benefits of its own. These so-called 'economies of concentration' take many forms, such as the attraction of ancillary trades which enable the main industry to satisfy its specialized needs more easily and cheaply. Thus the development of marine engineering on the Clyde and textile engineering in Lancashire not only facilitates prompt servicing and repair of specialized machinery but also, by allowing close contact between manufacturer and technician, encourages the design of improved machinery. In addition, professional and commercial services become closely geared to the needs of the industry. The establishment of joint research facilities becomes more feasible and economical and local educational facilities, particularly in technical colleges, are often designed to cater for the particular requirements of the major industry. If market trends are favourable all these agglomerative tendencies will result in a greater population density in the region, which thus also attracts those industries which are, for any reason, market-orientated. Public utilities and the service industries grow, and their growth, by offering wider medical, educational and entertainment amenities, further adds to the attractions of the region.

The strong impact of these advantages of industrial concentration have been well illustrated by an analysis of the West Midland conurbation.[9] This study also stressed another powerful economic influence. Concentration fosters the establishment, in close proximity, of a number of plants, the processes of which are highly 'linked'. This produces amongst firms the same sort of advantages which result from economies of scale in a single large firm. Firms engaged in similar and successive stages of an industry gain substantially from quick and easy contact with each other and from considerable specialization of functions as between firms. There are also close links between the different metal industries which are highly concentrated within the West Midland region. Each gains from the proximity of the others and can attract and draw upon other industries which perform processes (like metal founding and forging) which are common to all the main industries, as well as upon industries making tools and components (like lathes or steel tubes) which are required by all. Moreover, the high localization of these industries, which mainly employ male labour, probably encouraged the growth of such industries as cocoa and chocolate manufacture, which are also prominent in the region and which are predominantly female-employing industries.

Industrial complexes such as the West Midlands' metal trades probably benefit small firms rather more than large ones. A collection of interdependent small firms can each specialize on quite a large scale, so that collectively they show many of the features and economies of a single very large integrated firm. The tendency to conglomerate is an important factor explaining the survival of small firms in engineering, clothing, printing etc, even where the basic technology of the industry suggests significant economies of scale. Small firms inside such complexes will not transplant very easily to a new environment, and the whole complex will obviously be difficult to 'plan' artificially, since it will have evolved gradually over a very long period. It is therefore dangerous to conclude that because a firm is small, even if it uses little capital and apparently little highly skilled labour, it is therefore 'footloose,' and capable of locating anywhere. Very large firms are often less dependent upon their immediate environment and may survive, or benefit from, a move to a new location more readily than a small one.

Altogether the gains from industrial concentration are formidable and pervasive. They are further reinforced by the operation of the historical factor. When an industry has in the past settled primarily in one particular region there is a strong tendency for any new entrant into the industry to settle in the same district. The reasons for the industry localizing itself wherever it happens to be may be no longer operative, but the mere fact of localization, with all its attendant external economies, exerts a strong pull. It may be that if the industry as a whole could be moved some other region would now be more suitable for its development. But the individual enterprise has to take the existing industrial pattern as given, and the existing pattern, as determined by historical development, is always a factor influencing (consciously or unconsciously) the location decision of the new entrepreneur.

It is tempting to look to history to provide some of the answers which an imperfect theory of location has failed to provide. But there are dangers inherent in this approach as well as strong reasons why it should yield only limited results. It is not difficult to find historical confirmation of the broad trends. In the generation before 1850, for example, 'every traveller to Britain noticed the extraordinary way in which industry and population were being concentrated on or near the coal measures.'[10] But the more detailed movements are harder to discern. In the past, as now, it is rare to find any reliable and specific information on the reasons for individual location decisions. This paucity of precise evidence opens the way for two dangerous possibilities of misinterpretation. The first is that of *post hoc* reasoning. Because an industry has in fact been localized in a given area, plausible factors can be brought forward to explain this fact. But there is no assurance that the factors thus stressed *ex post facto* were the ones which were initially decisive. It is perhaps even easier to err in the opposite direction and argue that because there is no obvious explanation for an entrepreneur having chosen some particular location, the choice therefore was arbitrary. The conception that the cotton industry 'settled in Lancashire for largely fortuitous reasons', for example, is one that has to be considerably modified when the origins of the Lancashire cotton industry are pushed back beyond its spectacular rise in the second half of the eighteenth century.[11] The main point about the significance of historical factors of industrial location is not that they illustrate the extent to which the location pattern has developed as the cumulative result of historical accidents. Their significance is rather that historical inertia (well founded in the continuance of large external economies) tends to perpetuate the industrial importance of an area and, secondly, that there is none the less a continuous process of change in the location pattern arising from the influence of long-term trends.

4.4 Some other factors

The brief account given above of the more general influences bearing upon industrial location could be supplemented by an almost inexhaustible list of more specific factors. In view of the considerable uncertainties facing the entrepreneur it is likely that location decisions, which are essentially long-term in nature, are sometimes determined by short-term considerations. The shortage of factory buildings in the immediate post-war years, for example, led many firms to set up wherever they could find suitable accommodation. In many cases the ultimate decision has probably hinged upon more personal considerations. These may range over a very wide field, including such possibilities as the social ambitions of the entrepreneur's wife. The most important personal consideration, however, is probably the attachment of a person to his home locality. It is natural that a small business should be established where the entrepreneur happens to live and that, if successful, it should grow and develop on its original site. It is partly for such reasons that Oxford has become an important centre of the motor industry and York of chocolate manufacture.

It is easy to regard decisions grounded upon such factors as being mainly irrational, from an economic standpoint, but such a view would only be partly justified. The entrepreneur has to ensure that there is an appropriate site or building, that transport and power facilities are available, that the climate and water supply are suitable, and that there are no other factories nearby which are incompatible with his own operations (for example, a chocolate factory is unlikely to be established near a cement factory). More substantially, many of the so-called personal factors in location decisions are well based in economic terms. The particular difficulties facing small firms in raising capital may be more easily solved if the entrepreneur is well known in the district, whilst a personal acquaintance with a number of local businessmen may facilitate sales of the product or the procurement of raw materials.

The major point, however, is that although the ultimate decision might turn upon some apparently trivial personal considerations, this does not necessarily mean that other factors have been ignored. It may simply mean that transport and labour costs, etc. are relatively unimportant to the firm or show no significant variation at different locations. Normally the entrepreneur can only indulge his personal preferences if the estimated cost differences between possible sites are relatively small. But as we have seen, there has been a strong trend over a wide range of industry towards reducing the relative importance of transport and labour costs and hence removing the cost differences between alternative sites. To some extent, then, there is more scope for the ultimate choice being governed by less general factors, especially if market imperfections permit the neglect of minor competitive disadvantages.

Finally, it is important not to underrate the influence of ignorance and uncertainty on location decisions. The average entrepreneur will have limited personal knowledge of the possibilities open to him, and will naturally incline to stick to the area he knows. If he does have to move he will tend to stay as close as possible to his place of origin (It has been shown, for instance, that when firms have moved out of London, there has been a tendency for them to move to suburbs or new towns on the same side of the London area as their original location—for instance Crawley has generally received firms from South London, Basildon from East London, etc.) or go into an area which already contains firms similar to his own. It could reasonably be argued that the survival or success of similar firms is an indication that the location is at least not positively adverse, although if this line of reasoning were followed by too many firms of the same type, it would lead to congestion and increasing competition for labour in the area. The tendency may well be cumulative, since the more firms crowd into the area, the stronger would the case appear to the outsider that it must be a good location, otherwise there would not be so many firms there. Thus a line of reasoning which is logical for the individual may not apply in the aggregate.

Even for large firms, the research necessary for a detailed investigation of all possible sites will be very expensive. Analytical models of cost minimization generally employ a few variables which fall into a convenient mathematical form. In practice, since firms are usually multi-product with a very large number of inputs, the variables run into hundreds or even thousands, their mathematical form may be irregular, and some will not be directly measurable. Location decisions thus present severe problems in the field of operational research, and it is only recently that the appropriate techniques and the large-scale computers required to solve these problems have evolved. It has therefore been impossible for a complex firm to find the absolute optimum location except by chance, although in most cases this has not mattered a great deal, since the cost difference between the uniquely best site and a large number of others has been trivial. Only very large firms can afford to employ the personnel and equipment capable of this sort of analysis, but specialist firms of consultants have established themselves to sell their services to smaller firms as well. It seems to follow that over the course of time, the actual location of industry could begin to correspond with the theoretical explanations, but given the large proportion of industry in which costs are insensitive to location, there will always be a large random element in the geographical distribution of most industries.

4.5 Industrial movement
The location of industry is conventionally measured and discussed in terms of employment, firstly because the social implications are most readily apparent through employment, and partly because employment statistics are most readily available. However other measures such as capital employed or space requirements may be more relevant for physical planning, or output for transport studies. There will often be a tendency for capital, output and square-footage to move closely together, but employment can often diverge as industries become more capital intensive. It is important to be careful in using expressions like 'declining industries', when only the labour force might be contracting and everything else is expanding, especially as the

effect on associated industries of a general contraction, due to either falling demand on the one hand, or increasing capital intensity on the other, will be completely different.

The last two sections have stressed the force of inertia in retaining the *status quo*, but in spite of this, the pattern of industrial location does slowly change. Some change might be expected from firms actually moving about (e.g. building a new plant or an extension in another area) but the main influences will be the differential growth or decline of industries which have different location patterns. If an industry which is highly localized in an area reduces its total labour force, the pattern of employment in that area must be significantly affected, and if the industry expands, the area might become even more specialized than it was before. Thus changes in markets, products, technology, or materials will all change the pattern of distribution of the employed population even if no firms or establishments actually changed their location. Thus, very little of the shift in the relative distribution of employment towards the South-East actually involved firms moving from the North to the South (one of the main difficulties in producing spectacular results in regional policy is that in attempting to moderate or reverse this process, it has to rely very largely on moving firms to the needy areas, and in most cases cannot rely on what would in principle be a more natural process of encouraging the expansion of 'growth' industries already situated there); instead, the industries providing the employment in the north contracted, while the orientation of the market became more towards the South-East, with a consequent expansion of the service industries in that area. This may not apply directly to some of the new industries which grew up in the South, but often the new industries developed as subsidiaries of slightly less new industries in the same area— electronics from electrical goods, computers from electronics, and so on. This would then involve little, if any, change in locations for the firms involved.

Nevertheless, firms do change their locations on occasion, although the total effect of such moves is relatively small compared with the numbers involved in industrial growth and decline and the numbers of workers who change their jobs for one reason or another. A recent official survey[12] shows during the two decades after the Second World War, 3,014 establishments, employing 870,000 people had moved in the sense in which a move is defined in the report, i.e. the creation of a new establishment, employing more than ten persons, in a different region from the original location, purely 'local' moves thus being ignored.[13] Establishments which had moved in the previous twenty years, thus accounted for 9·7 per cent of the 1965 manufacturing labour force and about five per cent of establishments employing more than ten people. As a crude approximation, inter-regional moves affected less than half of one per cent of manufacturing employment in an average year. As some indication of the relative importance of different sources of change, over the period 1952–65, moves accounted for 497,000 jobs at the end of the period, whereas *net* growth in the growing industries in the same period was 1,531,000 and net decline in the contracting industries was 709,000. The gross volume of changes resulting in these net changes is unknown, but must be many times the net volume. Transfers (the shift of an existing establishment from one place to another) accounted for a third of all moves, with the creation of new branches (while the base establishment stayed put) covering the remainder. These proportions varied from one part of the country to another, three-fifths of all moves into the South-East were transfers, while in the outlying regions, five-sixths of incoming moves were new branches.

Firms will rarely change their location simply because they find that location factors affecting them have changed making costs significantly lower somewhere else. Movement is expensive. Equipment like blast furnaces and railway sidings cannot be moved and may have no value to any potential purchaser of the present site, and, although this may not be any great loss if the assets are old, most businesses involve continuous investment and replacement. Thus, at any given time, a lot of fairly new assets might have to be written off. Key workers might not be prepared to move with the firm or will require a high price to do so. Above all, a long running-in period is required in any new location and production costs will be high until the 'teething troubles' are over and the plant is up to full production.[14] Movement will thus tend to be associated with some other stimulus, and the most important such stimulus is growth in demand which leads to pressure on productive capacity on the firm's present site. The capacity restriction might be space or shortage of labour, but firms have often shown great ingenuity in overcoming such restrictions rather than move to a place where both were plentiful. Moreover the Howard Report showed that where firms did 'move' much of the movement was short-distance. For example, sixty per cent of the labour involved in moves out of the congested London area went to other parts of the South-East and East Anglia. However, nearly all of the movements covered in the Board of Trade enquiry affected firms in expanding industries. Substantial changes in the pattern of markets might also provide a strong incentive to suppliers to change their location pattern. The sudden creation of a large new motor-manufacturing area on Merseyside was expected to produce a very large influx of component manufacturers in its wake, although it seems in general that the component manufacturers have not followed unless they wished to expand their capacity, Merseyside being regarded as a suitable location for their expansion.

Firms may also respond to changes in the pattern of supply, although here again the timing of their response will usually be determined by a need to expand, and the changed conditions then help to determine where the expansion will take place. The slow response of the iron and steel industry to changing supply conditions has been strongly influenced by the slow overall growth of the industry and it could be argued that this has in turn been one of the causes of slow growth. Aluminium smelting, on the other hand, having few traditional roots and with an explosive rate of growth, has shown great sensitivity to the new situation created by new technology (nuclear power), government policy (investment grants), and the commercial policy of its suppliers (marginal cost pricing in the fuel industries) resulting in locations as diverse as Anglesey, North East Scotland and the North-East of England.

The post-war period has produced some specific influences on movement which have not necessarily been linked to the growth of the industries concerned. The rebuilding of city centres has displaced many businesses, the majority of them small and medium in scale. Such businesses often find movement a problem, even when they are fully compensated for their old site, since they may well be part of the characteristic conurbation complex and hence highly dependent on firms around them. Small-scale textile finishers in northern cities, or firms in the London tailoring trade may find survival impossible even in a brand new purpose-built factory on a trading estate some distance away. Most of the movements due to redevelopment will be short distance—so that relatively few will have been included in the Howard enquiry already referred to—but in the London area, owing to the size of the conurbation, many of these moves became inter-regional,[15] and this largely accounts for the high proportion of 'transfers' as opposed to 'branches' in movements from the South-East.

The development of firms in city centres may come about through the demolition of their old premises, or it may be because the change in the environment is so extreme as to outweigh the general rule that firms rarely change their location simply because of a change in location factors. The removal of some other firms making up the complex may weaken the hold of the central situation, and increasing traffic congestion may impose heavy costs on firms moving materials into and out of a factory. Moreover, the value of the site may be enhanced by the neighbouring developments, so that eventually the management realizes that it is using an asset whose value is entirely out of proportion to the other assets in the business. By realizing this asset (i.e. selling the land) and moving out to a cheaper site, the firm may have enough capital to begin again on a much larger scale. If the firm's own management does not appreciate what is happening, there are industrial holding and property companies which are aware of such situations and may acquire the land relatively cheaply by buying the whole company at something close to its book value, which will be below the true value of its assets. The new owners will then move the plant, or they may simply close it down. 'Financial' transactions such as these are often thought of as being somewhat separate from the 'real' world of production and the large capital profits which they may generate make them easy targets for criticism, but where existing owners are slow to respond to economic stimuli, a change in ownership may be a necessary condition for greater efficiency.

Any attempt to explain the distribution of any industry, or of industry in general, must take account of the long time-lags in the process of change, so that at any given point in time, the distribution will represent the effects of many influences, some of which will still be in the process of working themselves out. Thus many of the locational forces which were acclaimed as 'new' in the 1920s (such as electricity and road transport which could provide any firm with two of its principal requirements at almost any point on the map, instead of their being tied to the coalfields and the railway system) have certainly not exhausted all of their potential for changing the location of British industry. Similarly, the latest influences such as North Sea natural gas as a source of power and raw chemicals, and the European Common Market which will shift the marketing centre of gravity further towards the South-East, will produce gradual rather than sudden change.

Since changes in location are strongly associated with industrial expansion, the rate at which the distribution of industry changes will tend to increase if the rate of economic growth increases. Faster growth would also help to make it easier to deal with the consequences of change. Higher incomes and greater security may cause the population to become more mobile, more can be spent on housing and other services, and government location policies have more chance to work if there are many firms on the move. It has been the case in the past that governments have delayed action until recessions or depressions have caused acute problems and the lack of general expansion has made it almost impossible to produce significant effects. The obverse is also true. During the 1950s regional policy was allowed to lapse although this was a period of moderate but sustained growth when there was a fair amount of industrial movement amenable to channelling. The reappearance of acute symptoms of a regional problem in the late 1950s led to a revival of regional policy, but this has since been hampered by the generally less favourable economic climate of the 1960s. However, it is to the nature of the 'regional problem' that we must next turn.

4.6 The regional problem
The distribution of industry and the distribution of population are naturally very closely related, and, as a long historical process, population has generally adjusted to industrial distribution rather than vice-versa. However, as industry has become less orientated towards fixed sources of materials and power, population has become an increasingly important influence on the location of industry. The movement of both population and industry is a slow and uncertain process, and it is likely that a rapid change in one will tend to leave the other behind, perhaps for a very long time. The most rapid series of such changes in this century were those affecting employment in such traditional industries as coal, shipbuilding and cotton. These industries tended to be heavily concentrated in Northern England, South Wales and Central Scotland, and the reduction in their labour requirements through

113

declining demand and greater labour productivity was far faster than the rate at which the populations of these areas could adjust. The consequence was very severe unemployment affecting not just particular areas but also particular groups within those areas. The case of nearly one hundred per cent unemployment among shipbuilders and steelworkers in Jarrow in the early 1930s is still remembered, but similar percentages of unemployment occurred in some mining areas among coal miners.

The market economy is highly flexible in dealing with most adjustments by harnessing thousands of individual decisions to a particular end. Thus, when a group of workers become 'redundant', there will usually be a variety of consequential small changes which will help to re-absorb them—other employers each taking up one or two, a few deciding to leave the district and try elsewhere and so on. At the same time some workers (especially women) might decide to withdraw from the labour force, and some older workers (particularly unskilled) may find that in spite of all the changes, they are left stranded as 'hardcore' unemployed unless they are prepared to undertake very menial work. By and large, however, this process is an everyday event attracting relatively little attention. Only when the redundancy is very large and highly concentrated does it outrun the powers of the market economy to cope with it. Obviously, a great deal depends on the general economic environment in which it occurs. If economic activity is generally depressed, the high concentration of unemployment will persist, whereas adjustment may be relatively easy when demand is buoyant. The postwar history of the cotton industry provides the outstanding example of a region's adjustment to a continuous and very large decline in its staple industry. The old mills provide sound and cheap accommodation for a great variety of new industries, and the skilled labour force of the cotton industry is frequently ideal for the light assembly work and packaging which is characteristic of many of the new industries. Thus in spite of the rundown in the cotton industries' labour force[16] unemployment has not risen above the national average. Emigration from the area and some reduction in female activity rates (i.e. a fall in the proportion of the female population of working age actually in work) have contributed to this process of adjustment.

However, cotton is a rather special case, for in the heavy industries like coal the men do not have the kind of skills wanted in most of the new light industries and the capital equipment with which they work is highly specialized. When the assets and the skills are large scale, specific and indivisible, they are not amenable to a form of solution relying on flexibility and divisibility. In short, the market system is inherently weak in solving problems such as this except in the very long run. Thus, half a century after the end of the First World War when the problem really began to emerge, the old coalmining areas still suffer from unemployment persistently above the national average. The balance of unemployment is maintained between loss of employment and population growth on the one hand, and new jobs and migration on the other. Persistent unemployment in Britain's problem areas has generally arisen because new jobs have not been created at a rate adequate to overtake the rundown of the old, and outward migration has not been adequate to absorb all of the difference. The exception to the general rule is Merseyside, where rapid population growth has outstripped the creation of new jobs and outward migration, but the end product of persistent unemployment is the same.

Unemployment may be the most acute, and the most politically sensitive problem, but it is not the only one which particular areas may face as a result of the fortunes and decisions of industry. In most cases, unemployment is coupled with slow growth in employment (although in the case of Merseyside, there is unemployment and relatively rapid growth and in East Lancashire there is slow growth and relatively little unemployment), with relatively low incomes and a general air of depression which may inhibit new enterprise and help to perpetuate the problem. Such areas suffer very badly from the effects of dereliction, with old waste heaps, abandoned factories and generally obsolete social capital in poor housing and early Victorian schools and hospitals. The emigration from such derelict areas naturally tends to take the younger people, so that there is an ageing population to add to the other problems.

Such areas epitomize the classic dichotomy of private versus social costs. Nineteenth-century industry benefited greatly from the fact that it could concentrate in such specialized areas, but the market economy never obliged the individual firms to make any provision to deal with the social consequences. Even today, when a firm goes out of business, nobody in that firm has any obligation to deal with any resultant dereliction, although the

115

Redundancy Payments scheme forces each firm to make some advance provision for the unemployment which may result. The consequences of a very rapid expansion of some of the highly specialized industrial towns in Victorian times is thus a lingering, progressive and depressing process of degeneration which seems to call for vigorous public action either to reverse the trend or accelerate it and in effect write-off and disperse these communities around the rest of the economy where the normal adjustment processes may be expected to work.

There are a related set of problems of adjustment in the areas of growing industry—principally the Midlands and South-East of England. Here, the tendency since 1945 has been for the growth in industry's demand for workers to outstrip the growth in the working population, which in turn has tended to outstrip the provision of social capital in housing, transport, schools and other services. These areas are thus faced with the high social costs of congestion. With all facilities overloaded, each additional member of the population needs a full set of social assets created for him—additional housing, extra road space, extra school places for his children and so on—since there is no slack left for him to take up. Every time a firm creates a new job in such an overcrowded area, it simultaneously imposes on the community the obligation to provide this set of social assets. This is of course not necessarily a net *extra* burden on the community, since these assets might well have to be created somewhere, but if there are other parts of the country which have spare capacity, and particularly if the extra work is drawn from some other place which has this capacity then the community might reasonably object that it was being asked to pay out unnecessarily on this account. (It does not follow that workers drawn from semi-derelict towns to Coventry or London would always come into this category, since it has already been pointed out that much of the social capital they are leaving behind is worthless and would have to be replaced.) Extreme congestion, even with high wages, can create a very poor quality of life for those involved and can generate severe social and political stresses.

Inadequate adjustment of the distribution of population to that of employment also creates problems at the macro-economic level. The broad objective of economic policy is to maintain full employment consistent with reasonable stability of prices, an approximate balance of international payments, and an efficient use of resources. Centres of extreme congestion have long been suspected of 'leading' the inflationary process, since any increase in aggregate demand will first meet supply bottlenecks in areas where there is a chronic labour shortage. Since wages and prices tend to be fixed nationally, the inflationary consequences may spread to areas which still have unused production capacity, and the government may be forced into deflationary policies before all resources have been absorbed.

It is important to distinguish between those social consequences which arise out of *changes* in the distribution of industry and those which arise from the distribution of industry itself. The first may be termed dynamic effects and the second, by way of contrast, may be termed permanent effects. The dynamic problems are primarily those of imperfect adjustment which may be expected to disappear in time although the period may be very long. The permanent effects will not soften with time. Many of the textbooks examples of 'externalities', i.e. social costs and benefits, are of this kind. Some industries have an adverse effect on their environment because of the processes they employ, and any concentration of such industries must create inferior living conditions. Smoke and effluent are traditionally thought of in this respect, but the location of any new major airport will now be strongly influenced by consideration of the noise nuisance which it will create, as the recent controversy over the proposal to locate the new London airport at Stansted has shown. In other cases it may be much more difficult to distinguish between dynamic and permanent effects. Congestion costs come into this category. Congestion will eventually be overcome as extra facilities are provided unless the congested areas are above optimum size or badly sited in a geographical sense. The costs of overcoming congestion are also affected by these considerations. If the optimum size of a city is fairly large (optimum here being defined as that size at which its citizens can be provided with necessary services at minimum average cost) then ultimately it is economically desirable that industry and population should concentrate in a few large conurbations and congestion costs and dereliction are just transitional phenomena.

Such long-term judgments can only be made in the light of society's long-term objectives, and there is neither a political nor a market machinery for determining these. We therefore tend to judge regional problems by much shorter-term criteria. In these terms, problems exist now in both the declining and expanding industrial areas, but one must beware of the solutions, ignoring the long-term objectives.

1 Alfred Weber's *Theory of Location of Industries* translated C. Y. Friedrich (Chicago, 1958) was for a long time the most noteworthy effort to provide such a theory. More recently considerable advances have been made by such writers as Hoover, Greenhut and Isard.

2 Warren, K., 'Coastal Steelworks—a Case for Argument?', *Three Banks Review* (June 1969).

3 Hoover, *The Location of Economic Activity*, pp. 36–7 (New York, McGraw-Hill, 1948).

4 Luttrell, W. P., *Factory Location and Industrial Movement*, Vol. I (London, NIESR, 1962).

5 Florence, P. S., *The Logic of British and American Industry*, pp. 83–4 (London, Routledge, 1953).

6 *Report on the Scottish Economy* (Edinburgh, Scottish Council Development and Industry, 1961).

7 Luttrell, W. P., 'The Cost of Industrial Movement', *NIESR Occasional Papers*, XIV, pp. 2–3, 26–8 (London, NIESR, 1952); Hague, D. C. and Newman, P. K., *Costs in Alternative Locations* (*NIESR Occasional Papers*, XV), Chapters II and IV (London, NIESR, 1952).

8 Hague, D. C. and Dunning, J. H., 'Costs in Alternative Locations: the Radio Industry,' *Revue of Economic Studies* (1954–55), pp. 203–13.

9 Florence, P. S., *op. cit.*, pp. 85–8.

10 Clapham, *Economic History of Britain: The Early Railway Age, 1820–1850*, p. 42 (Cambridge, University Press, 1930).

11 *Royal Commission on Distribution of the Industrial Population*, Cmd. 6153, p. 32 (London, HMSO, 1940); Wadsworth and Mann, *The Cotton Trade of Industrial Lancashire*, 1600–1750, Chapter 1 (Manchester, University Press, 1931).

12 *The Movement of Manufacturing Industry in the United Kingdom, 1945–6* (London, HMSO (Board of Trade), 1968). Referred to as the Howard Report.

13 Fifty regions are defined for the purpose of this survey. The definition of more was rather restrictive, e.g. the opening of a new establishment in Region *A* by a firm mainly located in Region *B* was not a move if the firm already had establishments classified to the same trade in Region *A*. See Beacham, A. and Osborn, W. T., 'Movement of Manufacturing Industry,' *Regional Studies* (Spring 1970).

14 Luttrell (*op. cit.*) found that four years is a characteristic period over a wide range of plants and industries for this running-in period and that initially, production costs could be much higher than those in an established plant.

15 By inter-regional we mean movement between the fifty areas designated by Howard and not movement between the Standard Regions into which the United Kingdom is divided for statistical purposes.

16 The labour force in cotton and allied textiles fell from 710,000 in 1912, to 265,000 in 1958, and 126,000 in 1968. *Report on Cotton and Allied Textiles* (Manchester, The Textile Council, 1969).

CHAPTER 5

Growth of Firms

5.1 Theory of the firm

Economic theory is not much concerned with the growth of firms. Price theory sets out, on the basis of various assumptions about market conditions and conditions of entry, the way in which firms will determine their most profitable outputs. Under conditions of perfect competition it concludes that each firm will adjust its output so that marginal cost is equal to market price. This output will be the optimum output—the output which can be produced at lowest average cost. The optimum output will be different for different firms depending on cost conditions.

Under conditions of monopoly and monopolistic competition firms will produce less than their optimum outputs and marginal cost will be less than price. Since price measures the sacrifice required from consumers to obtain the product and therefore (in some sense) the satisfaction derived from it, it is argued that resources would be more efficiently allocated if larger outputs were produced up to the point at which marginal cost (a measure of the marginal productivity of the resources in the next best alternative use) equalled the price. Abnormal profits are earned which may persist if there are restrictions on freedom of entry.

It is clear from this bald summary that a theory designed mainly to elucidate the allocative functions of prices and markets cannot be expected to explain very much about the growth of firms. This will be the case more especially as we leave the abstractions of theory and explore the real world in which firms are commonly multi-product, where markets are never very clearly delineated, where average cost cannot be assumed to be the lowest possible average cost of producing a particular output, and where tastes, techniques and methods of organization are constantly changing. But theory does help to direct our thinking in a number of important respects. It traces the adjustment of firms to changes in tastes and technology. It also suggests that the main limitations to growth are imposed by upward movement of average costs (possibly because of increased difficulties of management) and in some circumstances by the tendency of price to fall as output expands. Finally it implies certain relations between the structural characteristics of industry and the conduct and performance of firms. If, for example, sellers are few (that is, conditions of oligopoly prevail) then firms will produce outputs which are too low and sell at prices which are too high. We shall be looking at this particular matter in the next chapter and it need not detain us here.

By structure we mean principally the relationship of sellers to each other and this will be mainly conditioned by their relative size (as we saw in Chapter 2 this is formally measured by the degree of concentration). We also include the relation of sellers to potential sellers (depending on ease of entry for new firms) and the pattern of relative numbers and sizes of buyers to sellers. But the term structure is often conveniently stretched to cover other aspects of the market environment which may be expected to affect the behaviour of firms such as product differentiation, the relation of fixed to total costs, and the rate at which demand for the product is growing. Obviously many of these factors are inter-related. For example, the extent to which, and the means by which, the product is differentiated may constitute a formidable barrier to entry.

These structural conditions may affect the behaviour of firms in many ways. We have noted the effect of relative size and numbers of sellers on price and output adjustment. But the stimulus to aggressive price competition caused by the cost structure of firms, the effect of rate of growth of demand on technical innovation and so on are also important.[1] It also needs to be remembered that the conduct of firms is affected in real life by a host of personal and institutional factors which are too varied to be taken into account in a general treatment of industrial organization.

The response of firms to what we have called structural conditions may promote inefficiency not only through misallocation of factors, but also through direct cost inflation, the protection of obsolescent capital which would have to be replaced in more competitive conditions and retardation of technical innovation. But where inefficient performance is predicted by theory it is difficult in our present state of knowledge to verify this by empirical enquiry and in some respects theory offers little guidance on likely performance of firms in different structural situations. Theory says very little about the conditions which may be expected to promote a high rate of technical innovation or about conditions likely to promote cartels and their effects on performance. But what we do have is a frame of reference which permits an orderly approach to the problems with which we are concerned[2] though we should not become obsessed with the importance of allocative efficiency.

5.2 Origins and growth of firms

The preceding section has enabled us to put the growth and size of firms into some sort of theoretical context. But the firm in real life is very different from the rather soulless price and output decision-taker of theory. It develops a personality reflecting the fears and aspirations of an often ill-defined management group. (Some American writers have referred to the power of large firms to mould the desires of consumers, to affect the general direction of research, and to espouse political causes.) Growth is not so much a matter of expanding output to some equilibrium point as a process of development as the firm continuously adapts itself to changes in its environment and changes many of its characteristics in the process.

We know very little about the origins of firms. Entirely new firms in the sense of a person or group of persons contributing capital to purchase and operate new capital equipment in new premises are something of a rarity. New firms are more likely to be formed to acquire and adapt existing capital assets. New establishments are more likely to be started by existing firms to exploit some new product or process which may be the invention of its own research and development department. Entirely new firms which are started are mostly small and many fail because of lack of funds or business ability. We know most about new firms which succeed and grow. Some of these are firms with a new idea for making traditional goods[3] (e.g. ready-made pills) or something entirely new like hovercraft or jet engines. Technical

121

factors will inevitably affect the success of new firms but chance (e.g. ability to find a backer at the right time) can also play an important part.

Once a new firm takes root what will determine its rate of growth and direction of development? There are many ideas about this but most of them are difficult to substantiate by reference to the facts. Galbraith[4] stresses the drive of technical development towards larger size of firms which alone can afford the cost of discovery and have the security to profit from it. Schumpeter[5] describes how, in a world where large firms predominate, a process of industrial mutation is produced by competition from the new commodity, the new technology, the new course of supply, and the new type of organization. Growth and adaptation to this 'gale of perennial destruction' are the price of survival. Downie's competitive process[6] is a variation on the same theme.

Professor E. F. Penrose[7] has developed what is perhaps the most systematic theory of the growth of the firm. She argues that the nature of the managerial process creates both opportunities for and limitations to, growth. Each firm at any one time is likely to see some productive opportunity provided the economy is buoyant and there is some elasticity in the supply of factors. This opportunity is based on a subjective appreciation of the position which may not be borne out in the event.

In any case the firm may not respond to the opportunity. Both the opportunity and the disposition to exploit it will depend on the quality of the management team—its ability to smell out opportunities, its willingness to take risks, work hard and inspire confidence.

The opportunity is likely to derive to an important degree from unused resources within the firm which it is economical to mop up. No firm is ever likely to be in equilibrium because of indivisibilities and this excess capacity (which may be an excess capacity of the management team) is a selective force determining the direction of expansion. As expansion proceeds further opportunities reveal themselves as further sources of excess capacity develop.

Growth may be limited by the capacity of management but since growth itself enlarges the supply and quality of management and permits the use of more sophisticated techniques the limits imposed by management tend to recede. (It is important to remember that although there may be much delegation of authority, final responsibility cannot be delegated. Considerable pressures towards diversification may be generated by the growth process and this is likely to intensify the strain on top management as the firm gets bigger.) The probability is that growth becomes more difficult as the firm gets larger but there is no absolute limit to growth. Some of the checks which are stressed in theory such as rising cost curves and falling average revenue curves would seem to be largely irrelevant or unimportant. But in practice growth may be limited by barriers to entry to particular trades or by inelasticity in the supply of factors. We shall see in a later section that these limits may be considerably reduced by amalgamation and combination of firms.[8]

5.3 Economies of scale and diversification

Firms may grow by a process of internal expansion or by external expansion, i.e. by combination with other firms. There is no certain way of knowing which is most important but there are very few large firms whose growth has not been considerably affected by absorption of or combination with other firms.

It is sometimes suggested that the motivation of internal growth is different from that of amalgamation. Amalgamations reduce the number of sellers and are likely to be motivated by a desire to increase monopoly power. Internal expansion, it is reckoned, is more likely to be prompted by a desire to achieve economies of scale. But this would appear to be a considerable over-simplification. Combination of firms does not necessarily increase the degree of concentration of control over particular markets and may even increase competition in some. Moreover the amalgamation of firms may yield important economies of scale and internal expansion, which is initially promoted by a desire to achieve economies of scale, may result in complete domination of the market. A desire to escape from restrictions imposed on growth by restricted demand for a product may promote either internal or external expansion into different product lines. But as we have seen such diversification may have been inspired by a desire to mop up a surplus capacity of some factors and this is clearly a form of economies of scale. It seems somewhat unreal therefore to try to associate particular motives for growth with particular methods of growth.

Economies of scale constitute what is probably the most

important impulse to grow. They are present if long-run expansion of output produces a reduction in average costs. (It is assumed that technical knowledge is given, the price of factors is constant and that the supply of all factors is variable. This does not preclude the possibility of introducing more advanced techniques and better methods of organization at higher levels of output. The fall in unit costs which normally takes place as a plant works up to its designed capacity is not evidence of economies of scale.) Under these circumstances growth will promote more economical use of resources, strengthen the firm's competitive position and lead to an increase in turnover and profits. (They may also constitute formidable barriers to new entry. The Monopolies Commission report on Cellulosic Fibres, p. 11 (1968) instances two potential competitors who were discouraged from entering the industry by fear that they could not compete after noting the scale of production achieved by Courtaulds.)

It does not follow however that, because economies of scale are present, growth will necessarily follow. Technical economies may be available whilst growth is precluded by limitation of the market. There are also many human and institutional factors which will inhibit firms from taking advantage of economies of scale.

The main sources of economies of scale may be briefly summarized. [9]

(*a*) *Indivisibility of factors.* A particular piece of equipment may be necessary to produce low outputs although its optimum capacity may be very high, e.g. a press for stamping out metals. As production rises the cost of the press is spread over more units of output and average cost falls. Many examples can be cited where factors have to be assembled to produce one unit (say a book) yet a large number of copies can be produced for only marginally more than the extra cost of raw material and labour. The general trend of technological development towards high capacity machines producing specialized products emphasizes the importance of indivisibilities as a source of scale economies.

(*b*) *Increased dimensions.* The capacity of a piece of equipment may increase much faster than the additional cost of labour and raw material going into its construction. Ships (e.g. the large oil carriers and oil tankers which have become common in recent years), gasometers, and double-decker buses are common examples of this.

(c) *Specialization.* As output expands labour and machinery can be employed and designed to do specialist jobs. The owner-manager of a small firm cannot be expected to purchase raw materials as efficiently as a person specially trained in the job and who does nothing else. A computer can handle a very large pay-roll more efficiently than a large number of pay clerks. As we have already noted this specialized labour and equipment has to be used to its full capacity to produce its maximum effect but it may produce considerable economy of resources at outputs lower than this.

(d) *Massed reserves.* This is the principle on which banking and insurance operates. A large bank with a hundred branches does not need to keep a cash reserve one hundred times larger than a small branch bank. The latter must make prudent provision against the possibility of a 'run' on it whereas the larger bank will proceed on the assumption that the chance of a simultaneous run on all its branches is much less. In the same way the large firm will make proportionately less provision for bad debts, spare parts, and so on.

(e) *Superior organization.* At certain levels of output it becomes possible to introduce a different method of organizing the work. The introduction of the assembly line in motor-car manufacture is a case in point. The initial cost of setting up the new organization may be considerable, but when this is spread over a large output, unit costs are reduced.

It is obvious that these factors overlap to some extent. Also it will have been noted how many of them seem to be related to technical factors. Probably for this reason some writers have discussed economies of scale in relation to the establishment rather than the firm on the ground that few economies are attributable to the ownership and control of more than one establishment by the same firm.[10] But, in principle at any rate, some of these economies attach as much to the firm as to the technical unit or establishment. The indivisible factor is as likely to be a countrywide marketing organization or a first rate management team as a piece of machinery.

From the point of view of the owners, large firms may have advantages other than those which derive from economies of scale. They may exercise considerable monopolistic control over the market for their particular products and raise prices and profits by restricting output. They may exercise considerable downward pressure on the prices of their raw material by using their power as large purchasers.

This and other factors considerably complicates efforts to check empirically on the prevalence of economies of scale. Like many other concepts in economics it gets very fuzzy around the edges when we try to identify and measure it in practice. An important category of difficulties derives from the prevalence of multi-product firms and firms which manufacture and assemble many products to make a fairly homogeneous product. If the scale of output of a multi-product firm increases in such a way that the mix of products is varied it is difficult to be satisfied that a reduction in average costs is evidence of economies of scale. If the optimum output of cylinder blocks is much lower than the optimum for car bodies then the optimum output of cars may be reached whilst there are still important economies of scale available in the production of car bodies.

A study of the average costs of different sizes of firm at a point in time may show that large firms have the lowest average costs. But this does not prove conclusively that economies of scale are available to the smaller firms. A study of the change in average costs as a particular firm grows is also of limited value as evidence for economies of scale. Many irrelevant factors, including the price of factors and the state of technology, are likely to have changed as the firm has been growing. Also, as has been previously pointed out, we have no unequivocal measure of size.

Since economies of scale are reductions in average cost which are solely a function of increased output many investigators have fallen back on engineering studies (that is, calculation of the probable average cost of hypothetical firms or plants at different levels of output based on technical information) to establish the existence or absence of economies of scale. But it would seem that the possibilities can never be fully known until someone has actually grappled with the practical problems of operating a plant of a given size.[11]

It is not easy to summarize the drift of the evidence. Over a wide range of manufacturing industry it would appear that average costs decline with increasing output, at least up to medium size of plant, if factor costs are constant. This is the more likely to happen if the product is fairly homogeneous, and if the product mix does not change as output increases. It seems to be quite common for average costs to diminish up to the limit of size set by the largest plants in operation.[12]

It must be admitted however that most of the studies on which these conclusions are based are concerned with establishments rather than firms. On the whole it seems probable that scale economies available to establishments will be available to firms though some of the much quoted limiting factors (e.g. entrepreneurial skills and capital resources) relate to firms rather than plants. Certainly the evidence for superior performance of large firms is much less clear-cut than is the evidence for falling long-run average costs in manufacturing establishments. Firms are financial and accounting units and, assuming the price to be given, lower costs will be reflected in higher profits. Whilst there is some evidence for better financial results for large firms[13] there is much more recent evidence which points in the opposite direction.[14] But the measurement of profits sets many problems which are not relevant to this discussion and there are many factors bearing on financial results which do not reflect the presence or absence of economies of scale. On the whole the evidence does not support the suggestion that average costs will continue to fall as firms expand beyond medium size if factor costs are assumed to be constant and technical change is ruled out. In practice there does seem to be a tendency for factor prices to increase at large outputs. On the other hand large firms frequently have a good record of technical innovation.

Diversification of output as we have seen may be a method by which surplus capacity is mopped up and may be deemed a variant of economies of scale. It is most likely to happen where the market for existing products is limited and where there is a desire to lessen the risk of dependence on too narrow a range of products though it may introduce risks of another kind (for example, competition from specialist producers and the difficulty of commanding sufficient management skills to supervise production of varied products). The kind of new product, if any, which is taken on as a firm expands is determined by the entire productive opportunity with which it is confronted. Pilkingtons facing an expanding market and with an impressive record of technical achievement have grown by producing what is basically more of the same thing. Firms like Hoover and Dunlop have expanded into different products requiring the same raw materials processes or sales techniques. Other firms like English Electric and Decca have expanded into different product lines which spring from a common scientific and technological base—computers, television, and navigational aids.

Diversification is another notion which lacks precision. If a firm is said to diversify by going into different products we should have some criterion by which product differences are measured. The official statisticians will measure diversity according to whether the products of the firm are allocated to the same minimum list heading. But for some purposes we would need to measure diversity between products by lack of substitutability in use. Also it is not at all clear whether 'enforced' diversification (as in the case of joint products) is to be categorized as such.

Diversification is rarely completely haphazard as we have already seen. There is nearly always some technical or market link between the products though the market link may consist only in the fact that the goods are usually consumed by the same sorts of people and purchased in the same sorts of places. Perhaps the nearest we get to haphazard diversification is where a group with adequate financial resources looks for firms which can be obtained on reasonable terms and which can be nursed into greater profitability by fresh injections of capital and management advisory services.[15]

It is not easy to measure the extent to which diversification takes place though it is generally assumed to be on the increase. In 1958 the Census of Production covered over 9,000 enterprises employing over 6·3 million persons and controlling 24,113 establishments. Of these establishments, 4,103 (employing over 950,000 persons) were classified to one of fifty-three industry groups other than the one to which the enterprise was classified. But this level of diversification probably understates the real position since some industry groups embrace a fairly wide variety product.

On the whole a firm is unlikely to diversify very much in the process of internal expansion except where it sets up a new establishment to produce an entirely new product. By taking over other firms (or particular establishments of other firms) the parent company acquires ready-made machines, technical skills and market contacts. But the significance of growth by combination of firms is much wider than this.

5.4 Acquisitions and mergers
Combination or amalgamation of firms may take various forms. There is no generally accepted nomenclature but when one firm (the parent) acquires a controlling interest in another (the subsidiary) we generally refer to this as an acquisition. When two firms combine (with or without loss of their own identity) to form a third firm to control and perhaps operate their combined assets, this is often called a merger. But other forms of combination are possible. One firm may take over part of another firm, or a group of firms may combine for certain purposes such as the design and construction of nuclear power stations.

Acquisitions are the most common form of combination and we have previously quoted figures to illustrate the extent of so-called 'take-overs' in recent years. (Chapter 1, p. 19. In recent years the term merger has increasingly been accepted as a description of any form of combination of firms.) The structure of joint stock companies undoubtedly facilitates combination in this way. Control of another company can be obtained by the acquisition of more than fifty per cent of its voting stock and this may be done by simple exchange of shares and without expenditure of cash.[16] Whilst some value related to their current market price and future profit earning prospects has to be put on the shares exchanged this is much simpler and less risky than an outright purchase of capital assets for cash. The shareholders in the acquired company are merely exchanging shares in one company for shares in another and if the former are over-valued this will simply reflect itself in lower dividend per share in the acquired company for some years to come. But a cash transaction will almost certainly involve borrowing and repayment. The valuation of the capital assets would have to be very carefully done and this can present formidable problems since the value of fixed capital is determined by expectations of future profits rather than by age and original cost.

With an acquisition the acquired firm retains its separate identity and so does not lose tax rebates on account of past losses and retains any good-will attaching to the name of the firm. On the other hand, since parent and subsidiary remain separate corporate bodies there may be some clash of interest (the interests of minority shareholders have to be safeguarded), the parent may lose control if profits are not earned and the preference shareholders acquire voting rights, and separate accounts have to be kept. For any or all of these reasons the acquisition may not achieve all the advantages of integration of operations that had been hoped for.

Mergers, which are much less common, minimize some of these advantages since the new company may operate the assets—the combining companies either disappearing altogether or continuing to exist only as holding companies, i.e. holding shares in the new firm, which it has taken in exchange for its working assets. In this case the new company will have a free hand to concentrate production, eliminate surplus and obsolescent capital, combine research and development establishments, and rationalize distribution networks. (This and the preceding paragraphs illustrate the flexibility and adaptability of joint stock companies as a form of business enterprise. But it is curious that the form of combination should be affected by the vagaries of the tax system as much as by the achievement of such purposes as reducing the costs of production.)

Combinations of firms are generally classified as vertical, horizontal or conglomerate. Vertical combination takes place where there is a union of firms operating at different stages in the production of a good, e.g. the combination of a textile spinning firm with a weaving firm. Horizontal combinations are combinations of firms producing the same or similar goods or services. Conglomerates are combinations of firms producing highly diversified products. It rarely happens that the products are completely unrelated. But some conglomerates are linked only by common managerial services and financial provision which are reckoned to produce significant economies. It hardly needs to be emphasized in view of what has been said previously that this classification is not watertight. Links between goods are extremely complex and not confined to goods which are substitutable in use. It is therefore a matter of judgment whether a particular combination can be classed as conglomerate or whether a very low use by a parent of some raw material produced by a subsidiary entitles us to classify it as vertical. But these distinctions are too useful to discard. The motivation for a union of two spinning firms is likely to be different from that for a union of a bank and a laundry.

There is a tendency to link conglomerate combinations with economies of growth where limitation of existing markets is important, to link horizontal combinations with pursuit of economies of scale and/or market power and to link vertical combination with a desire to ensure supplies of raw material and market outlets where those are in few hands. But it may be doubted whether motives can be so neatly assigned. A horizontal combination of aluminium firms may reduce competition in that industry but sharpen competition between steel and aluminium in the automobile industry and between aluminium and copper in the electrical trades. Vertical combinations by pre-empting the entry of other firms into trades supplying components may increase rather than diminish the risks of monopoly exploitation.[17]

Each combination is very much the product of circumstances peculiar to itself. The personal prestige of the promoters, pressures from the Industrial Reorganization Corporation,[18] and taxation[19] may be important considerations in particular cases. But the most powerful and persistent forces promoting combinations are

(*a*) a desire to increase seller or buyer control over a particular market by becoming bigger and reducing the number of buyers and sellers;

(*b*) a desire to reduce average costs; and

(*c*) market conditions.

We shall discuss these motives for combinations in turn without attaching them firmly to particular forms or categories of combination.

The desire to increase market power (i.e. power to affect price by restricting output) is often prompted by a prolonged period of sharp price competition. This may be sparked off by a long-term decline in demand (although the history of the cement industry indicates that this is not a necessary condition) and can be severe where the excess capital capacity is long lived and little affected by technical obsolescence, where fixed costs are a high proportion of total costs and the product is reasonably homogeneous. Under these circumstances a producer will be tempted to take any price which is above marginal cost, i.e. makes some contribution to overhead costs. The extent to which prices are cut will depend on producers' estimates of the elasticity of demand for their products (which in turn will depend on their estimate of competitors reactions to their price cuts) and the possibilities of price discrimination. Occasionally this competitive price cutting will not be informed by such rational considerations. It can become rather blindly imitative and force prices well below the costs of even the most efficient producer. This is sometimes called cut-throat competition.

Sooner or later there is likely to be an agreement between firms to restrict price competition (such cartel agreements are discussed in Chapter 6) and this will be immensely facilitated if the number of sellers is reduced by combination. Larger firms which frequently take the lead in promoting cartels will be particularly anxious to absorb 'weak sellers'—those firms which have taken the lead in making price reductions not justified by their average total costs. The latter quite frequently are not the most technically advanced firms in the trade. They are often firms with a limited future which are prepared to 'eat their capital' when it has been cheaply acquired or substantially written off. Amalgamations, under these circumstances, may be defended in spite of the fact that they are immediately aimed at increasing the degree of monopoly control. Severe and prolonged price competition can have a debilitating effect on an industry by reducing profit margins and by minimizing both the incentive and the means to improve technology. The textbook virtues of price competition are well known and generally valid. But there are circumstances under which it cannot be counted on to eliminate surplus capacity quickly or to eliminate the weak rather than the strong.

There are undoubtedly cases in which realization of economies of scale are dependent upon combination. Where scientifically trained man-power is scarce it seems likely that considerable economies can be realized from amalgamation of research and development departments. Much the same applies where a few commercial banks have developed a national network of branches which are not fully utilized or where in order to realize economies of scale in the manufacture of beer the brewers have to acquire more sales outlets which are virtully in fixed supply and largely 'tied' to other brewers. But more usual cases occur where

(*a*) under the impact of technical change there is room only for one or very few establishments producing specialized products; or

(*b*) where a firm needs to diversify in order to utilize more fully some spare capacity of its own but finds it difficult to branch into another trade except by acquisition of some well established producer which has ready made market contacts, technical knowledge and specialized equipment.

It is not only the most practicable way to expand but also the quickest and perhaps, as we shall see below, the cheapest method of improving efficiency.

Market conditions affect the pre-disposition to combine in very different ways. If the market for existing products of a firm is limited then, as we have seen, diversification is a condition of growth, and combination may be the quickest and easiest way to grow. If demand in the economy generally is high and resources are fully employed then the incentives to grow are enhanced whilst the possibilities of internal growth are limited. (This is not incompatible with the argument that combinations are promoted by secular decline of particular industries.) But the opportunity to combine must be present and this too may be affected by the general state of the economy.

What constitutes a favourable opportunity to acquire other firms? The parent firm, *A*, will need to be satisfied that the acquisition will be less costly than internal expansion. The proposed subsidiary, *B*, is not likely to agree a take-over price, in cash or shares, which is less than the present value of its expected earning power. But a deal attractive to both parties may nevertheless be negotiated. *B* may take a less rosy view of its profit earning power if *A* is in a position to make life difficult for it. *B* may own assets (e.g. freehold land and buildings) which *A* is in a position to develop in a much more profitable use. *B* may be forced to sell to pay death duties or *A* may derive substantial benefit by setting past losses of *B* against its tax liabilities. *A* may command management resources much superior to *B*'s which may have reached the point of becoming too complex for its existing management. If *B* is a family business and the supply of family management brains is drying up, the family may feel that the future of the business and their own income will be best assured by being taken over.

These are some of the reasons why a bargain may be struck. It explains why the causation of combinations appears to turn around circumstances peculiar to each case. It also suggests that these factors are likely to operate with special force when demand is high, employment is full, money prices and profits are rising and there is an active market for ordinary shares. Under these circumstances assets are likely to be seriously under-valued in many businesses and some combinations are likely to be inspired by the prospect of quick speculative gains.[20]

In these kinds of situation it is not easy to see limits to growth by combination. There is not likely to be any lack of opportunities but as the firm grows bigger the checks are likely to become more serious. The checks may be administered through anti-monopoly legislation, or they may be due to the increased strain imposed on management by the size of the undertaking. The most convincing proof that such checks exist resides in the fact that the economy is not yet completely dominated by a few giant undertakings. The extent to which trades (or industry generally) are dominated by few firms is measured by the degree of concentration. See Chapter 2, p. 43, where concentration is discussed and some figures given.

Some studies have been made of 'success' and 'failure' of combination of firms but the results are inconclusive. On the basis of six case studies Cook and Cohen conclude[21] that mergers have increased efficiency in all cases. Reports by the Monopolies Commission suggest that some large firms built up by amalgamation have an impressive record of rationalization of productive facilities and technical innovation, whereas others have built up a commanding position by buying up small competitors as they appeared and have not made much effort to minimize costs. Some firms have undoubtedly made themselves more efficient but this has not deterred them from organizing cartels to suppress price competition.

Evidence on the financial results of mergers is equally inconclusive and difficult to interpret. Financial success is not necessarily indicative of increased efficiency—it may reflect exploitation of a strong monopoly position. The significance of the results will also depend on the methods used to measure financial success. But it is certainly possible that financial success will reflect increased efficiency. Livermore[22] concludes that nearly half the combinations formed in the USA between 1888 and 1905 were failures. Most large firms have grown to some extent by a process of absorbing other firms and we have previously noted some evidence of association between large size and high productivity and earning power, and also more recent evidence of declining profitability with size. Some enquiries into the experience of recent amalgamations tend to confirm these results.[23] It is of course almost impossible to distinguish between what is due to amalgamation as such and what is due to the larger scale of operations which amalgamation makes possible. But on the very limited evidence available we would not be justified in concluding that combinations have generally justified themselves by improved economic performance.

5.5 The survival of small firms

The preceding discussion makes it difficult to understand why so many small firms persist. According to the Ministry of Labour,[24] now the Department of Employment and Productivity, there were about 140,000 establishments in manufacturing industry employing ten persons or less but they probably employ less than ten per cent of total employees in manufacturing. There were more than 55,000 establishments employing more than ten persons of which about seventy per cent employed between ten and a hundred persons but accounted for only twenty per cent of total employees. A firm may own more than one establishment but the average is only 1·3 establishments per firm and it is the largest firms which own most establishments. So the figures we have quoted for establishments reflect fairly accurately the proportionate importance of small firms in manufacturing. We need to remember also that very small firms are characteristic of many service trades, retail distribution and agriculture. (For further detail on the size of firms refer back to Chapter 2.)

Part of the explanation is that new firms are being born every day and most of them start on a small scale. There is considerable prestige and satisfaction attached to being in business on one's own; entry into some industries is fairly easy, and there seems to be an unending supply of potential entrepreneurs who are ready to take a chance on the exploitation of some new idea or favourable market opportunity. Some of the small firms of today will grow, by internal growth or merger, into the larger firms of tomorrow. Many will die but the ranks of the small firms are quickly refilled by new entrants. Moreover, as we shall see, some industries offer more favourable opportunities to small firms than others and if these industries are expanding the number of small firms will increase.

The main explanations of the presence of so many small firms at any one time can be assembled under two main heads.

Firstly, there are economies of small scale to be realized under certain conditions. The technical unit of production (e.g. the power loom in a weaving establishment) may be small and a small firm may operate quite economically with very limited overhead costs. This may make the firm less vulnerable in periods of depression and give it a degree of flexibility which is denied to the larger firm. Competent management is more easily found at this level of activity and small firms may be able to offer a wider variety of experience to able young executives than large firms. Also, in trades where quality, variety of product and attention to detail are important, the small firm can operate to great advantage. The small firm may also be able to exploit favourable opportunities provided by the existence of large firms. A number of large firms may require in the aggregate a great number of a particular component which it is not economical for any one of them to produce for itself. A separate firm may devote itself exclusively to providing this component and whilst employing only a small number of persons may achieve considerable economies of specialization.[25] Another factor which does not fit quite so well into this category is the tolerance shown to small firms in trades which are dominated by a small number of large producers. The small firms do not operate on a sufficient scale to threaten the quasi-monopoly of the large firms and a tendency of the small firm to cut prices may be ignored. The continued existence of the small firms is reckoned to be useful evidence that a state of near monopoly does not exist.

Secondly, there are limitations on the growth of firms. Some of these may be categorized as dis-economies of scale. With an increase in the scale of output there is an increase in risks involved, in the sense of the magnitude of possible losses. The firm will now probably be operating to a greater extent on borrowed capital and the risks of failure become more serious. This may incline management to discount its expectations of the future more heavily as the scale of output grows. In other words, the larger the firm becomes the less inclined it will be to expand output further. It is true that growth in size may reduce uncertainty to some extent, by diversification of output, greater flexibility of management, operational research, market research and so on. Nevertheless it seems likely that the increased risks attendant upon increased scale may keep firms smaller than would otherwise be the case.

Associated with this factor is the increasing strain placed on management as the size of the firm increases. In spite of all that has been achieved by management research and improved management techniques, there is some evidence of declining rates of increased efficiency or even of absolute decline as output expands above the range of medium-sized firm. There are more decisions to be co-ordinated, more people are involved in these decisions, and the problem of communication of information, ideas and decisions becomes quite formidable. There may be an increase in inertia—a growing feeling on the part of individuals that they cannot significantly affect the outcome of events. A serious decline in morale may follow as executives and others come to regard themselves as unimportant cogs in a very big wheel.

But perhaps the most important reason why so many small firms continue to exist arises from the many obstacles to growth. We have already referred to the difficulties experienced by small firms in obtaining the necessary finance for further expansion. Also, a firm (or establishment) may be able to produce larger outputs at lower average cost but these lower costs may be offset by increased transport costs as wider markets need to be tapped. If the necessary raw materials are widely dispersed and the finished product is heavy and expensive to transport, operation on a small scale in many different parts of the country may be more economical than large-scale production at a few points, although this may be offset by establishing branch factories in different parts of the country. This, of course, is only a particular example of market limitation. There are others. Production on a small scale may be possible because the demand for the product is very limited and any further increases in output can only be sold if prices are sharply cut. Competition, extensive advertisement, and demand for a great variety of products may also keep firms small.

So far we have been thinking mainly of the growth of firms by internal expansion. If growth takes place by absorption of other firms some of these restrictions on the size of firms become less serious. Management problems are reduced by allowing subsidiaries a great deal of autonomy and greater diversification of output reduces some forms of market risk and limitation.

1 George and Cyert, 'Competition, Growth and Efficiency', *Economic Journal* (March 1969), have called attention to the importance of growth as a determinant of efficient performance.

2 Bain, J. S., *Industrial Organization*, 2nd edn. (New York, and London, Wiley, 1968) makes use of such an analytical framework.

3 Edwards and Townsend, *op. cit.*, p. 2, express the view that most new firms start to do something that is already done.

4 Galbraith, J. K., *American Capitalism* (London, Hamish Hamilton, 1952).

5 Schumpeter, J. A., *Capitalism, Socialism and Democracy* (London, Allen and Unwin, 1954).

6 Downie, J. A., *The Competitive Process* (London, Duckworth, 1958).

7 Penrose, E. F., *The Theory of the Growth of the Firm* (Oxford, Blackwell, 1959).

8 'The prime reason for take-overs is that a company's assets are being underutilized and the new management could use them better. . . . Find the right management and cluster as much of an industry around them as possible.' *Economist*, p. 67 (12 October 1968).

9 This particular listing is taken from Pratten and Dean, *Economies of Large-scale Production in British Industry*, pp. 17–18 (Cambridge, University Press, 1965). See also Florence, P. S., *Logic of British and American Industry*, p. 48 *et seq.* (London, Routledge, 1953).

10 Bain, J. S., *Barriers to New Competitors* (Cambridge, Mass., Harvard University Press; London, Oxford University Press, 1956) finds no significant multi-plant firm economies additional to those available to single plant firms.

11 Good accounts of the difficulties involved in any empirical check-up on the existence of economies of scale will be found in Pratten and Dean, *op. cit.*; and Smith, Caleb, 'Survey of Evidence on Economies of Scale,' *Business Concentration and Price Policy* (Princeton, University Press, 1955).

12 Smith, Caleb, *loc. cit.*; and Pratten and Dean, *op. cit.* There are many other significant indications of widespread occurrence of economies of scale, e.g. Evely and Little, *op. cit.*, p. 97; and Rostas, *Prices, Productivity, and Distribution in Selected British Industries*, p. 45 (Cambridge, University Press, 1948).

13 Crum, *Corporate Size and Earning Power* (Cambridge, Mass., Harvard University Press, 1939).

14 Whittington and Singh, *Growth Probability and Valuation* (Cambridge, University Press, 1968); Samuelson and Singh, 'Variability of Profits and Firms' Size', *Economica*(May 1968); Boswell, J. S., *Small Firm Survey* (London, I.C.F.C., 1968).

15 The Thomas Tilling group would appear to be a good example of this, see Edwards and Townsend, *op. cit.*, p. 68.

16 Full details of consideration given by large acquiring companies to shareholders of acquired companies from 1964–68 will be found in *Mergers*, Appendix 2, Annex 4 (London, HMSO, 1969). Cash consideration during these years varied from six to sixteen per cent, loan stock from four to twenty-three per cent, and shares from thirty-six to seventy per cent.

17 *Mergers*, paras. 19–24 (London, HMSO, 1969).

18 The Industrial Reorganisation Corporation exists to encourage the rationalization of industry and since 1966 has been active in promoting combinations of firms where it is reckoned that this will increase the efficiency of production. (See Chapter 8.)

19 See, for example, *Monopolies Commission Report on Cellulosic Fibres*, p. 14 (London, HMSO, 1968).

20 Markham, *Business Concentration and Price Policy*, p. 141 *et seq.* (Princeton, University Press, 1955), states that in the USA a desire for quick speculative profits has been a more important factor promoting combinations than a desire to secure increased market control.

21 Cook and Cohen, *Effect of Mergers* (London, Allen and Unwin, 1958). It is very difficult to measure performance and the evidence is somewhat impressionistic.

22 Livermore, 'Success of Industrial Mergers,' *Quarterly Journal of Economics* (November 1935).

23 Reported in *Times Business Review*, p. 25 (9 September 1968).

24 *Annual Abstract of Statistics* 1966, Table 141 (London, HMSO). The figures relate to 1961.

25 'Some of the most successful British firms are relatively small because they go on doing one thing very well.' *The Economist*, p. 67 (12 October 1968).

CHAPTER 6

Monopoly

6.1 Introduction
Strictly speaking, monopoly exists when the supply of a commodity is controlled by a single seller. But this obviously does not take us far. Much depends on how narrowly or widely the commodity is defined. In the last analysis all commodities compete with each other for the patronage of consumers and pure monopoly can hardly exist unless one conceives of one firm supplying all goods and services. We need not waste time on this abstract limiting case which has no practical, and very little theoretical, interest.

It is equally true that the output of every firm to some extent is generally different from that of every other. Even if their outputs are physically identical they may be differentiated in the minds of consumers by branding and advertising. Firms may also be protected from competition of firms selling the same or similar goods by goodwill or by transport costs. To this extent these firms have a degree of monopoly or market power. That is to say they have a degree of power to fix price without losing their entire market—unlike the firm in perfect competition which has to accept market price and adjust its output and marginal cost to it. More explicitly the monopolist can raise prices and sell less in his quest for the output and price which will maximize his profits.

The extent of a firm's monopoly power will depend substantially on how sharply the commodity is differentiated from (i.e. is non-substitutable for) other commodities, the number and size of firms selling the commodity, and the possibility of other firms entering the industry if prices are raised and abnormal

140

profits made. The strongest monopolistic positions occur where one or a few firms supply the whole or the bulk of a commodity for which demand is inelastic, i.e. which is not competed against by close substitutes. Under these circumstances prices can be substantially raised without losing many customers. It is possible that because of transport costs a firm may find itself in a stronger monopolistic position in some part of its market than others.

Many theoretical measures of monopoly or market power have been suggested, for example, the divergence between marginal cost and price, and the comparison of the demand curve for the products of the firm with the demand curve for the product as a whole. These show the extent to which, if profits are maximized, firms will exploit their monopoly position by producing lower outputs and charging higher prices than they would do under circumstances of perfect competition. Another and perhaps more important aspect of the exercise of monopoly power can be measured by the extent to which low-cost firms have, over a period, enlarged their share of the market. But all these measures suffer from the serious defect that we lack the data and statistical techniques to calculate them with reasonable precision.

The measure most generally used is the concentration ratio which, as we have seen in Chapter 2, is a rather crude estimate of the extent to which supply is controlled by few sellers. But market power, its exercise, and its effects have to be evaluated in terms of the entire market situation. For example we will need to know not only the percentage of total output controlled by (say) the three largest firms but also their size relative to the remainder; the total number of firms; the vertical relationships of firms; actual and potential competition from new entrants, substitutes, and imports; practices designed to restrict competition; the extent to which technical methods conform to the best current practice; profit rates, and much else besides. In most cases the best we can hope to achieve is an impressionistic and qualitative appraisal of particular situations.

Strong monopoly positions are comparatively rare. They are never very secure and the more the monopolist exploits his position by raising costs or charging higher prices the less secure he is likely to be. The threat may come from new entrants, from imports, new products, new techniques, and from shifts in demand as the tastes and incomes of consumers change. Even where price competition is limited by price leadership or cartel agreements (e.g. by agreement on minimum prices) competition may be merely diverted into other channels—more elaborate service arrangements, showroom facilities, proliferation of models, and so on. Also the growth of monopoly at one stage of production may be the prelude to more fierce competition at another, or it may be checked by the countervailing power of a large buyer. For example, the growth of large artificial fibres firms may lead to stronger competition in markets where artificial fibres have not previously been demanded, or the monopoly power of a supplier of cables may be checked by the power of a very large buyer like the GPO. It is a mistake therefore to think of monopoly in terms of the number and relative sizes of sellers of a particular product, though this is an important aspect of the matter. The real strength of a monopoly position can only be assessed in terms of what we have called the total market situation.

6.2 Theory of monopoly
We see that monopoly is not easily defined or identified. But the condemnation of monopoly derives very largely from theoretical analysis of certain clearly defined market situations.

A state of perfect competition exists where many firms are producing a homogeneous commodity and no one firm can affect the market price by variation of its own output, and where there is free entry of new firms. Under these circumstances each firm accepts the market price and will produce that output for which marginal cost equals price. It can be shown that, when all firms and industries are in equilibrium under conditions of perfect competition, factors are ideally allocated between different firms and the production of different commodities, in the sense that any re-allocation is likely to make some consumers more worse off than others are made better off.

We are not here concerned with the niceties of theoretical models. So much has been said because this particular model has exercised a curious domination over our thinking despite the fact that most economists agree that it is too unrealistic to yield any worthwhile prediction about what happens in the real world. Monopoly in theory is by definition a departure from ideal alloca-tion which is one (but only one) of the conditions for efficient functioning of an economy.

The other principal models—such as monopoly, duopoly (two sellers), oligopoly (few sellers), and imperfect competition (many

sellers of a differentiated commodity)—in effect introduce monopoly elements by reducing the number of sellers or introducing
non-homogeneity of products. In some cases the models yield no
determinate results about price and output except on severely
limiting assumptions. In other cases it can be shown that firms
will produce outputs for which marginal cost is less than price and
in the absence of free entry will make abnormal profits. In other
words, outputs will be lower and prices higher than if perfect
competition prevailed. Resources are uneconomically distributed
between different uses and incomes may be less evenly distributed
as a result of a shift to profits.

This, very briefly and simply, is the nub of the theoretical case
against monopoly. Competition is equated with perfect competition. Competition is therefore 'good'. Monopoly is a departure from perfect competition and is therefore 'bad'. No one
believes, however, that it is really as simple as this. Nevertheless
public opinion is very sensitive to the evils of monopoly and the
Governments devote a lot of attention to controlling it. This is
partly due to the case against it established by theory. But
economists are nowadays inclined to treat monopoly as a term of
very general description—meaning only that some power exists
to affect the price. In the current jargon monopoly is not a dirty
word.

The perfect competition model is a considerable abstraction
from reality and it may be doubted whether static equilibrium
analysis is likely to throw much light on the behaviour of firms
constantly reacting to changing tastes, techniques, and organization. Also, firms do not, in real life, frequently aim at short-run
profit maximization, and complete homogeneity of product
between firms is rare. But there are two rather more important
reservations to be made about the theoretical case against
monopoly. In the first place the comparison between the equilibrium positions of firms in perfect competition and monopoly is
largely invalidated by the fact that the latter are likely to be
producing much larger outputs at very different levels of marginal
cost. Price under monopoly may exceed marginal cost but that
price may be below the competitive price. Secondly, cost curves
in theory are drawn on the assumption that they represent the
cheapest method of producing each output. Under monopoly
however there will be a diminished incentive to keep costs down.
As someone once remarked, the greatest of all monopoly gains is

a quiet life—the monopolist may take his 'profit' by inflating costs rather than by maximizing profits. In other words one of the evils to be most apprehended from monopoly is ruled out by theory.

Some doubt has also been cast on the logical consistency of the perfect competition model. Lack of information on the plans of other producers makes future prices indeterminate and each producer is unable to make the ideal adjustment assumed by theory. If this is so then it would appear that some forms of collusive conduct are more likely to promote ideal allocation of resources. This is not to deny that monopoly may promote misallocation by producing too little at too high a price. But by modifying the situation in a direction favourable to perfect competition one cannot be certain of improving matters.

Perfect competition presents us with a very odd view of competition. Most people think of competition in terms of rivalry, i.e. a course of action designed to better oneself at the expense of others. The firm in perfect competition is a passive price-taker. Whatever he does is assumed not to affect market price. He threatens no one and feels threatened by no one. It is true that by adopting some innovation he can reduce costs and improve his share of the market. If the innovation spreads to other firms, supply may significantly increase and the fall in market price will put pressure on marginal firms. Similarly if demand falls market price falls, all firms must adjust to the new price, and once again pressures are felt by marginal firms. But these impersonal market forces do not symbolize what most of us think of as competition—a deliberate attempt by price or product adjustment to cut into the markets of one's nearest rivals.

In some ways rivalrous conduct is more likely to arise where sellers are few and each is sensitive to the actions of others. Oligopoly is certainly not incompatible with fierce price competition. Where firms are few innovation may be encouraged because they feel relatively secure and large firms have the resources to finance the necessary research and development programmes and successful innovation will strike more heavily at the markets of rivals than shading of prices. Imperfect competition may be massive promotional campaigns and product differentiation which most people would regard as forms of competition though where they succeed they may form a basis for some degree of monopoly power.

It would seem then that competitive conduct is as likely to be associated with oligopoly as with perfect competition. But the point should not be pressed too far. Large firms which dominate particular trades, or associations of firms who act together to restrict competition, may choose to exploit their monopoly power by raising prices above the level which would otherwise obtain and restricting output, by protecting existing and obsolescent capital, by impeding innovation, and by trying to deny entry to new firms with new ideas, new methods, and perhaps a better product.

In an attempt to move away from the concepts associated with 'perfect competition' and to emphasize competitive (rivalrous) conduct the notion of 'workable' or effective competition has emerged. By this we mean the development of situations in which sellers have the maximum possible freedom to develop alternative market strategies—the essence of many monopoly situations being that firms lose or surrender their freedom of action. This releases the notion of competition from undue dependence on structural characteristics of the industry. It suggests a sufficient degree of freedom for efficient firms to cut prices and enlarge their share of the market, to enter other trades where a productive opportunity presents itself, and to introduce new techniques and products. The idea is that the efficient must be free to cash in on its efficiency and make life difficult for the inefficient.

Workable competition is not a precise concept.[1] Its formulation as a desirable object of policy derives from an intuitive belief that efficiency is likely to be promoted in an atmosphere of rivalry and emulation. It recognized the wide variety of market situations in which competitive and monopolistic elements intermingle and in which firms generally preserve some freedom of action. The whole situation is examined for elements which stimulate economic rivalry. Anti-monopoly policies are thus guided by an intention to modify situations in a way which will increase the firm's freedom to manœuvre. The notion of workable competition recognizes that similarities of structure may conceal wide disparities of market power and that in some situations (e.g. where economies of scale are pronounced) fewness of sellers may be a necessary condition for minimizing costs per unit of output. It releases the notion of competition from its association with perfect competition (e.g. abnormal profits may be compatible with workable competition) and stresses that efficient allocation is not the only important aspect of economic efficiency. Monopoly is equated to market power and this is not simply a reflection of fewness of sellers, restriction of entry, and differentiation of products though these are important elements in most situations.

Thus the approach to monopoly and competition becomes much more pragmatic. Each case is to be examined on its merits and judgments are likely to become rather vague and indeterminate.

It does need to be added that opposition to monopoly is not wholly based on its economic effects. The opposition to monopoly in the USA is partly prompted by concern for 'the little men' and a belief that concentration of economic decision-taking is not in the best interests of a democratic society. The opposition to some monopoly practices in Great Britain has been partly prompted by ethical considerations. The collective enforcement of re-sale price maintenance for example could deprive a man of his livelihood by withholding supplies and firms can be heavily fined for breach of a price agreement. It is widely felt that the imposition of such penalties by private courts for offences not known to the law is morally wrong.

6.3 Factors promoting monopoly

Various factors promote monopoly. Most of them have the effect of restricting the entry of new competitors. Monopoly may depend on some legal restriction such as will arise from conferment of patent rights though safeguards may be written in to prevent flagrant abuse. Freedom of entry is not permitted into nationalized industries though once again the State attempts to protect consumers in various ways (see Chapter 7). In some of these industries (e.g. gas and electricity) competition was never a real possibility and when operated by private enterprise they were granted exclusive rights of supply. They depend for their operation on an expensive distributive network of considerable capacity which it would be wasteful to duplicate. But in return for monopoly rights conferred by statute the operators were required to accept some control of prices and profits.

Economies of scale may be of such magnitude that one or a few firms of optimum size may be sufficient to meet the demand forthcoming at prices reflecting costs. New entry is effectively barred by the amount of capital needed to set up on the scale necessary to compete with established firms and by the risks arising from excess capacity. Concentration of raw material supplies may place a limited number of producers in a strong market position which they may combine to exploit more effectively. But such monopolies are rarely long lived since the search for new natural sources or synthetics is accelerated and is rarely unsuccessful.

Tariffs may also facilitate monopoly. Home producers are more likely to combine to exploit their stronger monopoly position in the home market if the threat of foreign competition has been removed. Tariffs imposed by other countries or the existence of strongly organized groups of foreign producers may induce home producers to combine in order to raise prices in the home market and so place themselves in a position to cut export prices.

Monopolies are frequently the outcome of agreements between otherwise independent firms to control in some way the marketing of the product and to discourage the entry of new competitors. These and the conditions which are likely to give rise to them will be discussed in the next section.

6.4 Types of monopoly—Cartels

Monopolies may be roughly classified under two headings. Firstly, we have agreements between firms controlling a substantial proportion of the total output of a commodity which restricts their freedom of action in disposal of their outputs. The general term 'cartel' is often used for such associations which are described in this section. Secondly, we consider in the next section of this chapter monopolies of scale (or dominant firm monopolies) where one firm (which may of course include parent and subsidiaries) controls a substantial part of the total output of a commodity. These distinctions are never very clear cut. There can be much argument about what is substantial, there may be collusion between firms without any formal agreement between them and dominant firm monopolies shade off into a wide variety of duopoly and oligopoly situations.

No brief summary of types of cartel and cartel practices will do full justice to the variety and complexity of arrangements found in the real world. The least formal type is found where no restrictive agreement in fact obtains. Firms by 'conscious parallelism' may keep their prices in step with each other or tacitly follow the prices of one of their number who becomes known as the price leader. Firms may also develop the habit of comparing notes on prices, customers and investment programmes, and though they are undoubtedly influenced by what they learn they do not bind themselves to any particular course of action.

It follows that collusion is very difficult to detect. It is often supposed that if a number of 'competing' firms pursue courses of action compatible with an assumption that they are influenced by knowledge gained of the intentions of their competitors then an arrangement to restrict competition exists. The existence of collusion is more obvious where there is a gentleman's agreement (i.e. unwritten agreement) underpinned by meetings between the parties the existence of which cannot be completely concealed.

Written agreements vary from information agreements to exchange trade information (which do not formally restrict the freedom of action of the firms but which may nevertheless restrict competition) to very elaborate agreements supported by various enforcement procedures and a secretariat.

The most common form of such cartels are agreements to observe specified minimum prices. In manufacturing industry minimum prices schedules for the chief grades of product are usually agreed which in some cases may run into hundreds of items and this makes control extremely cumbersome. The prices are often based on some sort of cost investigation and the application thereto of some more or less elaborate formula. For example, a weighted average of all costs (perhaps after elimination of some high-cost producers) plus the addition of some pre-determined rate of profit may form the basis of the price-fix. More complicated were the price-fixing procedures employed by the Yarn Spinners who took the cost of raw material at replacement cost, added a margin for spinning derived from cost returns submitted by a group of mills (of which the highest third was ignored) plus an addition for depreciation and interest based on what would be required to establish ring spinning mills of the most economic size and operating methods.

These elaborate procedures are often used to re-assure the critics of cartels that prices are based on the costs of efficient procedures and that the cartel is not exploiting its market power to charge monopoly prices. This is not the place to argue what is a fair and reasonable price and whether it can be determined by any administrative procedure. There are so many differences of accounting procedure, so much difficult argument about allocation of overheads, the percentage of capacity presumed to be engaged, the proper basis for depreciation, and what constitutes a reasonable profit margin, that it may be doubted whether any administered price (i.e. a price which has been arrived at by formula and has not emerged from processes of open competition) can be made to mean very much. The cartel price is most likely to be above the price estimated to prevail in the absence of the cartel—otherwise it would be difficult to see what advantage is to be derived by the associated firms. Nor is it likely that a cartel price will be agreed which does not offer some margin over average direct cost to the weakest firms.

The verdict of the Registrar of Restrictive Trading Agreements (see p. 159)[2] is worth quoting in this connection—

> There has not yet been before the Court any agreement comprising a formula or method for arriving at common prices which of itself provided assurance that prices would be reasonable; all left room for a considerable measure of flexibility and use of commercial judgment in fixing the common prices.[3]

What this amounts to, is that cartels in fact charge the (monopoly) price which they judge to be in the best interests of members taken as a whole and this is likely to be influenced by the availability of substitute supplies. A balance is struck between benefit of higher prices and loss of trade likely to result. In most cases, when a schedule has been agreed for some past period, prices are advanced by a uniform percentage equivalent to the estimated increase in average costs if this is not thought to exceed what the market will bear. This is simple and saves a great deal of argument but it does mean that as time goes on prices tend to get forced more and more out of line with the actual costs of producing various classes of the product.

Where goods are not standardized but individually designed and ordered (e.g. ships and most types of buildings) then some restriction of price competition and control over prices can be achieved by some form of level tendering. These vary in detail but the general pattern is that firms exchange information about tender prices and arrange the successful tender, the cost of tendering being remitted to the unsuccessful tenderer from the proceeds of a levy.[4]

Agreements for controlling output are more rare. The working of organized short time is an informal and flexible method which is employed when the nature of the product precludes more direct methods of control or where firms are reluctant to enter into any more elaborate arrangement. The more usual method is by means of the output quota. Each firm is given a standard output based on its performance in some past period and is permitted in each period to produce a certain percentage or quota of its standard output. Quotas are the same for each firm and are agreed upon in the light of the expected market demand during the period in question. The aim is to restrict output to a sufficient extent to permit sales at prices satisfactory to the firms making the agreement. Most output control arrangements permit firms to purchase quota rights from other firms. This partially meets one criticism of cartels, viz. that they hinder the growth of low-cost firms and keep all firms working below their designed and most economical levels of operation. It only partially meets the criticism because payment for quota rights is a burden on low-cost firms wishing to expand output and are in effect a subsidy enabling high-cost declining firms to remain in existence.

Where cartel agreements exist, pressures tend to develop in the direction of making them more elaborate. Thus output control is introduced as a support for price control since firms feeling some assurance of satisfactory prices will tend to over-produce. When price-control schemes are in operation each firm is exposed to a very great temptation to cut prices without appearing to do so. For a slight sacrifice of price a considerable increase in orders is likely if the other firms keep to the agreed price. Concealed price cutting may take the form of selling goods of higher quality than those invoiced, extended credit, giving overweight, giving excessive allowances for cash or for goods alleged not to be up to specification, and selling at cut prices through secret subsidiaries. For this reason most price-fixing schemes have supporting restrictions covering standard conditions of sale. A more satisfactory method of checking evasion is by controlled or central selling. In controlled selling schemes each firm continues to dispose of its own output but the joint marketing organization has to approve all orders. Each firm has some agreed share of the total trade and penalties are paid for excess supplies and compensation paid to firms supplying less than their trade share. In central selling schemes the selling agency (or syndicate) takes supplies from firms at some notional price and re-sells to consumers as a principal. The syndicate is in fact a complete monopolist and exercises complete control over price. The profits arising are shared in some agreed proportion between the constituent firms and this may be combined with trade share, compensation, and deficiency payments as in controlled selling schemes. Since firms produce only to the order of the syndicate and have no direct access to customers, evasion is virtually impossible. Central selling also reduces difficulties of quantitative regulation and detailed price control of highly diversified products. The central selling agency may also reduce marketing costs of firms by eliminating competitive advertisement and duplicate selling organizations.

The underlying purposes of cartels are to restrict competition between the constituent firms, to use their market power to keep prices above the level that would obtain in a free market situation and generally to live and let live. They will seek to protect their monopoly position by a wide variety of practices most of which are designed to limit the entry of new firms. These measures discriminate in some way in favour of some groups to the disadvantage of others and are often described as measures of collective discrimination. The cartel may deal exclusively with certain distributors who agree to support cartel price policies and handle only goods produced by the associated firms. New firms and existing firms outside the cartel will find themselves cut off from channels of distribution. The cartel may, by agreement with suppliers, seek to deny to rival firms access to supplies of machinery and raw materials. It may, by selective price cutting, try to drive competitors out of business or by offering rebates put customers in the position of making losses if they give some orders to firms competing with cartel members. (A loyalty rebate is paid on condition that the customer buys exclusively from the monopolist. Payment may be deferred and only paid if there has been continued loyalty. Aggregated rebates increase with the volume of orders. The purchaser is therefore always in the position of being better off if he continues to deal with cartel members rather than giving a trial order to a non-cartel member which may be a firm trying to break into the trade.) Where output is sold through retailers the associated firms may specify retail prices and collectively enforce them through refusal to supply price-cutting retailers. This could easily deprive a retailer of his livelihood and this particular sanction has always been subject to severe criticism. (Collective enforcement of re-sale price maintenance has been illegal in Great Britain since 1956. See p. 160.)

This short summary of protective devices is by no means exhaustive. Occasionally more subtle means are available to suppress new competition. A national cartel may be a party to an international cartel agreement and it may be able to deny access to foreign markets to outside firms. It may resort to unfair practices such as starting false rumours about the soundness of new technical processes and projects and try to influence financial interests against backing it.

It is true however that in particular circumstances some defence of cartels can be made. Loyalty rebates are sometimes deemed to be necessary (for example in shipping) where the associated firms undertake to provide a regular service and need to protect themselves against attempts to 'cream the traffic'. Exclusive dealing may be defended as necessary to ensure that distributors are qualified to handle and service the product and also to ensure that distribution channels are not unnecessarily duplicated. Re-sale price maintenance has been defended on the ground that it ensures provision of sufficient retail outlets to meet the convenience of the public.

This explains why investigating bodies are so much intent on close scrutiny of past history. They will wish to know what is the intention behind practices which appear to restrict competition. It is often difficult to decide for example whether particular price cuts or special low-priced lines are normal episodes in a continuing competitive struggle or whether they are designed to crush competitors and so bolster up a monopoly position.

It will be clear from what has been said that cartels are rarely very secure. Whilst cartels seek to take advantage of the relative inelasticity of demand for the product the individual member is always tempted to take advantage of the greater elasticity of demand for his output by shading the price if he can get away with it. Also the diverse interests of the constituent firms are not completely reconciled by the cartel agreement. Low-cost firms will become restive if prices are fixed high enough to satisfy the demands of marginal firms. Firms with important export interests will want greater freedom to dispose of this part of their output and vertically integrated firms will want to exclude sales to other parts of the undertaking from cartel restrictions. Other firms will naturally suspect evasion and oppose special treatment of this kind. Strains of a different kind will develop where there are elaborate classifications of goods. If there is overlapping the possibilities of evasion are obvious.

So it happens that although some cartel agreements are maintained over a long period they lead a very uneasy life and many break down. Not only is there pressure to underpin the loyalty of members by more elaborate restrictions and more watertight written agreements but also to introduce heavier sanctions for breaches of the agreement.

The circumstances likely to give rise to cartel agreement are extremely varied. In the circumstances of the inter-war period some industries (e.g. cotton and coal) sought relief in cartel organization from price competition induced by a long-term decline in demand and the emergence of considerable excess capacity (see Chapter 5, p. 131). In agriculture, chronic instability of output and prices produced demands for what was then called organized marketing. In a growing industry like cement changing technology and heavy transport costs produced severe price competition which culminated in the formation of a very tightly knit cartel. In the early days of road passenger transport by omnibus free competition produced wasteful over-capacity, serious social costs and much danger to life and limb which was only resolved by cartelization.

In some of these cases the state intervened to impose compulsory cartelization and from this we may suppose that in certain circumstances an economic case can be made out for cartels. Perhaps the strongest general case (there are, as indicated elsewhere in this chapter, various special arguments for and against particular cartel forms and practices) can be made out when industries experience a serious secular decline in the demand for its products. Under some circumstances the normal processes of price competition are not likely to produce the necessary adjustment through elimination of marginal firms in the short run. Weak selling may undermine the position of even efficient firms, profit margins disappear and new capital investment is inhibited (see Chapter 5, p. 132). We may also ask whether we need to worry unduly about misallocation of resources induced by monopoly when hundreds of thousands and perhaps millions of persons are unemployed.

It has also been argued that the security provided by monopolistic organization is necessary to encourage firms to engage in research and development and to take the risks of introducing new techniques and products (e.g. some cartels provide for the exchange of technical information and co-operation in research). The higher profits earned in some monopoly situations may result in a higher rate of capital investment. It has also been argued that in the absence of the risks of competition firms will proceed with projects on the basis of lower expected returns on capital employed and that cartels may therefore lower prices.

It is of course impossible to check up on these arguments except in specific situations. There is very little evidence associating innovation in general with firms which have sought the security of cartel argreements and whilst it may be argued that cartels are necessary to provide some protection for firms in conditions of severe depression and cut-throat competition it has to be admitted that necessary adjustment to changed market conditions may be indefinitely delayed by such agreements.

The general case against cartels is impressive. The most powerful argument is that they hinder the growth of low-cost firms and protect high-cost firms. Under circumstances of free competition the former would expand its share of the market by cutting prices and a more economical allocation of productive resources would result.

The high-cost firm is likely to be working a high proportion of old and obsolescent capital. The effect of the cartel is to protect the value of such equipment by the guarantee of some return. More efficient firms are also deterred from modernizing their equipment. This will be an economic proposition only if its full cost per unit of output is lower than the prime average cost of existing fixed capital assets. This is less likely to be the case if it cannot be worked to full capacity, which the restrictions imposed by the cartel may not permit. It may pay the more progressive firms to sit back and earn a comfortable profit on its existing equipment. It is, of course, true that given the cartel price it is still in the interest of each firm to keep its average costs as low as possible. But an important incentive to form cartels is the possibility of a comfortable and secure life rather than to maximize short-run profits. To get costs down may result in sufficiently high profits to attract public criticism and so force a revision of cartel prices. Perhaps the most serious economic disadvantage of cartels is not that it results in excessive profits but that it generates indifference to the level of costs.

6.5 Monopolies of scale

Monopolies of scale arise where a single firm controls a sufficient proportion of the total output of a commodity to exercise considerable power over the market. The exact proportion which confers sufficient monopoly power for us to worry about is a matter for judgment and will depend a great deal on the circumstances of individual cases (see p. 164). As we shall see later, British legislation specifies a proportion of one third as constituting a monopoly situation.[5]

To some extent the distinction between monopolies of scale and cartels is rather artificial. Many cases occur where an industry is dominated by one or very few firms but all firms in the industry may nevertheless be organized in cartels. Dominant firms frequently take the lead in promoting cartels. Also dominant firms may buttress their monopoly position by the same protective devices as cartels and we do not need to repeat what has already been said about this.

Firms which have acquired a strong monopoly position may not have been primarily motivated by a desire to acquire and exploit increased market power. But this is not the same thing as that when they acquire it they will remain indifferent to the commercial possibilities which it opens up. An equally plausible motive for growth is to increase efficiency, i.e. to exploit some source of economies of scale. When enquiry is made into the behaviour of monopolies of scale it is important to investigate the process by which dominant status was acquired to see if it will yield some clue about motives, and therefore about present and future likely behaviour.

So much depends on the circumstances of individual cases that it is not possible to say very much about monopolies of scale in general. The most important point is that, whilst they may promote economic waste like any other monopoly, both the opportunities and the incentives for cost reduction are much greater than in the case of cartels. It is very difficult to discern any motive for cartels other than exploitation of market power and they are designed to provide a reasonably secure place in the market for all the constituent firms. The latter remain as independent firms and in most cases there is no question of pooling resources (although some exceptions to this were noted in section 6.4). The dominant firm is a completely co-ordinated unit for the planned use of the resources it controls. If demand falls a complete establishment can be put out of use and the remainder worked to full capacity, whereas all cartel members will share the available trade and under-capacity working will be more general. A single firm monopolist may find it advantageous to increase output, reduce costs, and reduce prices. The cartel member has to accept the cartel price which is a crude reconciliation of the diverse interests and market positions of constituent firms.

It has been previously pointed out that cartel members are likely to be deterred from innovation by the protection given to existing capital and by inability to increase its share of the market when costs are reduced. But it is possible that the secure market position and monopolistic power of the cartel may increase the means and the incentive to innovate. In the case of single firm monopolies however the motivations which deter innovation are weaker and the encouragement to raise technical standards is strengthened. Because the cartel is always affected to some extent by internal dissension the dominant firm feels that its market position is more secure and permanent. The risks of going ahead with new technical development are much reduced and, if it is faced by competition from one or a few other large firms such innovation may appear to be the price of survival.

But there is always another side to the coin. Because competition is rarely completely suppressed in the cartel and because it lacks permanence, we are inclined to qualify the notion that the balance of economic advantage lies more with monopolies of scale than with cartels.

6.6 Control of monopoly—the legal background
We have already noted that even where a trade is dominated by one firm, a few firms, or a cartel of some kind, competition is rarely completely suppressed. Nevertheless, it has been found necessary in many countries to buttress these competitive forces with controls over monopoly which are backed by the forces of law. It may be doubted whether firms can be forced to behave competitively, but if the law is generally hostile to monopoly an industrial environment will develop in which competitive attitudes are more likely to develop. For example, the formation of highly concentrated structures may be hindered and entrepreneurs will be conditioned to think of competition as something to be desired rather than avoided. Certainly the existence of legal sanctions, if only in the form of independent enquiry and report, will make the entrepreneur pause before he exploits his market power by raising prices and restricting output.

Monopoly control by law may be quite specific. Before the

nationalization of the gas and electricity industries the monopoly powers of undertakings conferred by statute were circumscribed by various forms of price and profit control. Some safeguards of the public interest were also written into the officially inspired cartels of the nineteen-thirties. The post-1945 nationalization statutes provide for consumer councils, some price sanctioning bodies, and over-riding powers of direction by a minister of the Crown. The Patent laws also provide against abuse of patent rights.

General legislation against monopolies has taken various forms in different countries. Here we can only indicate the general trend of British legal action and experience.[6] Prior to 1948 the anti-monopoly law had three main facets. Firstly there were various statutes prohibiting monopoly going back to the seventeenth century and even before this. These statutes were virtually unenforceable mainly because they implied a definition of monopoly which excluded competition. Secondly, there was the law against conspiracy, i.e. an act (otherwise legal) done by two or more persons with intent to injure a third party. This was largely made ineffective by a number of rulings that the conspirators must be shown to be acting wilfully and maliciously to injure the trade interests of another. In other words if it can be shown that the real purpose of the 'conspiracy' is to defend the trade of those conspiring then the action is not likely to succeed. In monopoly cases this could almost invariably be shown.

There remained the common law doctrine that restraint of trade was contrary to public policy and that restrictive agreements were void and unenforceable. Obviously this could have weakened cartels since the constituent firms would be very likely to break the agreements if the prescribed penalties could not be enforced in a court of law. But in the half century prior to 1914 this common law doctrine was weakened by a series of decisions. Very briefly the effect of these decisions was to rule that agreements in restraint of trade were enforceable unless shown to be unreasonable as between the parties or clearly against the public interest. The parties to the agreement were considered to be the best judges of reasonableness and since they had signed the agreement they presumably found it reasonable. The onus of proof that it was against the public interest was on the parties alleging it. These presumably would be parties outside the agreement who would find it very difficult to substantiate such allegations and their difficulties were increased by the reluctance of the courts to hear economic arguments which they felt ill-qualified to adjudicate.

It was natural that the courts should to some extent reflect the prevailing climate of opinion which was that freedom of contract was more important than freedom of trade. After 1918 the courts were even more inclined to enforce cartel agreements since in circumstances of economic depression the Government was active in encouragement of cartels in some important industries.

But after the Second World War the trend of opinion again changed. A number of enquiries into particular trades were very critical of the effect on efficiency of various monopoly arrangements. Also it was felt that monopolies could be less easily tolerated in a society in which the Government accepted responsibility for maintaining a high level of employment and it was realized that the British economy, weakened by war, would need to be efficient and internationally competitive. The USA was regarded as the model of industrial efficiency and there was a general belief that its very strong laws and enforcement agencies against monopoly had contributed substantially to this.

In 1948 Great Britain made a new start with legal regulation of monopoly. Before reviewing its operation and effectiveness it will be most helpful if this legislation is briefly summarized from this point down to the present day (1970).

The Monopolies and Restrictive Practices Act 1948 set up a Monopolies and Restrictive Practices Commission of four to ten members. In 1953 this was increased to twenty-five thus permitting the Commission to operate in panels and to work on several references simultaneously. The supply of a class of goods could be referred to the Commission by the Board of Trade where certain conditions were thought to exist. These conditions were that one-third of the goods were supplied (or processed or exported) by one person (a 'person' would include a firm plus any controlled subsidiaries, i.e. a body corporate (firm) or inter-connected bodies corporate (firm plus subsidiaries)) or by a group acting together to restrict competition (e.g. a cartel). The Commission was obliged to confirm whether or not this monopoly condition did exist and, if it did, whether it (or things done as a result, or for the purpose of preserving, the condition) operated against the public interest which was defined in very general terms, i.e. full and efficient utilization of resources, the encouragement of new enterprise and innovation and the provision of goods in such amounts and at such prices as would best meet market requirements. The Commission could recommend action to protect the public interest and in the light of such report the Board of Trade could prohibit, or declare illegal, arrangements found to be against the public interest.

In 1955 the Commission reported on a general reference of measures of collective discrimination and declared these to operate generally against the public interest. The majority recommended that these practices be made illegal with exemption in specific instances where a case in favour could be made out. The minority recommended registration of agreements by virtue of which such practices were implemented and the setting up of a tribunal to adjudicate them. The Government compromised by declaring restrictive and discriminatory agreements to be *prima facie* against the public interest but provided also for registration of agreements and their adjudication by the High Court.

This compromise was embodied in the Restrictive Trade Practices Act 1956. Part 1 provided for the registration of agreements between two or more 'persons' engaged in the production, supply or processing of goods by which they accepted restrictions on their freedom to determine prices, quantities produced, conditions of sale, and/or persons or areas to be supplied. The Registrar was required to submit the agreements to a new division of the High Court—the Restrictive Practices Court—which would declare them against the public interest unless the Court was satisfied that they were necessary to protect the public from injury, that they conferred some substantial benefits on the public, or that they were necessary to counteract measures by other persons outside the agreement to restrict competition, to prevent substantial unemployment or loss of export earnings, or to support other restrictions found to be in the public interest. These became known as the seven gateways to approval by the Court in spite of the general presumption stated in the Act that such agreements were against the public interest. Even if the Court found that one or other of these conditions was satisfied the Court could not approve the agreement unless the benefit arising outweighed any detriment arising from the agreement, this became known as the tailpiece or balancing provision. If the Court found the agreement contrary to the public interest it was to be declared void and the parties forbidden to give effect to it or to any new agreement with similar effect. (In practice the Court has been satisfied with an undertaking from the parties to abandon the agreement).

The general effect of Part 1 therefore was to bring cartel agreements within the jurisdiction of the Restrictive Practices Court. Part III provided that registrable restrictive agreements were no longer to be referable to the (renamed) Monopolies Commission which in effect was now confined to the investigation of monopolies of scale, although export agreements (which were exempt from Part I) or any other non-registrable agreement restrictive of competition in the supply of goods were still referable to the Commission. Part II of the Act provided for legal enforcement of re-sale price maintenance (r.p.m.) by individual firms but collective enforcement of r.p.m. was declared illegal.

In 1964, however, the Resale Prices Act declared individual r.p.m. to be illegal unless the Restrictive Practices Court permitted it for any class of goods on the ground that without r.p.m. quality would be reduced, the number of retail establishments selling the goods would be reduced, retail prices would be increased, necessary servicing of goods would be reduced, and/or health would be endangered. The Court would not however exempt a class of goods from the general proscription of r.p.m. unless satisfied that the benefit arising under one or more of these heads outweighed any disadvantages arising from r.p.m. in the particular case under consideration.

In 1965 the Monopolies Commission was empowered by the Monopolies and Mergers Act to consider references covering the supply of services under the same conditions as applied to goods in the Act of 1948. Also the Commission was empowered to consider and report on the effect on the public interest of mergers and acquisitions above a certain size or where the merger created a monopoly as defined in the 1948 Act if these were referred to it by the Board of Trade (special provision was made for the reference of mergers and proposed mergers of newspapers). At the same time the powers of the Board of Trade to control monopolies adversely reported on by the Commission were strengthened by giving the Board power to make discriminatory practices illegal, to regulate prices, and compel publication of price lists.

This effort to control mergers which might result in monopolies operating against the public interest was however complicated by the setting up (in 1966) of an Industrial Reorganization Commission to promote industrial reorganization schemes. It was quite clear that such schemes would frequently take the form of mergers and acquisitions designed to increase industrial efficiency. The National Board for Prices and Incomes (PIB) which adjudicated the pricing policies of firms also over-lapped the Monopolies Commission to some extent. For example, the PIB in its report on bank charges reached conclusions which were at odds with those of the Monopolies Commission in its consideration of the proposed 'three banks merger'. There have been similar over-lapping investigations into Beer, Detergents and Professional services. In January 1970 the Government announced its intention to merge the PIB and the Monopolies Commission in a new Commission for Industry and Manpower.

The Restrictive Practices Act 1968 resolved some difficulties which had arisen with the operation of Part I of the 1956 Act. Certain agreements considered by the Board of Trade to promote industrial efficiency (e.g. agreements for exchange of technical information, joint research, etc.) and agreements designed to restrict increases or secure reductions in prices could be exempt from registration. (In some industries the Government has been pressing firms to reveal their investment intentions to avoid wasteful duplication of capital expenditure, but any agreement to do so would have been registrable under the 1956 Act. Similarly an agreement to carry out a Prices and Income Board recommendation on prices would be registrable.) At the same time the Board of Trade could direct the registration of agreements for mutual exchange of information on prices, quantities supplied, costs incurred, and classes of person or areas supplied (these so called information agreements could obviously be intended to restrict competition).

Agreements not registered in the time allowed were declared void without possibility of defence in the Restrictive Practices Court. Finally an additional gateway to approval of a registered agreement by the Court was provided. An agreement could be approved if it did not restrict competition to any material degree.

In bald summary, then, the position in 1969 was something like this: on a reference from the Board of Trade the Monopolies Commission could investigate and report on suspected monopolies of scale in the supply of goods, suspected cartel agreements on the supply of goods not registered under the 1956 and 1968 Acts, suspected monopolies of scale and cartel agreements in the supply of services, and on mergers and acquisitions believed to be above a certain size; if any of these conditions or arrangements were found to operate against the public interest (a report on the effect on the public interest only being made if the monopoly condition of one-third of the total supply was found to be satisfied) it could recommend ameliorative action and the Board of Trade had wide powers to implement such recommendations.

The Restrictive Practices Court adjudicates cartel arrangements (which may include information agreements) in the supply of goods. Unless certain conditions are satisfied they are declared void and the parties are required to abandon the agreement. The Court also adjudicates in similar fashion applications for exemption from the general proscription of individual r.p.m. Collective enforcement of r.p.m. is illegal under all circumstances.

No brief summary such as is provided here can do justice to this complicated legislation. But sufficient has been said to illustrate the complexities which develop when the legislature tries to define monopoly in practice and to control any harmful effects. We now turn to a brief review of these experiments. It will be convenient to consider separately the experience of the Monopolies Commission and the Restrictive Practices Court. In October 1969 the Queen's Speech promised further legislation on monopolies and restrictive practices which would *inter alia* provide for merging the PIB and the Monopolies Commission.

6.7 The Monopolies Commission

Up to the end of 1968 the Commission had reported on about thirty-five references made under the 1948 and 1956 Acts. Nearly all the references were to the supply of home manufactured goods. At this time no reports had been made on monopoly in the supply of services under the 1965 Act, though the supply of men's hairdressing services, estate agents services, and restrictive practices in the professions, have been referred to the Commission. Reports on estate agents services and hairdressing services were published early in 1969. Reports on mergers under the 1965 Act are considered later in this section.

The average time taken to produce each report has been about two-and-a-half years and this has attracted much criticism. At this rate it would take a long time to cover all sectors of manufacturing industry where monopoly is suspected. The original membership of the Commission was ten but this was increased to a maximum of twenty-five in 1953. It was difficult to find members with the right kind of experience and most members served on a part-time basis. This undoubtedly delayed the preparation of reports.

The reports have not been well received by businessmen who felt that some members of the Commission lacked practical knowledge of industry. Also, in spite of efforts by the Commission to persuade them that their approach was very open minded the manufacturers felt that they were being accused of some unspecified offence in the adjudication of which the Commission was both prosecutor and judge. The criticisms advanced in many of the reports were widely resented and this probably influenced the Government in deciding on a judicial approach with full adversary procedure in the 1956 Act.

References of classes of goods to the Commission were made by the Board of Trade and little is known about the basis on which references were selected. Complaints by Ministries, local authorities and members of the public had some effect but it is believed that the choice of the initial references was influenced by a desire to improve knowledge of the problem by sampling a wide range of trades, situations and practices. Since 1956 there has probably been more stress on cases felt by the Board of Trade to be potentially damaging to the economy. But there is always some risk of political considerations affecting the choice of reference and there would have been some advantage in permitting the Commission to choose its own cases. The suggestion has been made that a Registrar of Monopolies be appointed who would not only select cases but also prepare a brief for the Commission which would set out the main facts, establish that a monopoly condition exists, and clarify the issues which seem to involve the public interest.

Until 1965 the Board of Trade had little power to remedy harmful situations except to compel abandonment of practices found to be against the public interest. Even so it rarely used this power to the full and only one important 'cease and desist' order was issued. The Board preferred to initiate lengthy discussions with manufacturers and was very ready to accept assurances of future conduct in line with the Commission recommendations. Although the Board generally accepted these, this was not always the case, and occasionally the assurances secured fell short of what the reports required. The Board took a relatively tough line on measures of collective discrimination criticized by the Commission and in at least one case (colour films) where prices seemed exorbitant they persuaded manufacturers to make a considerable reduction.

This first approach to monopoly control after the Second World War was strongly influenced by a feeling that monopoly was not to be condemned out of hand. We needed to know more about it, to see what generalizations would emerge, and what principles could be applied to identify harmful situations. In the meantime each case was to be considered on its merits.

But no legislative approach was possible without defining the situations which required investigation. References were of a class of goods (not a firm or firms) where it was believed a 'monopoly situation' (one third of the goods supplied by one firm or cartel) existed. What constituted a class of goods was left to the judgment of the Board of Trade. It was obviously easy to produce monopoly situations if the definition of goods was sufficiently tightly drawn. Thus for example the reference of cellulosic fibres was in effect a reference of Courtaulds. Cellulosic fibres compete strongly with other artificial fibres. Also in considering the conduct of Courtaulds the influence of its other textile interests could not be neglected. Moreover the definition of monopoly situation was quite arbitrary—one could argue with almost equal conviction for twenty-five or forty per cent of goods supplied by one firm or cartel. Whatever proportion was taken, this was clearly a very partial description of structure. The total number and relative sizes of firms in oligopolistic situations are also relevant to market power and its effect on conduct. Also, as we have stressed previously, there are many other factors which in particular cases will determine the degree of monopoly.

The criteria by which the public interest was to be judged might have been lifted from an economics textbook and was of little practical use as a guide-line to judgment. One member of the Commission has called it 'a string of platitudes which the Commission found value-less'.[7] He goes on to argue that, nevertheless, if a number of people of different training and experience reached agreed conclusions they would probably be generally acceptable. Other people might argue that if little was possible by way of objective evaluation, if a group of intelligent people were to be left to make their own impressionistic appraisals or 'hunches' then the case for intervention was correspondingly weakened.

The *ad hoc* approach of the Monopolies Commission was not conducive to a general attack on monopoly. With one possible exception they were not given any opportunity to look back and synthesize their experience and to see what body of general principles seemed to be emerging for the guidance of the government. The one possible exception was the report on the only general reference to a group of practices (measures of collective discrimination) which formed the basis for the Act of 1956.

In considering the work of the Commission it is useful to distinguish between references made before and after 1956. Before 1956 most references were to 'cartel situations'.[8] The general line taken with all investigations suggested little pre-occupation with the theoretical case against monopoly with its emphasis on infringement of rules for the attainment of some welfare optimum. It did suggest a considerable commitment to the view that competitive (rivalrous) behaviour promoted industrial efficiency. The Commission was always critical of anything which reduced the freedom of action of firms and this no doubt accounted for its almost unqualified condemnation of measures of collective discrimination (selective price cutting, deferred and loyalty rebates, exclusive dealing, and so on) which limited the freedom of new entrants to break into the trade. It was equally critical of output quotas and market-sharing arrangements which limited the freedom of low-cost firms to enlarge their share of the market. In its recommendations to ameliorate harmful situations the Commission was mostly concerned to enlarge the area within which firms could take independent decisions.

This explains the particularly hostile attitude to cartels. There could hardly be any purpose in most such associations, except to restrict the market freedom of members. It was in effect an agreement on restrictive practices. It also explains for the most part the attitude of the Commission to particular practices. It was not generally hostile to individual r.p.m. and only recommended control of prices in the case of matches and industrial and medical gases. It looked sympathetically at agreements which contained provision for co-operative research, exchange of technical information and promotion of standardization although

165

these agreements are, strictly speaking, restrictive and would have been registrable under Part I of the 1956 Act. They may be exempted from registration by the 1968 Act.

There was no unqualified condemnation of price agreements. Where the agreed prices reflected the costs of the most efficient producers the Commission was inclined to feel that the restriction was not very damaging to the public interest. (This may have been tied in with the idea, for which some sympathy was shown, that security in matters of price often generated an atmosphere favourable to research and innovation.) Nor did the Commission feel strongly about price agreements where the cartel faced strong outside competition or was faced by a preponderant buyer.

After 1956 all the monopoly situations investigated were monopolies of scale since cartels for the most part were covered by agreements registrable under Part I of the 1956 Act. There was no *prima facie* assumption that such monopolies were harmful though only Pilkington (flat glass) and ICI (chemical fertilizers) escaped without some criticism.

In these cases the Commission were most concerned to discover how and why the monopoly situation had grown up. The showing of intent to acquire market power carried an implication that it would be exploited to the detriment of consumers and defended against new competitors. Thus for example British Oxygen and Courtaulds were criticized for their policy of deliberately buying up competitors; the latter were also hauled over the coals for selective price cutting to discourage new entrants and their policy of acquiring extensive interests in user (textile) industries. But no serious doubts seemed to be felt about the technical efficiency of either firm. It is difficult to say at what point an accumulation of detailed criticisms add up to an adverse report.

The Commission also investigated what competitive elements were built into particular situations, whether the size of the firm could be justified by economies of scale and whether its record in research, development and innovation looked good. Where some or all of these factors were favourable the Commission was not inclined to make too much of other criticisms. On the whole, dominant firms were not criticized much for technical inefficiency though one is inclined to wonder about the Commission's competence to make such an appraisal.

Where the achievement of market power was an object of the

firm's policy they were no less concerned than cartels to defend their position by discriminatory practices. Exclusive dealing (wallpaper manufacturers), price discrimination (Lucas and Champion Spark Plugs), refusal of machinery supplies to competitors (British Match), restriction on outlets (Kodak, Glaxo, Cow and Gate), all attracted criticism for reasons previously discussed.

One would have thought that abnormal profits would attract condemnation, this being the form of inefficiency which theory most leads us to expect as a result of exercise of monopoly power. But abnormal profits can also be a mark of technical superiority and a reward to successful innovation; they can be won in face of competition, and they may reflect abnormal degrees of risk. Only in four of the sixteen references reported in 1956–68 did the Commission feel that the level of profits could not be justified. It was implicit in their approach to monopoly that the earning of profits above the average would not automatically attract criticism. The prospect of greater profit is an important spur on competition and greater efficiency. Only in the unreal world of perfect competition and in the long run are all profits reduced to normal.

But the wariness of the Commission in its approach to profits was also probably a reflection of its awareness of the difficulties attaching to any objective evaluation of the performance of firms. Costs were looked at and if (in the case of cartels) there were wide disparities between the constituent firms the Commission was inclined to ask questions (for example, Imperial Tobacco were criticized for keeping high-cost branches in operation, but it was rare for the level of costs in individual cases to be queried) and, as we have just seen, some justification for high profits was also looked for. Also, in particular cases the Commission would interest itself in methods of fixing prices and in the relationship between particular prices and the cost of supply. (e.g. where uniform delivered prices are charged near consumers are discriminated against in favour of distant consumers, this can distort the pattern of demand and location of industry and impose additional social and private costs). But the Commission was disinclined to put too much weight on figures in view of differing accounting conventions employed (particularly the treatment of depreciation), the difficulty of comparing products between firms, and allocating overheads in multi-product firms.

167

Even if costs can be estimated on some comparable and meaningful basis there remain considerable difficulties in the quantifying of the resultant profits. Profits were generally expressed as a percentage on capital employed but there was much wrangling before the Commission about the computation of capital—what should be included, should it be computed net or gross of depreciation, should it be calculated on the basis of original cost or replacement cost, what were normal profits, and so on. We cannot go into those matters here but the Commission was probably right in not attaching too much importance to the financial evaluation of performance. Once again the evidence of Professor Allen is valuable. He describes these exercises as something of a ritual having little bearing on the findings and recommendations. [9]

It is difficult to assess the results of the work of the Monopolies Commission. Our knowledge of monopoly and restrictive practices has been much enlarged and it paved the way for the more spectacular success of the 1956 Act. Fear of investigation and unwelcome publicity may have acted as a deterrent though there is not much evidence that manufacturers feared the outcome of their subsequent negotiations with the Board of Trade. In particular cases there is some record of achievement—the freer importation of matches has probably disturbed the British match monopoly, Gallahers have felt themselves free to take an independent line with Imperial Tobacco and there has been a considerable reduction in the prices of colour films. Other cases could be cited. But overall it is doubtful if the Commission have done much to raise the level of industrial efficiency by stimulus of competition.

Since 1965 the Commission has also been empowered on a reference from the Board of Trade to investigate acquisitions and mergers where the assets to be taken over exceeded £5 million or where a monopoly condition (as defined in the 1948 Act) was created.

The purpose of the legislation is presumably to prevent the building up of strong monopoly positions. If this is so it is surprising that size alone should make a merger subject to investigation. Also the effectiveness of this new initiative in anti-monopoly policy depends very much on the Board of Trade. Up to the middle of 1969 the Board is believed to have examined about 430 actual or prospective mergers with a view to referring them to the Commission but only twelve references have in fact been made of which two were newspaper mergers where special considerations apply. Three mergers were found to be against the public interest by a substantial majority of the Commission. In the three banks case a bare majority was given against the merger. This was insufficient to activate the powers of the Board of Trade to forbid the merger, but it was nevertheless not proceeded with. The Board of Trade has published (July 1969) a guide to mergers which sets out the many and varied considerations which are borne in mind when deciding whether or not to refer a merger. The balancing of so many imponderables is necessarily uncertain and equally expert and well informed judges might give different decisions about whether or not to refer to the Commission. The Board of Trade emphasizes the pragmatic nature of its approach and the inappropriateness of specific guide-lines. A decision to refer to the Monopolies Commission would appear to constitute a *prima facie* case against the merger though the Board denies this.

The Board has probably been embarrassed by the setting up of the Industrial Reorganization Commission which sponsors mergers (i.e. the Commission is empowered to assist the process in suitable cases by investment in the amalgamated concern) with the object of eliminating wasteful duplication and achieving economies of scale in production marketing and research. The Board can hardly refer such officially sponsored mergers to the Monopolies Commission for investigation and report on whether they are in the national interest. These mergers have included such as the Leyland–British Motor Holdings and the Associated Electrical Industries–General Electric Company mergers. In each of these cases a considerable increase in market power must have been involved.

This illustrates a fundamental dilemma of monopoly policy. There is a widespread belief that if some British industries are to remain internationally competitive the constituent firms must be combined into fewer and larger units. How do we balance the risks attaching to increased monopoly power against the benefits of greater efficiency produced by economies of scale?

In three out of the ten non-newspaper references the Monopolies Commission has found that economies of scale are not likely to balance the dangers of exploited market power having regard to the fact that monopoly makes active pursuit of scale economies less urgent and less likely. In the third of these cases (the proposed Barclays–Lloyds–Martins bank merger) six members of the Monopolies Commission approved the merger and four disapproved in spite of there being no substantial disagreement on the facts.

It would appear that the risks attaching to increased concentration in particular markets must always be pretty conjectural. In the proposed three banks merger both the majority and minority agreed on the source and magnitude of likely economies but the minority also thought that competition would be increased by a reduction of the number of large clearing banks from four to three. (The National Provincial–Westminster bank merger which occurred about the same time and resulted in the number of large clearing banks being reduced from five to four was not referred to the Monopolies Commission.) One also wonders whether a body like the Monopolies Commission (or the Industrial Reorganization Commission for that matter) has the necessary technical expertise to assess the possibilities of economies of scale.

6.8 The Restrictive Practices Court

Up to mid-1966 about 2,550 agreements had been registered by virtue of the provisions of Part I of the 1956 Act. The word agreement has been very widely interpreted to cover not only written agreements but also informal understandings, the presence of which may be inferred from the conduct of the parties. This makes the tracking down of agreements an onerous task and in recent years the Registrar has been active in unearthing agreements which have not been registered. By the Act of 1968 such agreements are void without reference to the Court and any person affected thereby may sue for breach of statutory duty.

The number of agreements registered is impressive but no estimates have been made of their total coverage. Some cover the whole of important trades. Others cover some product which is a minute proportion of total output. The agreements vary a great deal in content. About three-quarters contain price restrictions and about four-fifths are between manufacturers.

Up to June 1966, 1,875 registered agreements had been terminated without being referred to the Court, 130 had been judged as of no economic significance and some 280 were referred to the Court. Most of the latter were abandoned before hearing and up to January 1967 only thirty-three agreements had come to judgment after a full hearing. Of these, eleven agreements were approved by the Court. The procedure in such cases has been for the undefended agreements to be formally declared against the public interest and an undertaking is given not to operate the agreement or any other agreement with like effect. It appears to be the case that no undertakings have been given in respect of the agreements which were abandoned before being referred to the Court. If replaced by arrangements which are non-registrable the parties concerned are in no peril.

About two-thirds of the thirty-three contested cases were price agreements. Other restrictions included common purchasing arrangements, market sharing, restricted trade outlets, and in one case only, resale price maintenance.

All the defendants pleaded the 'second gateway', i.e. that abrogation of the agreement would deny substantial benefit to consumers. The only other gateways pleaded were damage to exports (six cases), risk of injury (three cases), heavy unemployment (three cases) and need to counteract the bargaining power of a preponderant seller (one case). The very open second gateway permitted wide-ranging economic argument. Without the possibilities opened up by this it is doubtful if even thirty-three cases would have come to court. Nine of the eleven agreements approved passed through this gateway.

There is not much doubt that this phase of British anti-monopoly policy has been very successful. Assuming that all important agreements have been registered it is hardly an exaggeration to say that cartels in Britain have been swept away. It may be doubted whether it has been worth all the effort expended on registration and court actions in order that manufacturers can maintain price restrictions on a few odd commodities like nuts and bolts, cement, magnets, windows. In retrospect it would appear desirable to have made restrictive agreements illegal *per se*. But such legislation would need to be carefully drawn and might give rise to serious difficulties of interpretation by the Courts.

It is not known how many terminated agreements have been replaced by informal understandings having similar effect and not detected by the Registrar, although in 1965 and 1966 two groups of manufacturers (tyres and galvanized tanks) who had replaced their terminated registered agreement by arrangements to notify each other of intended price changes were heavily fined for contempt of Court for being in breach of their undertakings not to make a similar agreement. The continued charging of common prices is evidence supporting suspicions that an 'arrangement' still exists but the Registrar does not have the staff to police all abandoned agreements about which undertakings have been given. It is known that registrable agreements have been widely replaced by information agreements which may effectively restrict competition without being registrable under the 1956 Acts. But by the terms of the 1968 Act such agreements may, by order of the Board of Trade, become registrable.

So it may be too soon to congratulate ourselves on the demise of cartel agreements. We need also to remind ourselves that abandonment of restrictive practices is not the same thing as restoration of competition. Firms which have lived under the security of a cartel for many years are unlikely to be suddenly galvanized into competitive behaviour by its disappearance. In a few cases abandonment of registered agreements produced a short burst of sharp price-cutting but these were exceptional. One enquiry showed that in two-thirds of 262 cases of abandoned agreements it was considered that there had been no change in the degree of competition.[10] The Registrar's report on the three year period to June 1966 was rather more optimistic.

'In some industries (where restrictive agreements have been terminated) competition soon appears and, apart from the benefit to their customers, the stimulus it affords to keener buying of materials and components may well lead to increased competition and efficiency in industries supplying such materials and components. In other industries, particularly stable or slowly expanding ones in which common prices had existed for many years, the ending of the agreement appeared at first to have little effect, but in a number of these price competition has more recently appeared.'[11]

The work of the Court has not been impressive for its understanding of the economic issues involved and it has shown some impatience at having to listen to complicated economic argument.[12] One decision has been described as 'an aberration of judgment similar to that which occasionally causes weary examiners to award high marks to a mediocre script.'[13]

The sort of issue that arises can be best illustrated by the Deep Water Vessels judgment in November 1966. Here the argument was relatively simple. The owners of the trawlers operated a fixed price agreement. Let us call this reserve price x. The Court approved the agreement on the ground that without it the price would be higher, say $x + n$. The Court argued that in the absence of the agreement prices would immediately fall to $x - n$. This would cause withdrawal of trawlers, a reduction in supply and a rise in price to $x + n$.

The Court's argument implies that at price x supply exceeds demand—hence the fall in price if the agreement is withdrawn. It appears to follow that at $x + n$ the supply will exceed demand by an even greater margin and therefore this makes it a price which cannot be sustained in a free market.

When the facts of particular cases are examined, things are not quite as simple as the preceding paragraphs would suggest and in some cases the issues raised were such that experienced economists might disagree about the likely outcome of alternative courses of action. So the Court was given plenty of scope to 'follow its fancy' and reach conclusions which would be critically received by economists.

It has been suggested that the Court could have been aided by expert economist assessors and could have developed its own methods of objective appraisal, e.g. comparison of profit rates on some standardized measure of capital employed or measurement of the extent to which low-cost firms have improved their share of the market (although in practice both Registrar and the parties to agreements have been competently advised and a great deal of factual evidence of this kind has been presented). But this would have left many issues open to subjective evaluation and it is doubtful whether it could be reconciled with a judicial as distinct from administrative procedure.

The advantages of a judicial procedure are obvious. A clear cut decision is given—particular restrictions are approved as being in the public interest or disapproved. The Government was relieved of the necessity for considering long and closely argued Monopolies Commission reports which then have to be discussed with interested parties. Worse still it would still have to decide what to do about them.

But it may be doubted whether the Court was in fact presented with a justiciable issue,[14] i.e. an issue which sufficiently limited the discretion of the Court by giving clear guidance about what the public interest required. The Act stated that registered agreements were *prima facie* against the public interest and in the early days of the Court the presumption in favour of competition was given great prominence and a heavy onus was clearly placed on the respondents. In more recent years the Court has appeared to shrug this off and to concentrate on gateways to approval. Some of these such as liability to injury or the need to challenge a preponderant buyer were matters which were capable of reasonable objective evaluation. But the controversial second gateway, which was always pleaded, placed judges in an impossible position. They were expected to guess about the effect on competition of the disappearance of an agreement by oligopolists, to guess about the success of future government policy to control the level of employment, to assess the future trend of demand for goods or to weigh the benefit of lower prices against the detriment of higher unemployment.

The results of hearings before the Court have therefore become somewhat unpredictable. Any expectation of the emergence of a consistent body of case law embodying principles which could be applied in cartel cases have been disappointed.[15] Judges were careful to point out that an argument succeeding in one case could not be safely relied upon in others where some of the relevant circumstances would inevitably be quite different.

It is difficult therefore to offer any very definite verdict on the success of the 1956 Act. It has considerably enlarged our knowledge of the occurrence and functioning of cartels. It has forced a widespread abandonment of agreements covered by the Act. There is some evidence of more competitive attitudes and some evidence that restrictions on competition are merely taking different forms. The Court itself has proved to be a somewhat blunt instrument in the arsenal of anti-monopoly.

There is very little to add about the functioning of the Court under the 1964 Resale Prices Act. Up to the end of 1968 only two applications (Confectionary and Footwear) for approval of r.p.m. had been heard and both had failed, although the Registrar did not oppose an application in respect of books in view of the fact that the Net Books Agreement had been earlier approved by the Court in a case heard under Part I of the 1956

Act. There has been a widespread voluntary abandonment of r.p.m. and it seems probable that few further applications for exemption from the general prohibition of r.p.m. will be proceeded with. The standard arguments for r.p.m. have failed to win favour. These include the arguments that r.p.m. is necessary to provide an adequate number of properly serviced retail outlets, to prevent goods being used as loss leaders, to bring economies of branding, packaging and mass advertising, and to protect the public from higher prices than those enforced by manufacturers.

It now seems probable that a virtual abolition of r.p.m. will clear the way for the expansion of new low-cost methods of retailing and that price competition will increase in this field. Manufacturers continue the practice of recommending prices which of course they have no legal power to enforce against the retailer. They may nevertheless have some effect both on the retailer and consumer and the Monopolies Commission is currently looking into the practice.[16] So the battle goes on.

6.9 Conclusion

It would appear that the pragmatic British approach to monopoly has reinforced the feeling against laying down clear-cut rules which can be enforced and be seen to be enforced. One result has been to put more power into the hands of the Board of Trade which does not have to publish its reasons for what it does. The Board has always had power to select references to the Monopolies Commission and we have seen how much scope that gives them to refer whatever they think may be harmful. The Board has now been given similar power to single out merger cases for reference, it may order the registration of types of information agreement, it may exempt other agreements on grounds expressed in the most general terms. Many aspects of monopoly control thus pass into the realm of mystery.

In the United States the tendency has been to outlaw all restrictions on free competition. This, it is felt, is what is generally desirable, and to make the issue clear-cut it is worth taking some risk of harm to the economy in particular instances. In this country we have been so much obsessed by the need to look at each case on its merits that action against monopoly has come to depend on what are probably highly subjective appraisals.

To some extent this may be affected by the scale of state intervention in the economic life of the community. In Britain the nationalized industries are the strongest monopolies of all and the Government is currently engaged in supporting some large monopolies in private industry. Attitudes to monopoly are likely to be less coherent and consistent than in the United States and may even shift with changing emphasis in national economic policy. It may well be that some uncomfortably strong monopoly positions may have to be tolerated if more capital investment is to be forthcoming and more advanced techniques introduced more quickly. Something must also depend on the environment. The risks of monopoly are probably diminished in an economy where management is conditioned to competition, where there is a high rate of economic growth, and where trade union attitudes are not inimical to technical change.

Market power and the economic evils associated with its exploitation are real enough. We cannot afford to become too complaisant about it. But the underlying trend in this country has been for us to become increasingly uncertain about its effects and more conscious of the dependence of these effects on particular circumstances of each trade, the general economic environment and the objectives of current economic policies. Anti-monopoly policy has become very fuzzy around the edges. We are not so certain as we were in 1948 about what we are trying to do and why.

1 Lewis, Ben, *Monopoly Power and Economic Performance*, p. 100 (New York, Norton and Co., 1964), comments that 'the operating features and properties of "workable" competition defy identification except in terms that beg the question. . . . Workable competition rarely proves to be more definitive than the total indeterminate combinations of practices, motivations and forces operating in the market with which, nursing our confusions, we are currently willing to live.' On workable competition see Hunter, A. (ed.), *Monopoly and Competition* (*Penguin Modern Economic Readings*), Chapter 5 (Harmondsworth, Penguins, 1969).

2 Professor Allen comments that, 'It may be suspected that in many cases the elaborate cost-estimating procedure provided merely the façade behind which the price-making occurred. It lent an appearance of scientific respectability to what in the end turned out to be an estimate of market possibilities.' Allen, G. C., *Monopoly and Restrictive Practices*, p. 75 (London, Allen and Unwin, 1968), elsewhere referred to as Allen, *Monopoly*.

3 *Report of Registrar of Restrictive Trading Agreements to June 1966*, Cmd. 13188, pp. 13–18 (London, HMSO, 1967).

4 For a description of the method of tendering adopted by the London Builder's Conference, see Allen, G. C., *op. cit.*, pp. 65–6.

5 A list of dominant firm references to the Monopolies Commission, 1958–68, is given by Rowley, *Moorgate and Wall Street Review* (Autumn 1968). It includes such well-known examples as Imperial Tobacco, Pilkingtons (Glass), Courtaulds (cellulosic fibres), The Wallpaper Manufacturers, Rank (film distributors), and Kodak (colour film).

6 For a brief account of experience abroad see Allen, G. C., *op. cit.*, Chapter 10.

7 *Ibid.*, p. 66.

8 We have already stressed that the distinction between cartels and dominant-firm situations is somewhat artificial. Two references prior to 1956 were in effect investigations of dominant firms—matches (British Match Corporation) and industrial and medical gases (British Oxygen Company).

9 Allen, *op. cit.*, p. 87. Rowley, C. K., 'The Monopolies Commission and the Rate of Return on Capital,' *Economic Journal* (March 1969) severely criticizes the use of rates of return on capital as a measure of performance, and as a guide to the public interest by making comparison with some such norm or guide-post as the average experience of industrial companies. He discusses the different methods of measuring the rate of return which the Commission applied from time to time and *inter alia* suggests that different verdicts would have been reached if later methods had been applied in earlier cases. Sutherland, *The Monopolies Commission in Action* (Cambridge, University Press, 1969), contains a critical examination of the consistency of Monopolies Commission judgments, in particular, monopoly and merger references.

10 Heath, J. B., 'Restrictive Practices and After,' *Manchester School* (May 1961).

11 Cmnd. 3188, p. 6 (London, HMSO, 1967).

12 To examine these would take us too far afield. See Sutherland, 'Economics in the Restrictive Practices Court,' *Oxford Economic Papers* (November 1965).

13 Allen, G. C., *op. cit.*, p. 93.

14 Stevens and Yamey, *The Restrictive Practices Court* (London, Weidenfeld and Nicolson, 1965).

15 Brock, *The Control of Restrictive Practices*, pp. 166 and 136 (London, McGraw Hill, 1966).

16 The *Royal Commission Report on Recommended Resale Prices,* H. C. 100 (London, HMSO, 1969), recommended that Recommended Resale Prices be banned only in selected cases after investigation.

Chapter 7

Public Enterprise

7.1 Introduction

So far, we have been concerned almost exclusively with the structure and conduct of private industry, but, although private enterprise may be the dominant system in economies such as the United Kingdom, in terms of both the volume and variety of production for which it accounts, it is far from being the only system. The characteristic feature of private enterprise is that it operates through the price mechanism—an interlocking series of product and factor markets aimed ultimately at directing resources into forms of production which will yield the maximum satisfaction to individual consumers. It has always been accepted that there are certain services whose total benefits will exceed the sum of all individuals' assessments of their personal benefits from it, so that any voluntary system of payment would result in an inadequate supply—national defence and public order are two well-known examples. These are the so-called public goods and they are generally provided free of charge to individuals by the central or local government and paid for out of taxes. There is a good deal of controversy over which services are truly public goods, and it is now being questioned whether education and health services really yield benefits to society in general greatly in excess of those obtained by the individuals directly involved, but about fifteen per cent of the Gross National Product is currently accounted for under this heading.

There is another important category of public goods consisting of goods and services produced by public bodies and then distributed through the market system, i.e. *sold* to individual consumers. This is Public Enterprise, occupying a rather ill-defined and shifting territory between commercial private enterprise on the one hand and traditional public services on the other. The size and scope of the public enterprise sector varies greatly from country to country and from time to time in any one country. Railways and electricity production and distribution are public enterprises in Britain and France, but are privately owned and operated in the United States. Motorways are provided as public goods in Germany and Britain, although their early equivalents (the turnpikes) were in the hands of private enterprise, and currently in the United States, France and Italy, they are often operated by public trusts and financed by tolls.

There is thus no universal definition of the scope of public enterprise, although there are some general principles which provide a certain amount of common ground. However any attempt in this chapter to be completely comprehensive would involve so many exceptions and reservations that it would prove extremely tedious, and we therefore confine ourselves to British experience in this field, with only occasional references to other countries. Moreover, we cannot cover all forms of public enterprise in the space available as these include many local government services (especially transport and housing) and many miscellaneous bodies created *ad hoc* for specific purposes. We will concentrate on the very large public enterprises more generally known as the nationalized industries, which supply goods as well as services on a very large scale and which have developed a characteristic form and a distinctive set of problems.

Industrial organization is usually best explained in terms of evolution, but nationalization does not fit this pattern. It involves a sudden change, usually affecting the whole of an established industry and requiring the grafting of a completely new organization and set of objectives on to the old structure. It is thus a more drastic and sweeping change than would ever occur within the private sector and there is naturally a long period in which new systems are being established and the industry's management reorientates itself to the new objectives. This will be easier in some industries than in others. The great bulk of the public enterprise sector of the economy was acquired in a relatively short period from 1946 to 1951, during the period of the first post-war Labour Government. Some of the largest of these nationalized industries had a history of detailed regulations which made the idea of operating in the 'public interest' a fairly familiar one. The railways and the gas and electricity industries came into this category, and indeed the last two had been substantially owned by the public through municipal undertakings before they were acquired by the state. The electricity industry had been partially nationalized as early as 1926, when the Central Electricity Board was formed to operate the 'national grid' linking the principal power stations. The railways had been rationalized into the 'Big Four' companies in 1921 and were notable for their hierarchical management and apparent disdain for purely commercial values. Such industries adapted to their new form quite readily. Road haulage was a sharp exception, since it had previously consisted of a great miscellany of firms and had formed one of the main outlets for individual enterprise between the wars. The steel industry also consisted of a mixture of companies of all sizes, many of them with a strong 'family' element in ownership and management which would not adapt easily to the standardization and large scale organization implicit in nationalization. The process of reorganization may take a very long time to become effective unless the attitudes of the management adapt to the new situation. This is a problem which arises with company mergers and take-overs in the private sector, and its solution frequently calls for a degree of ruthlessness which is at odds with the gentle idealism of those who have pressed for nationalization as a cure to a wide range of industrial and economic problems, and indeed is hard to reconcile with the sensitivity to democratic principles which is such a feature of British public administration.

It is impossible to understand much of what has come about in the field of public enterprise without taking full account of these two pervasive influences—the intense conservatism of many of the industries concerned (this being shown not only by the management but also in the attitude of the labour force to traditional working practices) and the strong political pressure to run them with 'kid gloves', i.e. to try to introduce sweeping changes without actually disturbing anybody. A third critical factor in any assessment of British nationalized industries is the variety of reasons for which industries were nationalized. These are of more than just historical interest, since the initial analysis of the problems of an industry leading to the conclusion that nationalization was the appropriate cure would thereafter be reflected in the structure adopted in the industry, the policies it would be required to adopt and in its performance. For example, if the problem is defined as principally one of technical inefficiency, the form of organization selected would tend to give the maximum scope for standardization, large-scale production and the application of technical management skills. Its policies would be directed towards production and cost targets and this would determine the appropriate standards for judging its performance. This standard is not necessarily (and in the situation just described is most unlikely to be) profitability. If the problem is essentially that of monopoly, then the objective will be seen essentially in terms of providing a service to the public, and a form of organization set-up which will emphasize contact with the consumer. If the problem is one of inefficiency and uncompetitiveness, the organization would tend to lay stress on a marketing function. It would thus tend to be fairly close to that of a large private firm, and it may be reasonable ultimately to assess its performance in commercial terms. These hypothetical cases could be illustrated by the examples of coalmining (and up to a point, railways) for the first situation described, gas and electricity for the second, and steel and air transport for the third. However, since there were usually a number of separate strands of argument in each case, one must beware of oversimplifying this sort of analysis.

7.2 The nationalization argument

The industries nationalized in the post-war period fell into two main groups, transport, and fuel and power. The first included railways, long-distance road haulage and bus services, canals, scheduled air services and a trail of associated activities, many of which had formerly belonged to the railway companies—some docks, short-distance sea ferries, hotels and the Thomas Cook travel agency. London Transport was also brought into this group, but it had been taken into public ownership in 1932, and could be considered the prototype of the later measures. The fuel and power group covered coalmining, gas and electricity, but not oil, the Government's half share in British Petroleum Ltd having been acquired a generation earlier largely, it seems, to ensure priority for naval fuel supplies. The biggest nationalized industry outside of these groups was iron and steel, and this was also the most controversial. Other publicly owned bodies such

G

181

as the Bank of England (1946), the Atomic Energy Authority (1954), the British Broadcasting Corporation (1926), the Independent Television Authority (1954), the National Research and Development Corporation (1948), the Forestry Commission (1919) and the New Town Corporations (1946) are generally less self-contained businesses than those already mentioned. Some of them rely wholly or mainly on public funds, while none of them is selling a service in an established open market. Nevertheless, much of what will be written about the motives for nationalization applies to these special cases as well as to the more standard examples. The Post Office remained a rather odd exception, selling essentially commercial services (post, telephone and telegraph) but as a government department, until it became a public corporation in 1969. The privately owned Overseas Cable and Wireless company was nationalized in 1946, and although this was effectively an overseas extension of the Post Office telegraph service, it was formed into a separate nationalized industry.

The share of British industry operated by public enterprise has largely stabilized at the level reached in 1951. The steel industry was 'denationalized' after 1952 (with the exception of Richard Thomas and Baldwins) but the fourteen largest firms in the industry were then 'renationalized' in 1967, with the net effect of leaving the smallest and more highly diversified units in private hands. Road haulage was partly returned to private ownership, although some of the largest units (e.g. Pickfords) remained publicly owned. There are frequent discussions of other industries as candidates for nationalization, but the only serious prospects at the present time are major port undertakings and water supply, both of which are mainly publicly owned already, and neither of which would appear to introduce any new principle.

The nationalized industries represent an immense concentration of economic wealth and power. It was estimated in 1968[1] that they controlled net assets of £11,000 million and each year invested about £1,600 million—as much as the whole of private manufacturing industry. They produced about eleven per cent of the gross national product, and employed about eight per cent of the national labour force. If this power is held in relatively few hands, it confers upon the individuals concerned great potential power for influencing the rest of the economy. These figures in effect summarize the main arguments for nationalization and they lie at the root of many of the special problems with which these industries have to deal. It is immediately obvious that these industries are in general highly capital intensive. Since they are so capital intensive, there is little scope for genuine competition which would otherwise tend to disperse the control and limit the powers of any small group. In political debate, these industries acquired the label of 'the commanding heights of the economy', although this also referred to the fact that they sell basic services to all other industries, and thus have great indirect as well as direct influence over the general functioning of the economy.

Strong capital intensity normally implies increasing returns to scale in the long run, and this in its turn implies that marginal cost will be less than average cost. There are strong welfare arguments for producing outputs which equate marginal cost and price. In these industries therefore the ideal output can only be achieved if average cost (greater than marginal cost) is greater than price, i.e. losses are made. This is advanced as a further argument for nationalization since private enterprise cannot sustain continuous losses (see Section 7.6). On the other hand, in the short run the average cost function will have a pronounced U shape because of the high proportion of fixed costs. Both plants and enterprises will therefore tend to be large scale, and there will be a marked premium on operating at or near full capacity. The short-term cost structure may in turn contribute towards the pressure for large scale, since an irregular pattern of demand in one part of the market may make full capacity working impossible, but if the enterprise can expand into many markets, it may be able to find compensating fluctuations which will mean that on this larger scale, the variance (i.e. the spread around the average) will be smaller.

An industry faced with these problems will find that in order to achieve the minimum feasible average costs, it has to be able to control its operations as a monopolist, and where these circumstances occur in an extreme form, the industry concerned is often referred to as a 'natural' monopolist. Services such as railways, electricity production and distribution and postal services require a massive investment before any service can be provided, but once this indivisible investment has been made, its capacity will be very large and in the interests of economic efficiency the fullest possible use should be made of it. Thus even in the heyday of the 'Railway Age' there were few cases of separate companies offering parallel services, and where this did occur it tended to produce extreme and sometimes ludicrous examples of destructive competition. Parallel gas mains, electricity networks or postal and telephone services would not only tend to be more costly, but would also be a positive nuisance to the consumer.

The more bizarre examples of railway competition occurred in the United States, but a similar problem arose with the operation of competitive bus services in London. There is a smaller indivisible element in bus investment than in railways, but there was extreme competition on the popular services, undermining their profitability, and often inadequate services on the less busy routes. The London Passenger Transport Board was set up to regularize this situation. Similar examples may be quoted in shipping services, leading to the establishment of the Conference system, and in airlines, where the domestic scheduled airlines are closely controlled by a Public Board (Air Transport Licensing Board) and internationally there is an extremely powerful body (International Air Transport Association—IATA) to control competition and generally attempt to maintain profitable levels of capacity utilization for the very expensive assets which the industry employs.

Natural monopolies thus give rise to a direct clash between the interests of technical efficiency and the possible exploitation of the consumer through monopolistic pricing and managerial inefficiency. Public enterprise might thus appear a perfect compromise solution, since it permits as large a scale of operation as the market will allow, controlled marketing conditions to maximize capacity utilization, and no incentive to the owners (i.e. the public) to exploit the consumers (i.e. the public). The one thing which is not automatically provided is an assurance that the management will not exploit the public by inefficiency, although the risk of this is no greater when a natural monopoly is in public hands than when it is privately owned. However, it obviously has to be a focal point in designing policies for these industries after nationalization.

Public ownership is not the only solution. Prior to nationalization in Great Britain, and at the present time in some other countries, including the United States, a strong element of public control is preferred. In the United States, the industries designated public utilities are subject to detailed regulations by

State and Federal Commissions, and in a number of respects by City and County authorities as well. The regulations extend to pricing, investment, the quality of service, profitability, capital structure and any other point at which there could be a conflict between the interests of the consumer and those of the owners. A massive body of legislation and case law has grown up so that each utility company has to employ its own specialist lawyers, accountants, economists and engineers to match the corresponding experts employed by the various regulating bodies. It is an open question, very much deserving a definitive study, whether ownership of these utilities has actually conferred upon the British government a greater degree of control than, for example, the Americans have achieved with their public utility law, and whether the kinds of control thus achieved have tended to work towards greater efficiency. Judgment on this question is not eased by the fact that in Britain some industries have been subject to both nationalization and regulation at the same time. The Railway Rates Tribunal had been established to ensure that the public interest was safeguarded when the railway companies arranged their prices and services, but it remained in existence long after nationalization effectively in opposition to the Transport Commission, which on its creation had been charged with the task of operating in the public interest! Probably the main distinction between ownership and control lies in the negative character of control—it is easy to stop the companies from doing something which they may wish to do, but much more difficult to make them do something which they do not wish to do. However, this becomes important only at intervals when major policy decisions are involved.

Even when capital intensive industries are not monopolistic, they may generate economic problems for another reason, viz. their slow response to changing demands and technologies. This is partly inherent in the great expense, the longevity and the specificity of the assets employed in these industries, which will cause a 'gestation' lag before accepted changes can be made effective, but perhaps more important, will cause a resistance to change, since the assets previously created to meet old demands or use earlier technologies will have to be written off. It is ironic that the resistance to change could inhibit the development of monopoly in such cases, because the latest technologies demand such a large scale of production that the industry has become in principle, if not in practice, a natural monopoly. This is the essence of the case presented for steel nationalization and partly for coalmining—not that the industries were monopolies, but that they should have been! The coal industry had been subject to a secular decline in demand beginning in 1914, and this was far too rapid for either the number of coalminers or the number of mining companies to adjust, particularly when the cyclical decline of the early 1930s was superimposed. The result by 1939 was a demoralized and technically backward industry, which for a generation had not had a breathing space to adjust to the changes affecting it. The technical deficiencies of the industry were set out in great detail in the Reid Report of 1945,[2] and although the Committee did not specifically recommend nationalization, it laid great stress on the need for concentration, standardization and larger scale generally. The Trade Unions in the mining industry had long since come to the conclusion that their interests were in complete conflict with those of the owners. They had pressed unremittingly for the nationalization of the industry, and this became one of the first priorities of the post-war Labour Government.

The steel industry did not have the same history of secular decline, although it accounted for a continually diminishing proportion of world production. During the 1930s the industry had begun to suffer severely from foreign competition and was granted high tariff protection while it reorganized. It is impossible to say how effective this might have been, had not the war intervened to give a period in which the industry operated continuously at full capacity, but with little capital replacement and no major reorganization. After the war critics alleged that it was technically inadequate for post-war industrial requirements, and the industry was not capable of taking full advantage of the extraordinary export opportunities which existed then. In its defence, the industry's spokesmen have claimed that the threat of nationalization facing the steel companies during the late 1940s inhibited the industry from tackling its own problems comprehensively, and that the same became true after de-nationalization in the 1950s, when the Labour Party continually warned that on regaining office one of its first priorities would be the renationalization of the industry. It is certain that a political risk added to the business uncertainties of a capital intensive industry is likely to generate greater caution rather than more enterprise, so that the political future of the industry will have to be finally settled before it can show its full potential.

A further official enquiry[3] had shown the gas industry to be technically backward and organized in far too small units. Although this industry is a natural monopolist of this form of power, it had suffered from the competition of electricity, and was considered by many to be an anachronism. However, it had an important role in domestic supply and in some industrial processes, and its inefficiency would thus cause serious disadvantages to a large number of consumers. There was no very clear idea of how really large-scale units could be created outside the main conurbations, but this would be valuable in itself, and up until then was clearly restricted by the local government boundaries which arbitrarily divided these conurbations.

The railways were in many respects in a similar position to the gas industry. They were set in a nineteenth century pattern and suffering acutely from the competition of newer forms of transport industry, but were nevertheless providing vital services to the whole community. In 1921, the industry had been rationalized into four large companies each with a regional monopoly, but the possible benefits from this measure had been simultaneously denied by the restrictions imposed on the companies' commercial freedom, including a pricing system which was based on the assumption that the companies were pure monopolists, whereas road transport provided intense and virtually unrestricted competition. The railway industry stagnated, and although the 1939–45 war restored some of its former glories, it also led to over-utilization and under-replacement, so that again the situation existed of an industry with a large backlog of modernization and investment, and possibly a diminishing economic role. This is not a situation which private investors would greet with any enthusiasm.

The electricity supply industry was different in being one of the great growth industries of the twentieth century. Over a long period, demand has at least doubled every ten years, and constant advances in technology have produced a continuous series of 'new generations' in power technology, all involving a larger scale in return for lower unit costs. The problem here was to keep the industry moving fast enough to keep pace with these changes, and it was clear that an atomistic structure of small independent enterprises each running one or two small power stations would be entirely unsuitable for the kind of development required. This had been appreciated as early as 1926 in relation to the main transmission system, which was put into the hands of a public authority (the Central Electricity Board) but by the end of the war, it was obvious that the new generation required large scale organization in *some* form, and the success of the 'national grid' under the CEB seemed to suggest that a public authority would be appropriate.

Road transport appeared to be another industry which could benefit from large scale organization (which might minimize expensive cross-freighting and one-way loads) but had remained atomistic *and* commercially successful. An industry can often survive otherwise fatal faults if the market is sufficiently buoyant to keep floating it off the rocks. This was partly the case with road transport, but it is easy to miss the fact that an atomistic structure over at least part of the industry had a powerful economic logic in permitting the great flexibility which is much of the strength of this industry. It is very untidy, but on the whole it works.

For an industry to be a candidate for nationalization, it was clearly not enough that an industry was 'on the commanding heights of the economy', or that it was showing acute problems of adjustment to change—it had to be both. It is easy to identify industries such as petroleum refining and basic chemicals (e.g. sulphuric acid), machine tools and commercial banking which stand in a similar relationship to the rest of the economy as coal and steel. Similarly it is easy to quote examples of industries with immense problems of adjustment, such as cotton textiles and shipbuilding but none of these have been nationalized although they have frequently been proposed for this treatment. However, in some cases the distinction probably owes more to historical and political accident than pure economic logic.

As long as the motives for nationalizing an industry are of the kinds just discussed, i.e. micro-economic problems of faulty resource allocation and inadequate adjustment, then the criteria by which the industry will be organized and operated should also be micro-economic. The total objective of the criteria is greater efficiency—economic efficiency ultimately, but probably with technical efficiency as a necessary first step. The standard by which the industry's performance will be judged will then logically also be economic—their success in minimizing average costs and satisfying the consumer. Under certain conditions, this success may be measured in terms of profitability.

The picture is greatly complicated by the fact that economic efficiency was not the only consideration. At the end of the war, the dominant memory of the pre-war years was of the violent economic fluctuations which had played such an important part in the political developments of the period. Britain had avoided the hyper-inflation which had affected some other countries, but had suffered massive unemployment in the early 1930s and several smaller depressions and chronic deflation during the rest of the period. (Recent investigation of the trends in this period seem to show that there was an undercurrent of strong industrial growth, but this was not apparent at the time or for a long time afterwards.) The American New Deal, Swedish budgeting experiments and Keynes' rationalization of the principles of contra-cyclical public works programmes in his *General Theory of Employment, Interest and Money*[4] came towards the end of the period, but they all seemed to suggest that if the government directly controlled a central block of industry, it could use this in its macro-economic policies. The industries might be made to offer, in effect, subsidized employment during a depression, incurring accounting losses in doing so, but possibly skimming off excess demand by higher prices during the boom. In addition, timing of the industry's investment programmes might be varied to produce multiplier effects in the rest of the economy, and from this point of view, the capital intensive industries were the strategic ones to control.

This line of reasoning was perfectly consistent with most of the economic models produced at the time, but it begged a lot of questions. Was it actually feasible to change the commercial policies and investment programmes of these industries at short notice? If it was feasible, could it be made consistent with the micro-economic efficiency objective? These problems have since been encountered in practical form.

Finally, the motives for nationalization extended beyond the micro- and macro-economic into the social and philosophical. It is essentially a Socialist policy, even though there are numerous examples such as the BBC, ITV and AEA which have been created in an *ad hoc* fashion by Conservative governments. The central aim of socialism has always been to eliminate extreme inequalities of income and power, and it has already been pointed out that the capital intensive industries represent great concentrations of wealth and hence economic power. It seemed to follow that if these industries were taken out of private hands, it would tend to disperse this concentration, although it has never been clear exactly how this was to happen. It would obviously happen if the industries were simply expropriated, but this was contrary to most people's idea of natural justice—why should the owners of industries which on the whole had been performing an essential and often not very rewarding job be punished, while owners of other industries were unaffected? Compensation thus has to be paid, and this leaves wealth in the same private hands as before, although some individuals may now be denied a 'power-base' in a key industry. In fact the gas and electricity industries were already largely municipally owned, and the railways had traditionally been the 'safe' investment of the institutional investor. Steel and, to a lesser extent, coal supported some notable family fortunes and some of the larger steel companies retained a combination of large family shareholdings and family direction long after this had ceased to be the fashion in large companies. However, it is not easy to demonstrate that this structure gave the families concerned any more political power than was the case in brewing, where the same situation obtained, but where this was not seen as an adequate reason for nationalizing the industry. Compensation was made in government stock carrying a fixed rate of interest, with the basis for compensation being either expert valuation of the industry's assets or the recent market value of publicly issued stock. There was generally little complaint that the compensation terms were ungenerous and some critics maintain that they were extremely generous.[5] The compensation stock which was issued in the 1940s carried low rates of interest, and most of the purchasing power of the compensation has been eroded by inflation and rising interest rates. However, the same process would have affected the fixed interest stock of the companies to the same extent, and it is a matter of pure guesswork what would have happened to the equity of these companies in the past twenty years. On balance, nationalization has not proved to be an effective means of generally redistributing wealth and could even have produced the reverse effects, by forcing investors out of industries with poor prospects and enabling many of them to increase their fortunes by investing the proceeds of compensation in more profitable industries.

In spite of the over-riding aim of making these industries economically efficient in terms of 'market' criteria, much of the argument over nationalization has been on the question of the extent to which these industries should deliberately ignore or adjust market criteria in providing a 'public service' rather than economic goods. The public service principle may take many forms, but they all reduce to a redistribution of income between groups in the community, so that certain people have a higher real income than they would have if the distribution were left entirely to the price mechanism. The beneficiaries might be particular groups of workers (coalminers and lorry-drivers being favoured in the early debates) who are thought to deserve higher incomes and better working conditions than the market had created for them. To the extent that this is achieved as a deliberate policy, there will be some redistribution of income from consumers or taxpayers to the employees, and possibly as a result, some effect on the demand for the services involved. This may or not result in a less 'efficient' allocation of resources, since there will certainly be large elements of economic rent or quasi-rent in an industry with large indivisibilities and where consumer demands tend to be inelastic, so that the redistribution could principally affect these rent elements. In other cases, the argument may be that since these industries on the whole produce 'essential' services, the consumer is entitled to them 'as a right'. If he is charged the full cost of providing them, then some of them may be out of the reach of whole groups in the community. Electricity, postal, telephone and public transport services to rural consumers are cases in point, and such consumers are often provided with these services at a loss to the industry itself. This again raises many questions. What is an 'essential' service? Is everybody entitled to them regardless of cost? And so on.

Finally, there is the matter of costs and benefits which are external to the firm or industry, but nevertheless accrue to *somebody* in the community. Such externalities can be identified in every industry, but they will naturally tend to be more important in all-pervasive industries such as power and transport. Private firms will tend to ignore them, although very large companies may be anxious to impress the public and the politicians with their social responsibility and voluntarily undertake additional costs in landscaping, pollution control, product testing, etc. However, a private railway company would be unable to carry the cost of large scale unremunerative 'commuter' services for very long, even if it wished to do so, while their abandonment would create substantial extra costs through road congestion on the rest of the community. In principle a nationalized industry should be able to take account of such externalities more readily than a private concern, although it does not follow that the industry itself should be made financially responsible for such social costs, and it is arguable that a private company could also meet social needs if the taxpayer were prepared to pay it to do so. The question thus focuses on the issue of which form of organization makes such cost-benefit accounting more practicable—a subsidized nationalized industry or a subsidized private firm?

The special problem of the nationalized industries is that they have inherited this diverse set of objectives and therefore have to find some way of devising structures and policies which will enable them to strike the right balance between these aims. The balance has shifted over the last twenty years, and the policies have shifted with it, but further discussion of this will be reserved to later sections.

7.3 Structure

The Acts of Parliament creating the nationalized industries emphasized service to the public as their main task. The Coal Industry Nationalization Act, for example, in establishing the National Coal Board, laid upon it the responsibility to make coal 'available in such qualities and in such quantities and at such prices as may seem to them best calculated to further the public interest in all respects', and similarly worded statements of general objective are contained in the other Acts. An unrestricted commitment to the 'public interest' would be nonsensical, so that certain limits are set on this obligation. The most important restriction is financial, since the various Boards are only permitted to spend on satisfying the public interest what they can earn by selling their services. In short, the Nationalization Acts implied that each industry should at least 'break-even' financially. Typical wording, again quoted from the Coal Industry Nationalization Act, is 'combined revenues . . . (shall be) not less than sufficient to meet the Board's combined outgoings properly chargeable to revenue account taking one year with another'. Two special points may be noted at this stage, although we will return to a fuller discussion later. First, the statute stresses *'combined'* revenues and outgoings, and since the Coal Board and most of the others are diversified, then one activity may effectively subsidize another. Secondly, the industries are not obliged to break even every year, but could offset a surplus in one year against a deficit in another. Recent practice has moved away from a simple 'break-even' target to include a modest profit in the objective, but this will be examined more closely in Section 7.6. The nationalized industries thus appear to be less constrained by considerations of profitability than a purely commercial concern, but nevertheless they have to balance profitability against the other objectives.

This compromise objective is reflected in the form of organization chosen for the industries, which is the Public Corporation. The Public Corporation is a separate legal entity, like a company, but the government and not private shareholders owns the capital and appoints the members of the controlling Board. The Board is thus answerable to the government, as a Board of Directors is to its shareholders, and as the owner the government is in a position to determine the broad policy of the Corporation, leaving the Board to see to its execution. To simplify the relations between a Corporation and the government a particular Ministry is nominated as the Corporation's sponsor, and there is thus a particular Minister who acts as a direct link between the two, although in practice the relationship has been rather more complex than this.

The Public Corporation is thus a compromise body, and the central feature of the compromise is the distinction between policy and day-to-day management. In principle the government settles policy, i.e. it determines the ordering of priorities, but then gives the management the maximum possible freedom to exercise their commercial judgment and enterprise in carrying it out. Provided that the line between policy and management is correctly drawn, the result should be a combination of public responsibility and commercial efficiency, but it is difficult to define such a division of responsibility consistently and flexibly, where inconsistency and rigidity can both be very damaging. Different Ministers have taken a different view of their powers vis-à-vis the Boards, and if there is a rapid turnover of Ministers, the Boards may find it difficult to decide exactly what their own powers are from one year to the next. By and large, the Corporations with the severest commercial problems have also experienced most

Ministerial intervention, largely because these industries attract most public attention and may even need to be subsidized out of public funds (although this was never contemplated as a regular arrangement).

The outstanding exception to a Public Corporation structure for a major public enterprise in Great Britain was the Post Office, which was organized as a Department of State. This meant that all Post Office employees were Civil Servants, all income and expenditure passed through the Treasury, and as a result the Post Office was subject to continuous Parliamentary supervision and Ministerial control. It is possible to rationalize this distinction on the grounds that Post Office operations were largely routine and therefore there was less need for commercial enterprise than in the other industries. Also it was argued that it was an almost complete monopoly and that it performed a vast number of services for other branches of government. However, the principal reason is that the Post Office had been in the public sector long before the modern Public Corporation had been devised, and for a long time afterwards the task of bringing it into line with the other Public Enterprises never seemed particularly urgent. However, the industry has begun to find itself under pressure because the labour-intensive nature of part of its function (postal deliveries) has continually eroded the quality of its services in a period of rapidly increasing wages, while its telecommunications services are in the forefront of advancing technology and call for very large capital investments. Such problems as these call for business techniques and, it could be argued, a 'business approach' for their solution. In October 1969, the almost inevitable step of converting the Post Office to a Public Corporation was taken.

The Post Office had for a very long time been held up as the example of direct political control of a basic industry, a method of operation preferred by some supporters of nationalization who nevertheless suspected that the public corporation would always lean more heavily towards commercial rather than towards social criteria in its judgments. They lost their case on the grounds that the usual machinery of government is not geared towards a continuous succession of quick decisions in conditions of uncertainty—every decision is potentially subject to a public post-mortem unless the facts can be kept secret on security grounds. In addition, there seemed no simple way of avoiding a disastrous overloading of the machinery of Parliament and thus disturbing the entire political structure of the country.

Other alternatives which have been strongly canvassed have veered towards another extreme, that is, some form of workers' control, or control by 'syndicates' of interested parties such as workers, consumers and government. These proposals raise obvious (but not necessarily insoluble) problems of achieving technical efficiency, and even more difficult problems of sustaining maximum economic efficiency—for example how readily would capital be substituted for labour under such arrangements? In the event, the ready acceptance of the London Passenger Transport Board in the 1930s largely set the pattern for the future.

Although the *principle* of the public corporation was universally applied in the post-war period, the precise form of organization varied greatly from industry to industry. There seemed to be a shift of emphasis from a massive unitary structure, such as the National Coal Board, through looser federal forms such as the almost autonomous regional Gas Boards, loosely coordinated by the Gas Council, to the British Iron and Steel Corporation which retained the company structure of the privately-owned industry almost unchanged. It is debateable whether this reflected a change in principle, in response to the then fashionable doctrine of 'decentralization' as a supposed cure for all administrative problems, or whether it was simply an adaptation of the same basic principles to different circumstances in each industry. For example, the most monolithic of all the Corporations was the National Coal Board, but the problem for the coal industry immediately after 1946 was to increase coal output very rapidly, while controlling rapidly increasing costs. The Reid Committee had emphasized the need for standardization of equipment and for making the best use of the industry's scarce managerial talent, and the miners Union had long insisted on uniformity of wages and conditions throughout this industry. The structure which emerged was that of a powerful National Board, consisting mostly of functional specialists, with a pyramidal structure of Regions, Areas and Sub Areas beneath this. The structure exemplified the 'line and staff' form of management organization, with a line of executive managers through the middle of the organization chart, and technical specialists as advisers at each level. The system naturally did not function as smoothly as the organization chart would suggest, and colliery managers in particular often resented the fact that they now come about fifth in the general management hierarchy, whereas formerly they had been accustomed to a great deal of autonomy. But able managers could obtain very quick promotion within such an organization, and little was heard of this complaint after a few years.

It would appear to the casual observer that such a very large organization would raise very severe problems of management. An industry employing nearly three-quarters of a million men (initially) may involve a disproportionate number of administrative staff. The Coal Board was obviously extremely sensitive to press criticisms of excessive bureaucracy, and in 1955 it came as a surprise to most people when the Fleck Committee (the Chairman, Sir Alexander Fleck, was then Chairman of ICI), which had been set up to advise the Coal Board on its organization, in the course of a detailed set of criticisms and recommendations made clear its view that the NCB employed an inadequate number of management and technical staff. Far from the industry being overcentralized, the national Board had inadequate control of the operating units. The result was not a drastic change in the structure of the industry, but far reaching changes in the management techniques used to allocate responsibility between one level of management and another.[6]

If the gas industry is taken as an example of a decentralized industry, it is clear that although it shared some features with the coal industry (such as the need for standardization and better use of management skills) its central problem was one of marketing rather than production. Each gas undertaking served a local market, and the prospects of broadening this significantly seemed at one time technically remote. The traditional 'town gas' industry has now been overtaken by new sources and new technology—North Sea natural gas and liquefied methane are accounting for an ever increasing proportion of total supplies, and a network of large-bore pipelines is spreading over the country. The Gas Council has acquired greater powers than were orginally contemplated—it imports the methane, it purchases and distributes the natural gas and even shares with the oil companies in the exploration and exploitation of the deposits. In many ways, the technical structure of the gas industry is approaching that of electricity, and the organizational structure could well follow.

Air transport is another industry which has shown great stability in its organization, but in which technical factors could lead to drastic changes in the future. For a brief period, the nationalized airlines consisted of three Corporations—Overseas, European and South American—but the last was too small and not sufficiently differentiated in its aircraft and operations to survive alone and was merged into BOAC. Since then the rationale of maintaining separate Corporations for short- and long-haul operations has been questioned frequently, since each has to maintain administrative and maintenance staff and facilities, and the industry appears to be one which yields increasing returns to scale. The structure has survived because it could be argued that the two kinds of service involve different sets of problems, and they employ completely different aircraft. However, there has been a progressive reduction in the number of aircraft manufacturers producing large civil aircraft, and each of these is under strong pressure to produce a full range of aircraft using many standard components, including engines. In addition, the new generation of 'airbus' aircraft are highly flexible, and may cover both short and medium-to-long hauls. The case for a single Corporation offering a comprehensive service with standardized aircraft will thus become increasingly strong. The situation is complicated by the obligation of the nationalized airlines towards supporting the British aircraft manufacturing industry. If British manufacturers can produce a range of competitive aircraft with a degree of standardization comparable to that of Boeing or Douglas in the United States, it may be possible to reconcile this obligation with the airline's commercial objectives. But if it involves the use of a miscellany of designs, the scope for gaining economies of scale would be obviously limited.

In some of the nationalized industries there have already been sweeping changes from the initial structure. The corporate structure for electricity started as a sort of compromise between the coal and gas organization, with a single central authority (the British Electricity Authority) and twelve semi-autonomous Area Boards to manage local distribution. The organization had to meet the powerful demands for centralization and large scale in production with flexibility and sensitivity to local conditions in distribution, but these conflicting needs were difficult to reconcile within a single body. The industry was reorganized after the report of the Herbert Committee[7] and the two problems were separated and given to two independent bodies. The Central

197

Electricity Generating Board was set up to control production and main distribution of electricity, selling power in bulk to the Area Boards which were federated under the new Electricity Council. The conflict between the diversity of local needs on the one hand, and the technical case for mass production and the highest possible levels of capacity utilization can thus be resolved as a commercial battle between the Corporations.

The industry which has experienced most change is surface transport. This is not surprising in view of the range and severity of the problems in this field, and the rate at which circumstances change (for example, the rapid growth of private car ownership). The initial emphasis was on 'coordination' of different forms of transport, and this objective was given corporate expression in the Transport Commission, a Corporation responsible for all nationalized transport (excluding the airlines). Within the Commission there were separate 'Executives' for railways, road haulage, canals, docks, hotels and various miscellaneous activities. Each Executive had, in fact, a great deal of autonomy, although the Commission returned consolidated accounts. The different Executives adapted their organization to their own circumstances. The Road Haulage Executive had acquired a powerfully commercial set of companies and retained a decentralized structure highly geared towards selling road transport. The Railway Executive had inherited an industry with great technical traditions but with practically no experience of *selling* railway transport. The railways thus acquired a highly centralized functional organization which gave great power to technical specialists, but which was essentially geared to the problem of a monopolistic public service aiming at the highest possible standards of safety and reliability, rather than a commercial enterprise fighting for its life against the effects of new technology.

The Commission organization was not able to achieve significant results because there was never any clear idea of what was meant by 'coordination' or how to achieve it. Nor was there any will to 'coordinate' if this involved firm exercise of authority. The partial de-nationalization of road haulage in 1953 could not be expected to help in this. Coordination was left to the market, with each segment of the transport industry attempting to meet consumer demand in the ways which seemed appropriate to it. The railways fared very badly in this situation—the Railway Executive had started with an annual deficit and in the course of a little over a decade this mounted rapidly to over £100 million per annum. Increased capital expenditure on modernization and more flexible pricing procedures were brought in during the 1950s, but the strong engineering traditions of the railways still militated against an aggressively competitive approach by the industry. The Transport Commission was dismantled in 1961, and autonomous corporations created for the railways, London Transport, the docks, inland waterways and a holding company to operate the road haulage and bus services and miscellaneous activities such as hotels, travel agencies, etc. The railways remained the biggest problem. A regional structure was introduced into the British Railways organization and as a powerful gesture indicating the new commercial orientation, the first Chairman of the British Railways Board was a man with no railway experience whatever, but with a very successful business record in private industry. Dr Beeching, the new Chairman, was paid a commercial salary at double the standard rate for the Chairmen of large public corporations. (It is debatable whether this gesture was well managed, since the Chairman's salary distracted attention from the other more fundamental changes involved, and created a great deal of public suspicion of everything that he proposed thereafter.) The Railways Board was allowed to write off a large amount of obsolete capital liabilities and accumulated deficits, and given a fresh start, but with reduced services the deficit continued to climb to an annual rate of £150 million.

A further re-organization was brought in by the Transport Act 1968. This split up the transport industry by function rather than by mode of transport. The National Freight Corporation manages long-distance express freight movements by road or rail. The large conurbations each have their own Transport Authorities controlling the whole range of public transport in their areas. The Railways Board is thus left principally with an inter-city transport function, and a minimum of 'social' obligations. The logic underlying this Act thus appears to be one of management. Each of the Boards or Authorities is given a defined area of responsibility, and the task of balancing social and commercial objectives is effectively removed from the executive bodies and passed to political authorities, i.e. the Ministry or the Local authorities as the case may be. At the time of writing (1969) this new system is still not fully effective, so that it is not possible to judge its efficiency, but in principle it appears to come closer to an economist's criterion for effective organization than any of its forebears.

In the face of the diversity revealed above, it is difficult to sum up briefly the relationships between organization and objective in public enterprise. Certainly the generalized discussions on 'centralization' versus 'decentralization' which break out from time to time are quite irrelevant to the special problems of each industry. The Public Corporation structure is adaptable to a variety of conditions, and although the sheer size of the nationalized industries makes frequent structural changes difficult, experience has shown that a certain amount of experimentation is possible, making it possible for them to adapt to significant changes in their circumstances.

7.4 Public accountability

Since the nationalized industries are expected to operate 'in the public interest', means must be found of informing the public of their activities and ensuring that the wishes or needs of the public are taken fully into account in determining their policies. There are two main problems involved here: one is to take account of the interests of individual members of the public, the other is to discover and act upon the collective interests of the public at large.

The first of these is mainly a matter of commercial policy. The nationalized industries are powerful monopolists, so that they may quite easily ignore the legitimate needs of weak groups of consumers. This danger is increased when the industries become a means of redistributing income between one group and another, by charging prices above or below the cost of producing particular services. A corporation may find itself making arbitrary decisions on who should receive a service and who should not and this can generate resentment even when the corporation does all in its power to be 'fair'. The withdrawal of unremunerative railway services and electricity and telephone connections to outlying areas are cases which from time to time leave some people with a sense of grievance.

At first, it was thought that these problems could be solved institutionally, partly by making the various Boards (particularly the Regional or Area Boards) 'representative' of various interests through part-time members, and partly by creating special bodies specifically to look after the consumers interests. These bodies, with a variety of titles but known generally as Consumer Councils were established for each industry, and occasionally for each main group of consumers. They were intended to be consulted on matters of policy, including future plans and their views taken into account, but they were also to be a channel through which complaints from the public could pass directly through to the Board and even to the Minister if they were not satisfactorily dealt with at a lower level. In practice, they have been more active (but not necessarily more influential) in their consultative than in their 'watchdog' role. The public in general remains unaware of their existence and complaints are more usually aired through newspapers or local Members of Parliament, who will usually write directly to the Chairman, or raise the point as a Parliamentary Question. Since nationalization has been a basic political issue, the particular complaints of individual consumers could always be used as ammunition in the general political battle on the principle of nationalization. It is possible that the publicity given to nationalized industry's prices and services has led consumers to demand a higher standard than they might have done from private companies in the same situation, but this is not necessarily unreasonable if nationalization is offered as a way of improving an industry's performance.

The second problem involves the political process of bringing the public interest to bear on general policy making. This involves a difficult balance between excessive interference by politicians and public officials, which could restrict the commercial initiative of the management, and such a degree of freedom from public control that there would be no point in having these industries in the public sector at all. This is not the kind of problem for which there is a single, once-for-all solution.

The principal representative of the public interest is the elected government of the day, and the main means of communication between the nationalized industries and the government is the sponsoring Ministry—Transport, Power, Board of Trade, etc. (At the end of 1969, a number of sponsoring Ministries were merged into the Ministry of Technology, leaving only transport and the Post Office with other sponsors.) The Minister concerns himself with matters of policy and may influence the policy of the Corporation in a great variety of ways—by discussion, suggestion, persuasion and ultimately by directive, whereby he orders a certain course of action and takes full responsibility for the consequences. In practice, the directive is not used and the various indirect methods of exerting influence raise an important constitutional question in fixing the political responsibility for the policies of the Corporation. On occasions, the nationalized industries have pursued policies which were not of the Board's choosing, but the Minister has been able to deny final responsibility for them, and this has enabled him to avoid detailed questioning on the issue in Parliament. An extreme example of this was discovered by the Select Committee on the Nationalized Industries in the case of the National Coal Board, where the Minister of Fuel and Power had used the device of a wartime regulation to control coal prices for more than a decade, although the NCB retained statutory responsibility for the consequences.

The public may also influence the policy of the nationalized industries on sensitive issues by the general weight of 'public opinion' expressed through the press, television and the actions of backbench MPs. The Boards may respond directly to these pressures, or the government may be the first to feel them and be led to influence the Boards in the ways indicated.

If public opinion is to be effective it should be well informed, and this involves devising some procedure whereby well-informed representatives of the public can put searching questions to the responsible people. Each Corporation publishes a very detailed annual report, but this necessarily tends to gloss-over the background to many of the decisions it has taken. Parliamentary Question-Time is frequently used to obtain information from the sponsoring Minister, but its usefulness is usually limited by the questioner's lack of expertise and the procedural rules governing the form and scope of questions. Full-scale debate on Amending Bills, the receipt of the Annual Reports, etc., have occurred fairly frequently but irregularly, and they have suffered from discursiveness and the pervasive problem of lack of expertise. The usual solution to such Parliamentary problems is to use the Committee system, and this was done in this case. A Select Committee was established, initially in 1953, and after a period of trial and error it began effective work in 1958. The Select Committee uses the Annual Report of one of the corporations as a starting point, and then proceeds to examine in great detail the issues involved, calling as witnesses members of the Board, employees of the Corporation, Ministers and senior civil servants. It may make recommendations, based on its findings, and these are debated in the House of Commons, but ultimately the main value of the work of this Committee lies in the volumes of detailed evidence. The members of such a Committee will usually become highly expert in their field, and this has helped to overcome one of the main fears concerning this Select Committee—that it would be a perfect vehicle for busybodies to explore the details of the Corporation's business, while missing the main problems. A recent development has been for the Select Committee to take a general issue spanning many or all of the industries—for example, the whole question of Ministerial Control—and subject this to the same form of examination.

The enquiry just referred to has revealed much about the relationships between a public corporation and the government. In theory, each corporation has a sponsoring Ministry which acts as the sole link between a corporation, other interested Ministries, and the Cabinet, but the situation naturally turned out to be rather more complicated. Apart from the sponsoring Ministry, two other Ministries, the central economic departments in the form of the Treasury and the Department of Economic Affairs (DEA), were closely interested in the activities of the nationalized industries, since they are bound to have a strong impact on the short and long term prospects of the economy (see Chapter 8). The Treasury is in a position to exert a direct influence, since it provides the greater part of the funds for long-term investment and finances the deficits of the loss-making industries, and it now determines the overall level and composition of public sector investment by setting the 'test discount rate' (see p. 213). The DEA was responsible for long-term National Planning, and was interested not only in discovering the plans of the corporation, but also in influencing their plans in the interests of achieving a given rate of growth in the economy as a whole. In 1965 and 1966 the electricity industry based its expansion plans on a four per cent rate of growth in the economy, and as a result later found itself with considerable surplus capacity.

Other ministries may be involved on specific issues, such as manpower policies or tariffs. The sponsoring Ministry should act as a buffer between the Boards and the other agencies of government, but it is impossible to avoid all direct contacts between the Boards and other Ministries, and one of the main tasks of the sponsoring Ministry is therefore to represent the interests of their industries inside the machinery of government. This has created problems from time to time in maintaining a balanced approach to the corporations, since the sponsoring Ministry is simultaneously representing government authority to the industry, yet at the same time acting as a defender of the industry inside Parliament and inside the machinery of government. In one capacity the Ministry has to identify itself with its industry, in the other it has to be sternly objective. Not surprisingly, history shows some variations in emphasis as one Minister replaces another.

These relationships have now become further complicated by the introduction of a new representative of the public interest into the situation. In 1967, after a series of substantial price increases in the nationalized industries, the Prime Minister promised that the National Board for Prices and Incomes (PIB) would investigate and report on all further major price changes in these industries (see Chapter 8). The Board had already conducted specific enquiries on particular prices and pricing methods in the public sector, but it was now introduced as a permanent part of the public accountability machinery. The obvious danger is that the various Ministries, Committees and Boards will overlap and produce the excessive degree of control which the Public Corporation system was designed to avoid. It is argued that the PIB has a different kind of expertise from the other bodies and a fundamentally different approach—it is apolitical and attempts to answer the questions it deals with on the lines of 'what would be the answer which a properly functioning competitive market would produce in this situation?' It could even be argued that since private industry is subject to investigation by the PIB then exceptions for the nationalized industries would be discrimination in their favour. However, the arrangement is too new for its effect to be judged, and it may prove to be politically ephemeral.

7.5 Policies

We have already seen that the Nationalization Acts laid upon the newly formed Corporations the responsibility for operating these industries in the public interest, subject to the general condition that revenues would cover costs. The statutes did not lay down in detail how the public interest should be defined, nor how the financial objective was to be achieved, although the latter was qualified in three main respects:

(*a*) The Corporations were not necessarily expected to break even each year, but over a period—'taking one year with another' or 'on an average of good and bad years'. The length of this period was not specified, but it was understood to be fairly short.

(*b*) They were to charge prices 'related' to costs, although the nature of this relationship was not specified.

(*c*) The costs included depreciation and interest on all capital, including the original compensation stock. The capital structure consists exclusively of debt, so the interest payment is a fixed commitment, not varying with the prosperity of the enterprise. This does not apply to the nationalized British Steel Corporation or BOAC (see below, p. 212).

The first of these could be interpreted in several ways. One possibility is that it was intended to give the nationalized industries the commercial freedom to pursue a Keynesian counter-cyclical policy, by in effect subsidizing employment in a depression and compensating by profits in the subsequent boom. However, since at the time at which these Corporations were formed, the trade cycle was expected to follow the pre-war pattern, i.e. averaging nine years between peaks, this interpretation could hardly be consistent with the assumption that the break-even period would be fairly short. It seems more likely that it was intended simply to give the management a small margin of flexibility, given the impossibility of hitting a financial target (a zero profit is a financial target) precisely every year. Recent directives requiring the nationalized industries to earn specified surpluses include a similar provision.

The contra-cyclical theory was never put to the test, since the post-1946 period has been one of unbroken inflation, with a number of minor recessions resulting from periodic attempts on the part of successive governments to check the inflation. If the nationalized industries had attempted to prevent unemployment in these circumstances they would have been acting directly against central government policy. However if they had used periods of excess demand as opportunities to make a profit, they would have accumulated very large surpluses. Such surpluses would be deflationary in the same way that indirect taxes are deflationary, i.e. they draw off purchasing power from the public and therefore tend to reduce demand for other goods. Unfortunately, to the extent that such surpluses would be associated with higher prices for coal, electricity, transport, etc., than would otherwise have been the case the immediate effect is to *raise* the general price level. In a situation of general excess demand and easy credit, where consumers could relatively easily offset their loss of purchasing power due to these surpluses, the effect of the higher prices could therefore be simply another twist in the inflationary spiral. This dilemma is often dramatized as 'demand' versus 'cost' inflation, so that according to whether the government currently accepts a demand or cost theory of the continuing inflation, the nationalized industries might be required to increase their profits or reduce their prices—the alternative of doing both not usually being feasible.

Up to the late 1950s, successive governments leaned heavily towards a 'cost inflationary' policy in dealing with the nationalized industries. The industries were then under constant pressure to delay price increases. The National Coal Board in some years was making a deficit while at the same time the demand for good quality coal was persistently in excess of supply, i.e. the price was below the market equilibrium level. The demand for electricity also persistently exceeded the supply at peak hours, and although the industry did not actually incur losses, its surpluses were certainly smaller than they could have been. The railways suffered chronic and increasing deficits, and attempted with great regularity to recover part of these by price increases. These were invariably deferred and occasionally refused, and these delays contributed significantly to the eventual large accumulated deficits. (The Transport Tribunal was required to adjudicate on all applications for railway price increases, against which there would naturally be objections by various interested parties. This procedure was lengthy, so that even without Ministerial intervention, railway prices could be safely left to lag behind the general pace of inflation.)

Persistent losses or small 'profits' made these industries very easy targets for criticism, since probably a majority of the public have been accustomed to equating losses with inefficiency. At the same time, the public has also been ready to complain about higher prices (to reduce losses) or the removal of unremunerative services (to reduce costs). There is an obvious problem in maintaining morale and retaining first-class managers in such a situation, and this problem has not been eased by the relatively low levels of salaries paid to the senior management in these Corporations (see p. 220).

If this had been purely a problem for the nationalized industries themselves, they may have been left to deal with it as best they could. However, these losses, or negligible surpluses, were also creating severe problems in the central management of the economy. Losses had to be financed, and if they were cumulative the Corporation would have to borrow the necessary funds. A more serious problem was that these industries are generally highly capital intensive, and either expanding rapidly, or modernizing and becoming more capital intensive, or both at once. The nationalized industries are thus very heavy investors, but unlike private industry, whose savings have been generally comparable with their investment, the Public Corporations have been obliged to borrow on a very large scale in order to meet their investment needs. To take one year as an example, in 1956 gross domestic fixed capital formation by companies was £1,228m, with company saving £2,083m, while the Public Corporation invested £589m on fixed capital, but saved only £205m. In 1961, the company sector figures were £1,982m of investment and £2,460m of saving and the Public Corporations were £905m and £364m.

The major Corporations were initially responsible for raising their own capital, although their issues were backed by a Treasury guarantee and were thus effectively gilt-edged. This system created difficulties for the Treasury and the Bank of England, which were continually attempting to reconcile the conflicting aims of controlling an inflationary economy while keeping the servicing costs of the National Debt as low as possible. Their delicate manipulation of the capital and money markets could easily be disturbed by the appearance of the Transport Commission or Electricity Authority attempting to sell off a large block of long dated stock. Hence, in 1953, the Treasury took over the responsibility for providing long-term capital, although the Corporations continued to arrange their own bank overdrafts.

The new arrangement was temporary in the first instance, but soon became permanent. However, although it eliminated a number of difficulties, it did not solve the main economic problem, which was the sheer volume of the Corporation's borrowing requirements. The Radcliffe Report[8] pointed out that nationalized industry borrowings were largely responsible for the regular and large annual increases in the National Debt during the 1950s, and in some years accounted for more than half of the net government borrowing. In attempting to prevent this heavy demand for long-term funds from pushing long-term interest rates too high, the Bank of England was obliged to issue large quantities of Treasury Bills. This in turn added to the liquidity of the banking system and continuously undermined the government's control of the monetary system, thus restricting its ability to control the level of demand. It is indicative of the importance of these industries that the inconsistency of treating them for symptoms of cost inflation while the economy at large was being treated for excess demand could have such disastrous consequences for the national policy.

The White Paper on *The Financial and Economic Obligations of the Nationalized Industries* followed in 1961, quite soon after the Radcliffe Report. This White Paper signified an important departure in principle from the previous understanding of the nationalized industries financial obligations, although the practical consequences took longer to emerge and resulted in a further White Paper in 1967 to clarify some issues and rectify certain omissions. The main point of the 1961 White Paper was that the nationalized industries were now to be required to earn an annual 'target' rate of return on the capital they employed, this target comprising interest, depreciation and a surplus which would correspond to a profit in private industry.

The principle of bringing the commercial policy of the nationalized industries into line with that of the private sector has a long academic lineage. Apart from the advantage of having the nationalized industries as an additional source of saving, there is a case to be made for generally higher prices in the public sector as a means of improving resource allocation. Very briefly, the point is that if the private sector charges prices which yield a profit to the firms, while the public sector just breaks even, then the public sector goods are consistently underpriced, in terms of the resources put into them, compared with the private, and this will 'mislead' the consumer and cause a misallocation of resources. Since the private sector cannot be forced to forego profit, there is no real alternative to having the public enterprises fall into line, at least up to a point. The problem then arises of how far the public corporations should go towards imitating private companies, or in other words, how big a surplus should each corporation aim at? The 1961 White Paper sets out the considerations which the government believed relevant to this question, the main one being the rate of return on capital employed in private industry. The average gross return on capital in the private sector in 1959 was 14·9 per cent, whereas the nationalized industries, ranging from 8·6 per cent to minus 1·3 per cent, averaged 3·1 per cent. However, it was argued that the return on capital in the public sector *should* be lower than in the private sector, if proper account were taken of the monopoly status of the Public Corporation, the generally lower levels of risk which they faced, the fact that they were obliged to carry substantial unremunerative services, and the fact that the public expected low prices in the public sector. The last point is not as naïve as it might appear. The public are the final political arbiters of policy, and they would have reacted very violently to a large price increase designed solely to make the nationalized industries profitable (this was clearly demonstrated in 1967, when gas and electricity prices were sharply raised to help the respective corporations to meet their targets when demand had expanded at less than the rate previously expected). These were general considerations affecting all nationalized industries, but, account had to be taken of the individual circumstances of each corporation. For example, it would have been nonsensical to expect the railways to emerge from an immense deficit simply in response to a 'target'. In this case, no target was prepared until the railways had shown that they had finally adjusted to the new competitive conditions of the transport industry. For the others, there was a process of negotiation involving the Boards, the respective Ministries and the Treasury which produced a miscellany of targets expressed in various forms. The Electricity Boards were to aim at 12·4 per cent gross (i.e. including interest and depreciation), although the rates varied from one Area Board to another. The Gas Boards were set 10·2 per cent gross, the difference between Gas and Electricity being partly accounted for by the difference in depreciation costs, but also taking account of the fact that *at the time*, the gas industry was nearly moribund while electricity was vigorously expanding. BOAC had a high target of 12·5 per cent net of depreciation but not interest, while the Coal Board was required to break even, plus a round sum of £10 million to allow for the under-recovery of replacement cost implied by the accounting convention of basing depreciation on historical costs. This mixture of methods made comparisons between the performances of the nationalized industries very difficult, although greater comparability was one of the aims. However, even if it were applied uniformly, the technique is entirely at the mercy of accounting conventions in the measurement of capital and income. There is no unique and universally accepted way of measuring the value of capital employed, particularly where the capital is long-lived and represents a succession of different technologies—for instance, steam, diesel and electric, on the railways. Also earnings may be affected significantly by the treatment of particular items in the accounts. Variations in accounting methods can therefore produce widely different results from the same basic figures.

It is difficult to make a case that the financial obligation has much bearing on the efficiency of the industry. However, it can be argued that provided the target is agreed to be attainable in the circumstances facing the industry, but not too easily attainable, then the management has a clear objective to aim at and their success or failure in attaining their target is then some indication of their efficiency as business managers. However, the system can not be expected to operate mechanistically—the results need careful interpretation if they are to have any meaning at all.

The 1961 White Paper was a decisive step in ranking the *economic* obligations of the nationalized industries above the other considerations. From then on, these industries were to be thought of first and foremost as bodies responsible for handling a very large proportion of the nation's scarce resources rather than as instruments of social policy. However, many problems remained. The Corporations were left with some social obligations, but these were undefined and vaguely compounded into the target return—the greater the weight of 'social' services, the lower the target. The targets were to be revised every five years even though competition and technology could change very quickly, as in the gas industry. Finally the target rates related to the existing capital stock, and the relationship between the average return and the marginal return on new capital can vary greatly according to particular circumstances. Yet from the point of view of efficient resource allocation it is new capital investment which is important. The existing stock is already committed and 'bygones are bygones'—it will often have no alternative use and therefore in economic terms no opportunity cost. The implied guidance to new investment was that each year's batch of investments should have an average return which would enable each corporation to maintain its overall average target. There is no theoretical justification for such a criterion. An investment is justified when its yield[9] exceeds the cost of the capital.

In a market economy, the yield on an investment will be determined by what the consumer will pay for the future products of the investment. Therefore, in principle, the investments attracting the greatest future expenditure from consumers will also be supplying the goods which the consumers most desire, and in a competitive economy, the most profitable investment will also be the most socially valuable. (The argument depends on the assumption of highly competitive behaviour in the rest of the economy, and can only be theoretically *proved* in conditions of universal perfect competition. In the real world of varying degrees of imperfection in the private sector, it can be at best a broad rule of thumb.)

In private enterprise, only the returns and the costs directly affecting the company would be brought into the reckoning. In public enterprise, a broader definition of costs and returns *may* be used, as in cost/benefit analysis. In cost/benefit analysis, an attempt is made to measure the indirect effects of any particular project, and thus bring the total flow of extra benefits and costs to the community as a whole. The cost of capital in such an analysis should be the 'social opportunity cost', which is not necessarily the same as the current market rate of interest.[10] Cost/benefit analysis is slow and costly, and is unlikely to be widely used in the foreseeable future in the nationalized industries, although the Victoria Line project was undertaken by London Transport after it was shown that the value of the indirect benefits to *road* traffic in North-East London was likely to be much greater than the actual operating losses which the line was certain to make.[11]

The task of bringing public enterprise into line with private is complicated by the treatment and assessment of risk. Public enterprise in general is considered to be low risk, and this is reflected in the policy of making all of their capital charges a fixed obligation, whereas private industry, with a majority of its capital in the form of equity, is able to adjust its payments to its owners according to its current success or lack of success, and the value of the enterprise will vary with the amount which the business can afford to pay. The actual returns which private enterprise earns on its investments are not necessarily closely related

211

to the returns which were expected when the investments were made, nor to the returns which the firms would have required to induce them to invest. The public corporations were thus in some respects set a stiffer management task than the private sector, since the target was more precise than most firms would care to set themselves, and each year the public corporations were faced with rigid capital servicing charges without the flexibility which variable equity dividends can give.

After the 1961 White Paper, further important changes came in quick succession. In 1965, the principle of equity capital was introduced in BOAC. BOAC had become highly profitable, but it is engaged in international competition in an industry with high capital costs, while a fairly small decline in the rate of growth of international air travel could leave its high fixed costs uncovered. BOAC, therefore, pays the equivalent of a dividend to the Treasury, although it is not the final arbiter on the size of this dividend—the Treasury has the last word on this. The steel industry is seen to be in a similar, if not so extreme, commercial risk situation, and the capital structure of the new BSC contains a majority of public dividend capital. This principle is obviously capable of further extension.

The 1968 Transport Act distinguished between economic and social railway services, i.e. between those that might be expected to pay their way and those which almost certainly never would, but which would be retained for the sake of isolated communities, regional development plans, urban planning or other causes where the benefits would accrue outside the railways themselves. The Railways Board would be fully responsible for the first, whereas specific subsidies would be paid to support the second. Again, the principle introduced here is likely to be further extended in future, although further clarification is needed on where the initiative in providing and financing social services will lie.

However, the most comprehensive set of further changes were introduced by the 1967 White Paper. The sheer volume of public corporation investment had continued to grow (from £905m in 1961 to £1,447m in 1966) but the saving (surplus, depreciation and other reserves) was also showing a marked increase as well (from £364m in 1961 to £630m in 1966) so that the gap in average saving/investment rates between the public and private sector had closed somewhat. It was now decided that in assessing

212

the desirability of any new investment, each corporation was to measure its return against the cost of capital, by the process of discounting future net revenues to a net present value. (If this present value is equal to or exceeds the amount of the new investment the project should be proceeded with. The rate of discount used represents the estimated cost of the capital as measured by its yield in the best alternative use.)[12]

The sponsoring Ministry and the Treasury would judge the investment programme of each industry primarily in these terms. Government departments would then specifically avoid becoming involved in the technical details of each industry's programme, but instead employ a simple economic criterion. In theory, it is not necessary for the Treasury to understand much more of the technology of the nationalized industries than investors in private capital markets know of the technology of the vast range of industries in which they invest. By adopting a uniform discount rate for all industries, the collection of government departments involved may be said to be imitating the function of the capital market. The 1961 White Paper had standardized the procedure whereby the corporations would submit five-year investment proposals for approval every year, with the government making a firm commitment for the two years immediately ahead, but there was considerable doubt about what form the Treasury examinations of these proposals should take, apart from the obvious assessment of the implications of the total programme for the national economy. The Treasury does not employ a large team of engineers or marketing experts to advise on particular schemes, and indeed it would be obviously wasteful of scarce talent to attempt to duplicate the expertise of the corporations themselves.

The cost of capital, to be used as a test discount rate, was set at eight per cent, this being judged as 'broadly consistent, having regard to differing circumstances in relation to tax, investment grants, etc., with the average rate of return in real terms looked for on low risk projects in the private sector in recent years'. It was also a rate slightly higher than the current market long-term rate of interest. It was not intended that the test discount rate should alter frequently in line with market rates, but during 1968 and 1969 interest rates rose strongly all over the world, and by the middle of 1969, the yield on gilt edged stock had risen to over nine per cent. The 1967 definition of the cost of capital had now been overtaken by events, and in August 1969, the test discount

H

213

rate was raised to ten per cent. It will remain at that level until there is a further substantial change in market rates of interest.

The test discount rate is not to be applied rigidly. Some projects with a satisfactory yield may be deferred for macro-economic reasons, while certain projects with a low financial yield but a high net social benefit may be accepted. The latter point still leaves the social obligations of the industries obscure. It seems to imply that the public corporations must submit their unremunerative projects and the Treasury may approve them, but there is no specific commitment in this document to relieve the corporations of the financial consequences of such social obligations. However, it has already been suggested that this change may be coming about in a piecemeal fashion, for example in the 1968 Transport Act.

7.6 Pricing

It has already been shown that the method of pricing is inseparable from the investment and general economic policies of the public corporations. The 1967 White Paper[13] recognizes this in the statement, 'The use of correct methods of investment appraisal will only be effective if the nationalized industries also adopt, within the context of national prices and incomes policy, pricing policies relevant to their economic circumstances.'

The original statutes had laid down that prices were to be related to costs, without being specific about the nature of this relationship, and the public corporations subsequently employed a great variety of pricing methods, not all of which were cost related. These have been individually and collectively criticized as damaging and misleading and a large and complex literature has grown up on the subject, mostly concerned with applying the principles of Welfare Economics to the pricing policies of public enterprise in general, or to particular industries.[14] This concerted attack did not produce the impact which it might have done because many of the authors tended to oversimplify the assumptions they made about costs in these industries, leaving a very large gap between theoretical principles and practical applications which has only begun to be bridged by the application of sophisticated operational research techniques on both sides of it. However, the 1967 White Paper was an important landmark in that it selected one of the theoretical options available, and declared this to be the principle which should be applied thereafter.

214

Prices may be related to average costs or marginal costs, and there are a number of alternative ways of measuring either. Average cost pricing is the simplest way of ensuring that total costs equal total revenue, and, moreover, ordinary accounting data can be used to determine the prices provided that the fixed costs of the enterprise can be divided among the different services it offers. If the fixed costs cannot be allocated accurately, then one service may be required to recover more than its share and in effect subsidize the other services sharing the same overheads.

Marginal costs are more difficult to identify and will usually require special accounting studies. We cannot go fully into the theoretical justification for, and the practical difficulties of, equating price with marginal cost. Very briefly it is argued that productive resources will be most efficiently allocated when the outputs of all commodities are such that their prices are equal to their respective marginal costs. If the price of a commodity, X, is above its marginal cost (and the prices of all other commodities are equated to their respective marginal costs) a shift of resources into the production of X will produce output of a higher value to consumers than is lost by the withdrawal of resources from the production of other commodities. If the price of X is below its marginal cost there will be net advantage in shifting resources out of the production of X. Only when all prices are equated to marginal cost will resources be ideally allocated in the sense that no further shifts will produce any advantage. Such equalization of marginal cost and price is a feature of perfect competition and this is the basis of much criticism of monopoly as we noted in the previous chapter.[15]

The biggest problem in marginal cost pricing is to define what is meant by 'marginal cost'. In Professor Lewis's terms marginal cost is the 'escapable cost', i.e. the cost which could be avoided by not supplying one additional unit of output. In the short run, escapable costs would be entirely variable costs—fuel, raw materials and some labour, but over a longer period of time, more and more costs become variable, and hence escapable, so that the definition of marginal cost depends on the period of time which is chosen for the exercise. At the extreme, over a very long period, *all* costs are variable—it is possible to avoid replacing a power station or a railway bridge when they eventually become due for renewal, but at any time before then, maintenance and depreciation will undoubtedly be fixed costs. There can thus be short-run marginal costs (immediately variable costs), long-run marginal costs (the cost of adding and operating an additional unit of productive capacity including both fixed and variable costs), or any number of hybrids in between. There is a case in the short run for ignoring fixed overheads on the principle that bygones are bygones and once the fixed asset is installed the only rational thing to do is to get as much use out of it as possible—it costs the community nothing to allow one extra person to cross a bridge, so why charge him for it and possibly deter him from using capacity which could otherwise lie idle? However, if the price is thus set very low, the consumer may then be led to increase his demands to an extent where additional capacity is required, and this will be a major cost to the community in real terms. This dilemma has been elegantly resolved by the economists of *Electricité de France*, who have demonstrated in a number of papers[16] the fact that long- and short-run marginal cost will be the same as long as the industry is in equilibrium. If the SRMC exceeds LRMC it is a sign that the industry is short of capacity, and if LRMC exceeds SRMC, then the industry has over-invested and needs time to mark time on further expansion.

This is theoretically tidy, but in practice it is most unlikely that any industry will be in long-run equilibrium except by accident, so there is still a choice to be made between a long- and short-run basis for pricing. The 1967 White Paper opts firmly for long-run marginal cost pricing, on the grounds that this will indicate the future direction of relative costs and therefore offer the consumer better guidance so that he in turn, by the demands he makes at these prices, will offer the industries better guidance on the commitment of long-term resources. As a concrete example, natural gas costs are falling as exploitation develops on a larger scale, so the consumer should be encouraged to consume more gas so that the economies of scale can be reaped and costs will actually fall. If the first consumers of natural gas are faced with prices which would recover all of the overheads of exploration and initial development, very few of them would buy any and the industry would remain small scale and high cost.

This leads to another dilemma which the White Paper does not resolve. If long-run marginal costs are falling (owing to increasing returns to scale, or technical progress over time) then LRMC pricing will mean that prices are below long-run average costs, and therefore the corporation must deliberately operate at a loss.

It can readily be demonstrated that such an accounting loss would be in the public interest, but it is a policy which could not be pursued by private enterprise, unless it were subsidized (see Section 7.2, pp. 191–2). The 1961 and 1967 White Papers, which laid such emphasis on the overall financial target, both took successful private enterprise as the model for nationalized industry policy but there is no equivalent private-sector policy to be imitated in these circumstances. Private firms will be prepared to face initial losses on major projects, but not losses lasting indefinitely as long as costs are falling. It would be feasible to set a *negative* target but it is doubtful whether the target would have much value or meaning in this case.

The Select Committee on the Nationalized Industries examined at great length[17] the problem of how the three criteria of the financial target, the test discount rate and long-run marginal cost pricing could be reconciled. If the prices and the discount rate are taken as given, then the surplus (or deficit) would tend to follow, similarly if the surplus and discount rate are pre-determined, then prices may have to depart from long-run marginal costs. If the three criteria are set independently of each other, it would be coincidence if they should happen to prove mutually consistent.

This problem must be solved eventually, but meanwhile a good deal of 'slack' is built into the system by business uncertainty, so that exact guidelines become rules of thumb in practice. In particular, the measurement of long-run marginal cost offers many unsolved problems, and it will clearly be some considerable time before this principle is applied comprehensively.

7.7 Efficiency

There is no universal measure of efficiency in public enterprise. Efficiency is a measure of success in achieving an objective, so that only where there is a clearly defined objective can efficiency in its broadest sense be discussed. Only if the objective is to maximize profit is profitability a measure of efficiency, and only then if the market is competitive. If the objective is not clear, or if it includes non-measurable 'social' elements, then any single measure of efficiency will be misleading.

However, in its everyday sense, efficiency usually refers to the minimizing of costs of production and distribution. This is best defined as technical, as opposed to economic, efficiency. The

217

public corporations, relieved of the need to minimize production costs in order to survive the effects of competition obviously face particular problems here, both in devising appropriate measures of technical efficiency, and then in setting incentives to the managers. The nature of their problem is such that a completely satisfactory answer is unlikely to be achieved. It is difficult to devise a means of making the industry generate its own technical efficiency standards although decentralization has often been proposed as a way of breaking up an industry into smaller units which may be compared with each other. Decentralization is unfortunately *not* synonymous with competition. Other industries are unlikely to offer any true basis of comparison, and while comparisons with the same industry in other countries may be more relevant there are serious problems in making due allowance for the special factors affecting different countries.

The closest approach to an objective standard of technical efficiency in present circumstances must be a professional one. Firms of business consultants with international experience in large organizations should be able to specify what can and should be achieved with the available resources in the given circumstances, although there may be difficulties in involving such firms in 'political' situations. The National Board for Prices and Incomes seems to be expected to perform most, if not all, of the functions of business consultants in addition to applying the criteria of the Incomes Policy in their dealings with the nationalized industries. They have the advantage of being part of the political machinery and this makes intervention on sensitive issues easier than it would be for private consultants. On the other hand it is unlikely that they will normally have the time or the full range of management experts to study the problem in the necessary detail to be able to set definitive standards.

The early proponents of nationalization tended to rely on the sense of communal and community service which public ownership was expected to evolve to provide continuous incentives to both management and labour in these industries. This should not be discounted entirely, but stresses created by commercial and inflationary pressures on the industries quickly undermined the idealism with which some of the nationalized industries (particularly the National Coal Board) began their existence. However, the management may be expected to respond to

218

another set of incentives which apply to the public corporations as they apply to large private companies. These are personal rewards to managers (e.g. promoters) in return for efficient performance. They can generate competition *within* a monopolistic body, provided that it is organized in such a way as to be able to control and direct the energies created by the managers' personal ambitions.

It is also easy to underestimate the extent of external competition facing most public enterprise. Some corporations are engaged in international competition (the airways), some are involved in competition with the private sector (road haulage, and coal versus oil) while there is an element of competition between many of the corporations (gas and electricity, or road and rail transport). This effective competition is not perfect competition which is ruled out by the scale of each business in relation to the market. In some instances, competition develops some of the features of oligopoly and duopoly (e.g. competitive advertising of gas and electricity, 'tying clauses' in connection charges and so on), but experience in the private sector has shown that it is extremely difficult to legislate for a particular kind of competition. None of the industries is in a position to feel complacently secure however.

The financial target has its principal rationale in this area. If the target is set fairly high in relation to the general level of prices which a corporation is permitted to charge (or can charge without a sharp fall in demand), then the management will be put under severe pressure to reduce costs. However, cost reductions are also known to take the form of abolishing unremunerative services, and the logic of the situation demands that the management should be limited in their freedom to adopt this line by a clear directive as to which social services they should carry and proper payments made from public funds for this purpose.

The cost item which has attracted most political attention in the nationalized industries has been wages and salaries. A public corporation might be expected to have a special relationship with its employees, especially when the men have been largely instrumental in getting the industry into the public sector. Nevertheless, they have not, in general, paid the highest absolute levels of wages in the economy. The difficulty has been that these industries are so large and important, and attract so much political attention, that each new wage negotiation could become a political crisis. It was suggested in the 1950s that the railway unions were used by the rest of the Trade Union Movement to lead the annual inflating wage round. However, they were dealing with a management which did not have the funds to award higher wages without adding to the railway's deficit. The result was a regular process of a threatened national railway strike which would be settled at the eleventh hour by a compromise settlement. This cumbersome procedure left railwaymen's wages trailing behind other more prosperous industries where more effective and less conspicuous pressure could be employed. This did not improve the atmosphere for negotiating new working methods and quickly eroded the initial goodwill of the Trades Unions in these industries, and relatively low wages made recruitment of able staff much more difficult. Both the management and the men might have found their position improved if the industry had been smaller and less strategic. The prices and incomes policy has also probably had a greater impact on the employees of the nationalized industries than the rest in that large-scale formal negotiations are easier to control than a multitude of separate agreements with individual small employers. If the consequence of achieving a small immediate reduction in the possible wage bill is to lower the average quality of the labour force and retard the process of modernization, this cannot be in the interests of efficiency. If possible, some way must be found of taking the nationalized industries out of the front line of the fight against wage inflation.

The need for high quality labour is most acute in the top levels of any organization, among Board members, and senior management. The public corporation, being the largest and the most vital of all business enterprises might thus be expected to take extraordinary measures to attract the very best managerial talent. However, top managers are likely to go to the position offering the best salaries and conditions. The conditions for senior men in the nationalized industries have not been as good as for their counterparts in private industry. Their job has been fundamentally more difficult, involving a wider range of consideration in every judgment, and they operate under close and sometimes hostile public and political scrutiny. Salaries have been restricted by the British tradition that public service offers non-pecuniary rewards, and the difficulty of paying senior management in socialist-inspired enterprises salaries comparable to those in large-scale private enterprise. An investigation by the Prices and Incomes Board into top salaries in the public and private sectors of industry showed that 'whereas the average pay of the highest paid executive in the six (sample) companies in the private sector is over £34,000, the average pay of the six highest paid executives in nationalized concerns is below £15,000, even though the average turnover of these national industries is above that of the private concerns.'[18] This restricts the supply of top management talent to the corporations. In some cases, special salaries have been negotiated in order to attract the particular individual wanted for a particular job. Lord Beeching's salary of £24,000 as Chairman of the British Railways Board more than doubled the current rate for the job at the time and became a long-standing *cause célèbre*. Lord Melchett, in the position of Chairman of the BSC was prepared to accept a salary of £16,000 (above the rate in other public corporations, but less than his earnings as a merchant banker) but the salary for the Deputy Chairman and full-time Board Members were fixed higher than this. It may still be feasible to pay less than the private sector at the very highest levels, especially since surtax will reduce very large differences in gross salaries to relatively trivial difference in 'take-home' pay. However, middle management is trapped in a narrow band between low top salaries and increasing wages, and the public corporation thus becomes uncompetitive in this vital area. Cost minimization rests essentially in the hands of middle management, and any circumstance which dilutes the quality of middle management in the corporations must adversely affect their efficiency. This was the main reason for the PIB's recommendation of large increases in top salaries.

The Nationalized Industries have been in a constant state of evolution since their inception. Present policy is that the public corporations should be judged principally according to their efficiency in allocating resources according to commercial criteria, but experience suggests that all policies are subject to change. As the political climate and economic problems change, the nationalized industries could well find themselves being pointed in new directions in the future.

1 *The Select Committee on Nationalized Industries*, 'Sub Committee A' (London, HMSO, 1968).

2 *Report of the Technical Advisory Committee on Coal Mining*, Cmnd. 6610 (London, HMSO, 1945).

3 *Report of the Committee of Enquiry into the Gas Industry* (Heyworth Committee), Cmnd. 6699 (London, HMSO, 1945).

4 Keynes, J. M., *General Theory of Employment, Interest and Money* (London, Macmillan, 1936).

5 Robson, W. A. (ed.), *Problems of Nationalized Industries* (London, Allen & Unwin, 1951).

6 Robson, W. A., *Nationalized Industry and Public Ownership*, Chapter 4 (London, Allen & Unwin, 1960).

7 *The Report of the Committee of Inquiry into the Electricity Supply Industry*, Cmnd. 9672 (London, HMSO, 1956).

8 *Committee on the Working of the Monetary System*, Cmnd. 827 (London, HMSO, 1959).

9 *Treasury Memorandum to Select Committee* 'Sub Committee A', pp. 291–8 (1966/7).

10 Peters, G. H., *Cost Benefit Analysis and Public Expenditure*, 2nd edn. (London, Institute of Economic Affairs, 1968).

11 Beesley, M. and Foster, C. D., 'The Victoria Line,' *Journal of the Royal Statistical Society*, Series A (1965).

12 *Investment Appraisal* (London, HMSO, 1965), contains a simple account of discounting techniques. See also Chapter 3.

13 *Nationalized Industries. A Review of Economic and Financial Objectives*. Cmnd. 3437, para. 17 (London, HMSO, 1967).

14 Turvey, R. (ed.), *Public Enterprise (Penguin Modern Economics Readings)* (Harmondsworth, Penguins, 1968).

15 For further explanation see, Lewis, W. A., *Overhead Costs*, Chapter 1 (London, Allen & Unwin, 1949); and Brown, E. H. Phelps, *A Course in Applied Economics*, 1st edn., Chapter 8 (London, Pitman, 1951).

16 Nelson, J. R. (ed.), *Marginal Cost Pricing in Practice* (Englewood Cliffs, N.J., Prentice-Hall, 1964).

17 *The Select Committee on the Nationalized Industries* 'Sub Committee A' (1967/68).

18 *N.B.P.I. Report*, p. 43, para. 14 (London, HMSO, March 1969).

CHAPTER 8

Industry and Government

8.1 Introduction

Most countries in the world have an economic system which is neither completely private enterprise nor state controlled, but operating at some point in between. This is now generally known as the 'mixed economy', with the exact mixture depending on the political system, the stage of economic development and many other influences. The archetype of the mixed economy is the Western European industrial nation, with its mixture of private businesses, central and local government services and public enterprise, and governments which span a fairly narrow range between left-wing conservatism and right-wing socialism. Great Britain fits this pattern exactly, although it has its own unique mixture of public and private enterprise and its own style in economic management. The central feature of the mixed economy is that the government takes the responsibility for the country's total economic performance, but generally attempts to carry out this responsibility without intervening more than it thinks necessary in the business affairs of its citizens. This clearly begs a lot of questions (especially about what is thought necessary), but it is important to recognize that there are very few hard and fast lines in government-industry relations and the system evolves rapidly with new political ideas, changing industrial problems and new lobbying factions.

The relationships between government and industry are not all in one direction, with the government forcing industry to follow unwanted policies. Industrial interests (including the workers representatives) have their own means of exerting influence on governments; and the largest representing bodies, such as the Confederation of British Industry and the Trades Union Congress, have their main raison d'être in the collective pressure which they can exert on the government. Thus, although in this chapter we will be concerned mostly with specific laws and policies, it would be misleading if this gave the impression that relations were strictly formal. The great majority of the contacts between government and industry are informal, consisting of a 'sounding out' of views, appeals for and promises of cooperation and so on. It could almost be said that when a new law is passed in this area, it represents a breakdown of the normal processes. Having made this reservation, however, the main purpose of this chapter is to analyse the more formal relationships expressed in laws, regulations and institutions. There are so many of them, in such a variety of forms, that there are many possible classification systems which could be applied. The approach which is most consistent with modern developments in industrial economics[1] is to separate them according to whether they are aimed at affecting the structure, the conduct or the performance (labour productivity, rate of growth, exports, price levels etc.) of industry. This classification is somewhat arbitrary, since a change in an industry's structure (e.g. the size distribution of firms or establishments) will probably affect its conduct (i.e. the relationships between firms, or with suppliers and customers) and eventually its performance, since economic theory and practice specify certain casual relationships between structure, conduct and performance. However, the classification used here will rest on the point at which the government approaches the industry, although there will inevitably be particular cases (such as regional policy) which defy simple classification.

8.2 Government and the conduct of industry

Industry exists in order to produce, and production means the conversion of a miscellany of basic resources into an infinite variety of forms in which they will be more useful, or valuable or generally desirable. In any rational society, the total economic objective is to use the available resources to produce the maximum benefit to its members: but there is no general agreement on what is meant by maximum benefit and still less on how to achieve it. These issues form the great dividing lines in politics, within countries where different political parties offer their own definitions, and between countries espousing different economic systems. Industry is therefore inescapably part of political life since it produces and distributes the goods and services and generates the incomes that account for the majority of political differences.

The definition of maximum benefit can never be unique and 'scientific', since it must depend on the values of each society, and these values will be the result of history, tradition and ideas as much as physiological needs. It is probably true that at low levels of real income, the physiological needs for food, warmth and shelter are most pressing and real output is the dominant aim, but as bare subsistence levels are left behind, more subjective and essentially unmeasurable objectives will come to the fore. An influential critic of American society[2] has argued at length that qualitative objectives may be thwarted in advanced industrial societies, since the apparatus of production and distribution which made them affluent generates a momentum and values of its own, and controls the means of propagating these values through advertising. Against these the unorganized supporters of a rather vaguely conceived 'better way of life' find difficulty in gaining much support. Advanced countries therefore continue to measure their success in terms of the size of their Gross National Product, which takes no account of additional leisure through shorter working hours, or the contribution of education to a greater enjoyment of leisure (rather than its contribution to higher productivity), and industrial efficiency becomes an increasingly important political objective.[3]

Society's material aims consist mostly of the aggregated wants of individual consumers, and the price mechanism has evolved as the principle means by which individuals can make their wants known, and by which industry is able to draw together the factors of production to satisfy them. There are also certain needs which most people experience which are difficult or impossible to supply on an individual basis, and probably security is the most important of these. A simple approach to the organization of society is therefore to leave the market mechanism to cope with individual wants and to have some collective agency (i.e. a government) to identify and satisfy the collective wants, while interfering as little as possible with the market system. It is impossible to seal off the two sectors from each other completely since the government has to compete for its share of resources, and in order to pay for them it taxes people and thus interferes with the distribution of incomes which the market creates. The principal of *laissez-faire* would imply, however, that the government should make a positive effort to interfere as little as possible with the rest of the system in carrying out its basic functions. (The most comprehensive and competent attempt to relate this objective to modern conditions is to be found in the series of publications of the Institute of Economic Affairs.)

However, industry is much more than a collection of scientific and engineering processes; it is also the focus of a vast complex of human affairs. For most people, their lives are shaped by the work they do and most of the property in an advanced society exists because of industry. Any attempt to tuck industry away into a separate compartment, where the sole purpose is to produce and the only criterion is consumer demand is therefore unrealistic.

The need to regulate industry in its social, as opposed to its productive role has always been accepted, even at the height of nineteenth-century *laissez-faire*. Laws were established and progressively elaborated, governing the conduct of business affairs, between one business and another, between one property owner and another, and between the business and its owners. These naturally extended to the relationships between an industry and its suppliers and its consumers. This growing body of law could be held consistent with the principles of *laissez-faire* provided that the law is simply creating a set of general rules within which market relationships can function and these laws are intended to facilitate (rather than interfere with) the working of the market, e.g. the succession of Company Acts (see Chapter 1) were designed to make successful dishonesty more difficult and thus to generate greater confidence in business contracts. The government is thus seen as 'holding the ring' within which the economic battle is fought, but within the ring, the combatants are expected to be able to look after themselves. Much of the law concerning monopoly and restrictive practices (see Chapter 6) is of this nature, since here the government is attempting to create conditions in which firms will act competitively, competition being seen as a condition where the various parties—factors of production, firms and consumers—are fairly matched and market forces can be allowed to work themselves out freely.

However, it is clear that competition between producers will not always guarantee that *all* interests will be equally strongly represented. Governments have thus been prepared to depart from the principle of impartiality in order to correct an obvious imbalance of economic strength. The early Factory Acts granted special protection to women and children, since it was apparent that their economic bargaining strength was negligible compared with that of their employers. Trades Unions were gradually given greater legal freedom than corresponding institutions in recognition of the fundamental imbalance in bargaining strength between an individual employee and a large employer. (The existence of such an imbalance is debatable in the case of skilled labour in full employment, but it is true of any situation where labour is not in short supply.) By means of Wages Councils the government intervenes in industries where Trade Unions are weak or non-existent, for example where the industry consists of a very large number of small firms. One vital element of employer-employee relations—health and safety—is not normally left to be determined by market forces at all. Trades Unions will concern themselves with these matters, but ultimately if there is a serious hazard involved, as in the handling of certain materials such as lead or asbestos or in a great variety of mechanical processes, regulations will be drawn up to specify minimum safety conditions. It would be feasible to leave these to be negotiated between employers and trade unions along with wages, hours of work, canteen arrangements and the rest but by now there is a well established tradition that these are subject to different considerations, and a vast set of special regulations for particular industries has grown up, and is added to almost monthly as new products and processes appear.

The laws and regulations we have mentioned so far probably provide the greatest volume of formal contact between private industry and government departments. They are in a way the 'small change' of industry-government relations. They do not attract a great deal of attention and they do not change a great deal with changes in government. From the analytical point of view, they are interesting because they nearly all fall into a single category—they are policies designed to influence the conduct of industry. Industry is seen as a social or legal entity whose conduct in relation to other such entities must be regularized and placed on a 'fair' legal footing. They have economic consequences, but these tend to be secondary or accidental.

227

There are other detailed laws and regulations aimed at affecting conduct which are more directly related to the economic performance of the industries concerned. The consumer has always been protected by civil law, in that he has the right to expect the goods he purchases to meet the stated or normal specifications for such goods, and he can seek redress if they do not, but the average citizen is chary of going to law and this right often goes by default. As in employer-employee relationships a special case has been held to exist where there may be physical dangers or health hazards. Some goods are prohibited entirely on this account (e.g. narcotic drugs) and some are subject to restrictions on their distribution (alcholic drinks) and certain ingredients in foods and drinks are banned. The public are not judged to be wholly competent to look after their own interests in these matters, and the intention of such regulations is to prevent firms from exploiting ignorance and gullibility, where these may have obviously damaging results on the consumer.

The industry most obviously at risk in any further extension of such specific regulations is the tobacco industry. Some may argue that the government has done all that is required of it in giving the maximum publicity to the dangers of cigarette smoking, although they may concede that the government is also entitled to prevent the industry from trying to persuade the public to buy more cigarettes and thus ignore the medical advice. However, direct restrictions on cigarette sales could meet stronger objections, particularly since a very large established industry, employing large amounts of capital and thousands of people in production and distribution, would be affected adversely. Moreover, the public are unlikely to co-operate in making direct restrictions on such a long established good effective. The American experience of 'prohibition' (of alcohol) suggests that there are strict limits to a government's powers to control the public's pattern of consumption.

However, the principle of protecting the consumer has also been extended in a number of significant respects. Economic development has brought in more complicated goods and marketing arrangements and considerable developments in marketing techniques, especially in advertising. It is possible to argue that while the average consumer may be able to exercise his discretion quite adequately in simple purchases of basic goods, he is badly matched against a large firm producing sophisticated products and employing many specialist advisers in the arts of persuasion. The average consumer is assumed to be dangerously naïve in financial affairs. A purchaser is now given three days in which to have second thoughts on a hire-purchase contract, and the owner of the property cannot automatically enforce the full conditions of the contract.[4] Of possibly even wider significance, the Trade Descriptions Act 1968 has lifted from the buyer the obligation of treating all sellers with suspicion (the *caveat emptor* principle), since the vendor must be able to substantiate every claim, or vague assertion, that he makes. It does not prevent him from trying to persuade, but it restricts the firm's freedom to use a practice which previously had long been accepted as normal behaviour of the man in the market place—that of making loud but unspecific claims for his wares.

Industries may be obliged to take account of external costs by regulations governing pollution (e.g. smoke control and the disposal of effluent) and siting. Such measures as these introduce a new principle, in that they extend beyond the direct relationships of two interested parties, e.g. employer-employee, seller-buyer, to bring in the interests of third parties. In principle, it has always been possible for those adversely affected by an industrial process to take proceedings under civil law, but the burden of proof and the cost of litigation were powerful deterrents. Local Medical Officers have had great powers where a clear hazard could be shown, but they were frequently in a weak position where local employment might be threatened. In spite of the increased powers of the Central and Local governments in local and regional planning, few could claim that the law yet provides fully for the 'third party' relationships embodied in the economists's 'externalities'.

The most comprehensive attempt to control the pattern of producer-consumer relations was during war-time and post-war rationing. Rationing was introduced as a substitute for the price mechanism in conditions where it was assumed that the price mechanism would not work without severe inflation and intolerable inequality in the distribution of basic necessities. Rationing was accepted as reasonable during a national emergency, when collective interests may over-ride individual wants, but with the passing of the war-time emergency, it caused increasing dissatisfaction and was clearly politically unacceptable. It was difficult to operate a rationing system, which allocated equal quotas of food, clothing, fuel, etc. to each member of the population (subject to special cases, such as nursing mothers, workers in heavy industry etc.) alongside a price mechanism governing the allocation of all other goods, and an unequal distribution of incomes. The price mechanism encroached on the rationing system in the form of the 'Black Market', in which rationed goods could be traded at scarcity prices, and this helped to undermine the public's acceptance of it. The rationing system gave the government an overwhelming degree of control of the distribution of resources, and in particular it helped in channelling resources into war production. This was also backed by direct control of the factors of production, through conscription and the direction of labour, and very tight control over the raising of money capital, through the Capital Issues Committee, and the purchase of physical capital assets (such as factory building and machine tools) through a system of permits. The gradual recovery from a war-time to a peace-time industrial footing permitted the gradual dismantling of this apparatus, but the pace was set by the public's growing dissatisfaction with such detailed controls during peace-time. It provided the strongest possible evidence that a government must have the support of 'public opinion' if the steps it takes in intervening in the market are to be effective.

8.3 Government and industrial performance

One of the outstanding features of the post 1945 period has been an increasing government responsibility for the performance of the economy. It is ironic that the great increase in 'intervention' aimed at performance should occur in the 1960s after a long period of industrial expansion and rising living standards which represented a sustained level of economic performance unequalled in Britain's previous history, and bore little resemblance to the acute problems of the inter-war years. But the period was not free from problems. Inflation had become endemic and economic growth in Britain was slower than in most comparable industrial nations. Successive attempts to accelerate the growth rate by increasing effective demand generated further inflation and Balance of Payments deficits. Above all, these problems had not proved amenable to purely macro-economic policies, aimed at manipulating the level of aggregate demand, although there had been a long series of experiments with various combinations of macro-economic weapons. It is arguable that difficulties associated with slow economic growth may be more properly attributed to faulty industrial performance than could the pre-war problems. Prior to 1939 there were acute structural faults and genuinely macro-economic problems in the contraction of world trade and the over-valuation of sterling. An improvement in industrial performance would have been some help (particularly in offsetting the over-valuation) but would not have cured the crises. After 1945 greater international competitiveness would have made a major contribution towards overcoming the post-war difficulties.

The traditional view of economic performance was that it could be left to the market—the economy would produce a growth rate consistent with its resources, the level of saving and investment and the state of technical knowledge, provided that normal economic incentives are allowed to work. The government's responsibility for macro-economic performance thus lay principally in setting the proper conditions for competitive conduct, including in this a specific duty to control the money supply to avoid inflation, which will inevitably tend to upset the balance of market forces. The balance between imports and exports was also seen as essentially a function of the price mechanism, through either the internal monetary consequences of the Gold Standard, or through variable exchange rates. Particular industries might run into trouble, and particular measures be invoked to assist them, but these would usually be aimed at their structure (e.g. the railways, coal mines and ship-building) or their conduct. It is arguable that tariff protection was aimed directly at the industry's performance, but by relieving it of the pressure of foreign competition it inevitably affected its conduct. In iron and steel for example, it was used to give the industry an opportunity to reconstruct itself.

An attempt to summarize in a few paragraphs a historical process involving a succession of economic crises, rapid political evolution and several wars must inevitably blur most of the finer points and special cases, but the main point is that direct and detailed government involvement in economic performance is of recent origin, at least in the context of an industrial society. It has therefore tended to attract more attention than the other forms of intervention, which affect most firms far more closely, and in which the government usually acts in a far more authoritarian manner.

231

The problem facing any democratic government is that measures aimed at performance seek a positive result, whereas those aimed at conduct are generally negative, and it is easier to use laws and regulations to stop a firm from doing something than to force it to do something else. If a firm does not wish to expand, or reduce its costs, or export, and market forces are not sufficient to make it do so, can a government in a democratic society, most of whose laws are concerned with the rights of property, *force* it to do any of these things? The short answer is 'no'. There may be some aspects of performance where the government wishes to be restrictive rather than creative, for example in a cost inflationary process where prices are seen as a macro-economic phenomenon, contributing to the general price level, rather than as micro-economic and helping to allocate resources. Here the government uses legal powers to intervene and prevent firms from passing on its cost increases in higher prices, or from incurring higher costs in higher wages, or from distributing increased purchasing power in higher dividends. However, to say that this is easy in principle is a far cry from saying that it is highly effective in practice. In special cases, like public utilities the government may so limit the industry's conduct that it effectively controls its performance, and from this it is a relatively short step to actually taking over the ownership of the industry (see Chapter 6). However, there are clearly limits to how far a government may go in imposing special public-utility regulations on private industry or in nationalizing it, without altering the whole political balance of the country. Ultimately, then, the direct approach to performance reduces to exhortation and assistance, and much of what is termed national planning in industrial countries consists of these.

A more limited application of the same kind of approach is to impose selective restrictions on industries or firms where performance is in some sense unsatisfactory or undesirable, and to relieve the others of such restrictions, or actually help them. For example, in periods of financial stringency, banks may be directed to make credit readily available to industries with large exports and this is basically similar to the method of influencing the geographical structure of industry by severe restrictions on the granting of industrial development certificates (IDC) in prosperous areas. However, such methods are fundamentally lopsided—you cannot make the exporting industries borrow and expand, and you cannot force a firm to build in a Development Area if it has decided that it will expand its operations in the Home Counties or not at all.

If the government wishes to improve the performance of industry generally, it must be in a position to decide what kind of improvements are wanted and what are feasible. Significant changes take time to achieve, and they can rarely be confined to a single industry. An increase in output of, say, steel will presuppose greater purchases by steel using industries and increased supplies of ore and scrap as well as processing plant and possibly skilled labour. The internal changes in the steel industry necessary to produce this result may thus be, in economic terms, a relatively minor part of the whole problem. A serious involvement in industrial performance therefore commits a government to detailed economic planning, requiring a vast amount of information about inter-industry relations, the development of techniques for handling this data (e.g. input-output analysis for a group of industries, and mathematical programming for individual industries), many detailed decisions and a great deal of informed judgment.

The idea of economic planning has been subject to notable swings of political fashion. It was a popular idea in the years immediately after the Second World War, but it was then a name which was attached to the collection of policies associated with the Labour Government of the time—nationalization, physical controls and above all rationing. The unpopularity of the last discredited the concept of planning, although comprehensive planning in the sense of integrating and co-ordinating the various items of policy was never really tried. There was neither adequate data, nor adequate theoretical technique nor specialist personnel for such an exercise. The Treasury produced an annual Economic Survey which, subject to these limitations, went as far as possible in drawing the threads together, but this was essentially short-term in its approach. Economic planning almost disappeared from the political vocabulary until the late-1950s when, as has already been suggested, there was growing disillusionment with a purely macro-economic approach to economic policy. The first moves were very tentative—for example the Council on Prices, Productivity and Incomes was asked to comment on the general direction in which they thought the economy might be moving[5]—but in 1961 the National Economic

Development Council was set up, and this marked an important turning point in the management of the economy.

The Council itself was entirely conventional in its form, consisting of representatives of employers, Trades Unions and government with a Civil Service staff attached. This is the standard formula for all official or semi-official bodies involved with industry, and is aimed at securing the co-operation of the interested parties. However, the central role given to NEDC gave it an unusual degree of importance, and it could be taken as indicative of a future concentration of policy on neither macro- nor micro-economics, but on the dividing line between them, i.e. the relationship between individual company or industry performances and the national performance. The Council recruited a staff of economists, econometricians and various industrial specialists to undertake basic research in this area, which had been rather neglected by academic economists, and in due course published its preliminary diagnosis of the problem and some suggestions for their treatment.[6] The Council was a strong supporter of the policy of trying to break out of the series of short cycles of expansion and deflation, which militated against long-term planning by companies, and was possibly influential in bringing into effect the 'Breakthrough' policy of sustained full capacity working, regardless of the short-term consequences, which began in late-1963 and was finally peremptorily halted in July 1966 after a series of severe currency crises.

One of the main ideas underlying the formation of NEDC was that British industry consistently took too short term a view, and that this was an important factor in keeping industry short of capacity and excessively labour-intensive, and with too little of its capacity devoted to new products. This in turn would help to explain slow growth and apparently diminishing international competitiveness. Industry's reply was invariably that continual short bursts of expansion and contraction made caution essential. However if this caution led to chronic capacity shortages and excessive imports, it was a major *cause* of the continual quick reversals of government policy. A logical solution to this dilemma would be to change the way in which the important decision-takers in industry actually think about and assess the future. Earlier performance suggested that on the whole, industry worked on a short time-horizon, so that a current or imminent deflation could lead to the postponement or abandonment of projects which might not start work for well over a year, and would then last for several decades. It was important therefore to persuade industrialists to think in terms of *a trend* rather than the current situation or a specific forecast one or two years ahead. Secondly, caution is more restrictive when it is combined with uncertainty. Therefore if firms could be given more information about the future, this should encourage more of them to start taking a longer view, and gradually this might encourage more of them to become more adventurous.

These ideas are now usually combined in the notion of 'indicative planning'. The name, as well as the ideas, were borrowed from France, where the marked improvement in industrial and economic performance coincided with the development of a system of industrial committees, which pooled their ideas of the future and developed a consensus view of the total industry outlook. Those committees could supply information to other industries which might supply or be supplied by them. Here we have the combination of the long view and better information. (The French system in fact had further elements, especially a strong but hidden element of government direction, which could have a bearing on its effectiveness, but which could not be copied readily in a different political context.)

In 1964, there was a further change in the political climate, with the return of the Labour Party to government. Of all the principal British political parties, the Labour Party is most ready to 'intervene' in the market place. Its basic philosophy is against the allocation of resources according to the pure market criteria of effective demand or purchasing power (although in practice the vast majority of transactions would remain on this basis even in a highly developed Socialist state) and partly as a result it is much readier to suspect that particular markets may be performing inefficiently and that these inefficiencies will not be self-correcting, at least within a short period. The party's desire to override the market system is most conspicuous in its welfare and taxation policies, affecting the distribution of income. In dealing with the creation of income through production, policies have more generally operated through the market, either by changing relative prices or in some cases by supplementing the existing market structure.

The concept of indicative planning embodied in NEDC, and above all the idea that it is possible to encourage more logical behaviour by providing better information was therefore embraced wholeheartedly by the new government. A new Ministry —the Department of Economic Affairs (DEA)—was set up to develop and extend the NEDC, and also gather together many of the interventionist functions scattered about other government departments. The DEA was disbanded at the end of 1969, but the principle of concentrating the interventionist activities of the government under one roof (metaphorically speaking) was extended, since the Ministry of Technology acquired a higher proportion of them than the DEA had operated. The principle that there will be one main Ministry to deal with the government's relations with industry now seems to be established, and this is of more than just administrative significance. It now seems to be recognized that there are important elements of industrial performance—investment, the rate of growth and labour productivity for example—which may change only over a considerable period of time, so that they cannot be switched up or down according to the country's short-term economic situation, and attempts to do so may be positively damaging.

DEA's efforts to switch the emphasis of economic policy from short-term control to long-term planning, particularly in relation to industry, failed because the attempt was made in a period of short-term economic crises, which had immediate priority. The National Plan,[7] produced in 1965, was an extension of NEDC's tentative efforts at econometric projection, and attempted to examine the detailed implications over five years, for particular sectors of the economy, including the principle industry groups, of an increase in the rate of growth of the Gross National Product by over half to 3·8 per cent per annum. It was not a Plan in the sense that it set a series of targets and specified the actions necessary to achieve them, but it simply attempted to use available data to determine the conditions required to achieve the specified growth rate, and predict some of the consequences. However, it was presented, and universally accepted, as a working blueprint and almost instantly discredited when short-term policies to deal with the Balance of Payments eliminated the assumptions on which the exercise had been based.[8] One of the few positive effects of NEDC's and DEA's 'planning' exercises was to persuade the Central Electricity Generating Board to gear its investment programmes to the assumed higher rate of growth. However, there is an exceptionally long time lag in electricity investment, and power is basic to industrial expansion, so that it is debatable whether this effect (which later resulted in surplus capacity in the industry when the higher national growth rate did not materialize), really resulted from the general planning exercise, or whether additional power was so obviously a condition for faster growth that a government interest in this objective would have resulted in higher electricity investment in any case.

Subsequent projections have been more clearly presented as tentative and probabilistic and aimed rather more at improving forecasting techniques than guiding policy. If the National Plan were overpublicized and misunderstood, it nevertheless pushed growth, rather than stability and possibly even equity, into the forefront of thinking and discussion, and may have helped to change the personal and political scales of values which ultimately determine all policies. To the extent that the main economic objective is now accepted as faster growth, mostly through private enterprise, the implication is that policies would become increasingly helpful, rather than restrictive, to ambitious companies.

After the creation of the DEA, the NEDC continued to function mostly through sixteen Industry Committees, consisting of the representatives of principal firms, associations and Trades Unions involved with the industries concerned. These Committees are intended to allow for an exchange of ideas, for the identification of problems and the making of suggestions aimed at improving the industry's growth potential. This arrangement recalls the industry Working Parties of the early post-war years. The latter tended to be concerned with the detailed working methods and processes of their industries, making much use of American comparisons, whereas the Industry EDCs are more interested in broader economic and business policy questions. An examination of business policies in an industry is bound to touch more sensitive spots than a detailed study of particular working practices but will often be more relevant to the real problems of the industry. Nevertheless, reports have to be worded tactfully if the industry's co-operation is not to be withheld, so that the Committees have to rely mostly on offering guidance rather than sharp public criticisms as a spur to action. Indicative planning appears ultimately to depend for its effectiveness on persuading firms to *want* to grow and become more profitable

237

particularly by changing their assessment of future risks. Economics offers little or no guidance on how effective a policy of exhortation might be, whereas more direct inducements and restrictions may be rather more predictable in their results. This is true in principle, although in practice the research necessary for such prediction is often lacking, or inconclusive. For example, there is no firm evidence on the fundamental question whether heavy marginal tax rates are an incentive or a disincentive to effort.

Subsidization of the use of business consultants is a minor example of the use of those financial inducements or deterrents which are much more fully developed in the tax system as a whole. In an economy fully committed to *laissez faire*, the tax system would be designed to be as far as possible neutral in its effects, not discriminating between one industry or forms of conduct and another. But such a neutral system is not feasible in practice. A choice has to be made of the kinds of distortion which are acceptable or desirable, and from there it is not a big step to imposing taxes specifically to affect a particular industry or activity. Purchase Tax and Excise Taxes discriminate against the commodities taxed, reducing demand and hence the size of the industry if the demand is not infinitely inelastic. The industry might respond to the tax as an incentive to reduce costs, although if the tax is extremely high (e.g. petrol and whisky) the difference which the industry can make to the retail price might be proportionately so small that there is very little incentive left. These indirect taxes discriminate deliberately against 'luxury' goods on grounds of equity, and as a result the luxury industries probably attract a smaller proportion of total resources than they otherwise would. The Selective Employment Tax levies a tax on all employees in service industries (although it is also used as a method of subsidizing manufacturing industry in Development Areas), and might thus be seen as a way of discriminating against service employment and making more labour available for manufacturing. It can be argued that it is simply a method of bringing service industries into line with manufacturing, and thus partially correcting a bias which existed previously. But the reason offered at the time it was introduced was that manufacturing industry accounts for most exports and import substitutes, and, whatever its effect on the total balance of taxation, the SET itself favoured manufacturing.

Given an emphasis on growth a government may be expected to take a particular interest in investment and research. These are strictly aspects of conduct rather than performance, but the government's interest in these derives from their assumed effect on performance and especially growth and exports. In a free market economy, the price mechanism would be left to determine levels of investment and research, with the rate of interest playing a principal role in representing the cost of capital. For the levels so determined to approach the optimum, firms have to be far-sighted profit maximizers highly sensitive to changes in market conditions, and there would have to be a minimum of other imperfections, including taxation, in the system. Governments have clearly believed for a long time that left to the market, and given all the circumstances, the free choice of firms would lead to inadequate investment and research, and they have therefore attempted to tilt relative prices further in favour of both.

Investment is favoured by investment grants which are a subsidy of twenty per cent of the cost of new industrial plant and machinery. These rates are higher in the Development Areas as a convenient means of paying an extra subsidy to firms in these areas. Prior to 1966, firms were given capital subsidies by means of allowances which they could set against their tax liability, and an important factor leading to a change in the system was a survey of investment appraisal techniques in use by British firms which showed that the great majority failed to take proper account of tax relief in deciding whether to invest in new capital equipment, whereas if the subsidy were actually paid over in cash, they could hardly fail to take account of it. The fact that firms cannot fail to be aware of investment grants does not guarantee that they will apply the correct principle in taking these into account. A firm which is convinced that its existing investment policies are correct in any circumstances may simply treat them as a welcome bonus for its profits. It is unlikely that there are many firms in a position where a major shift in relative factor costs can really be irrelevant, and the extent to which allowances and grants are ignored thus becomes partly a reflection of inadequate accounting procedures and financial expertise within the firm. If this is the case, it shifts the diagnosis of and prescription for low investment one stage further back—to improving the quality of the management and its systems.

An advantage of allowance over grants is that a firm had to be

239

sufficiently successful to earn enough profit to claim the allowance, whereas the grant system is quite undiscriminating in this respect. This could possibly lead to a waste of capital, but nobody has yet shown that the investment grants paid to firms which would have been too inefficient to be able to claim the equivalent allowance amounts to a large sum.

The complement of investment is saving, and even though the two activities are separately motivated, the availability of investible funds is a factor in investment decisions. Corporation Tax (see Chapter 3) has among its objectives the encouragement of corporate saving, since the shareholder pays Corporation Tax and Income Tax (and Surtax) on his dividends, whereas he does not pay Income Tax on profits retained by the Company. (He will eventually pay Capital Gains Tax on the appreciated value of his shares due to the ploughing back of profits, but this is at a lower rate than Income Tax and much lower than income tax plus surtax.) In theory, shareholders are being encouraged to accumulate wealth within the company, rather than draw it out, and possibly spend it, as dividends. It is still too early to judge how effective it has been in this respect (see Chapter 3). A potential weakness of this system is that by encouraging more profit retention, it reduces the total mobility of capital between industries through the capital market, and this may militate particularly against smaller growing businesses. This would be true if the capital market were the dominant factor in capital mobility, but in reality, the multi-product and multi-industry firms and mergers and takeovers are probably already the main means of switching resources from one product or industry to another, and nearly all new product and process development occurs inside existing firms, or will be acquired by them from their initiators for full exploitation. Nevertheless, the system does tip the scales in favour of the large established business, and seems to call for some counterweight for the energetic newcomers. This is an interesting example of how difficult it is for a government to intervene in industry in such a way that the effect is confined precisely to the one which was intended.

The factors which may be expected to deter investment could be expected to affect industrial research even more strongly, since it is more uncertain and risky than investment in fixed assets and may involve just as large an outlay of cash for the individual firm. Aircraft, electronics and atomic energy are the most obvious cases of very rapidly growing industries demanding heavy investment in research and development, but basic research can often produce new technologies even in old industries— textiles and ceramics for example—which may call for large development outlays at fairly short notice if they are to be fully exploited. Research is a case where the total benefits should normally exceed the benefits to the successful researcher, even when he is given the protection of a patent. Society as a whole may thus be considered to have an interest in industrial research larger than the aggregate combined interests of the industrial firms which might engage in it. There is thus a strong theoretical case for at least basic research to be state subsidized, although the subsidization of an individual firm's development costs may be more questionable. In practice, however, development, i.e. bringing a new idea to the stage where full production can start, may well cost ten times as much as the original research[9] so that this is the stage at which subsidization is likely to be most effective, even though the benefits are likely to accrue much more directly to the particular firm than is the case with basic research. (The National Research Development Corporation was set up by the Board of Trade in 1948 to secure the development of inventions resulting from public or other research which were not being sufficiently exploited. Fears had been expressed that inventors often lacked support and that there was insufficient liaison between research centres and industry. The experience of the Corporation suggests that these fears have been exaggerated.)

Collective industrial research through Research Institutes has a long history, and the government has subsidized such institutes since the First World War, but on a small scale initially. In 1927 the Department of Scientific and Industrial Research (DSIR) disposed of £61,000 this way, and this had risen to £2·6 million in 1964, when DSIR was disbanded. However, even this was a trivial proportion of the total sums involved at the later stages. In 1966–67, it was estimated that total industrial Research and Development expenditure was £882·9 million, and of this the government provided £484·3 million, or slightly over half. Private industry accounted directly for 63·5 per cent of the spending but provided only 39·9 per cent of the money.[10] Slightly less than half of the government's spending was attributable to defence research, but much of this (e.g. in electronics and aircraft) could eventually have civil application. Government spending in civil industrial research had risen from £4 million in 1939 to £243·3 million in 1966–67, and was continuing rapidly upwards, while defence spending had levelled off.

The scale and exponential growth of this spending raises many questions. Can the government keep it under adequate control, or is this not one area where it faces a combined set of industrial, military and university interests which no democratic government is properly equipped to resist? Is industry perhaps too featherbedded in being sheltered from these risky, but vital decisions, to commit resources to long-term development? Above all, can the disposition of these funds between their different uses be accounted for rationally. The aircraft industry stands out as a special case, being expected to receive £69·5 million for civil aviation research in 1967–68, plus an unknown but obviously large amount of defence research and possibly more through university research grants. In addition, the nationalized Air Corporations have contributed towards the development costs of large civil aircraft. Can this one industry justify its very large share of the total research and development funds available to all industry? This question may be answered on defence and prestige grounds as well as the economic arguments of a very rapidly growing international market, but nevertheless there is an uncomfortable gap in the normal criteria of resource allocation to cover this situation. Finally, there is the problem of whether the government's stake on research encourages a false division between research and development. Contrary to generally accepted notions, Britain spends almost as high a proportion of its National Income on research and development as does the U.S.A. (2·7 per cent against 3·2 per cent) and higher than most other countries,[11] but there is likely to be a bias in government assistance towards research (i.e. science) whereas the main costs are incurred in development (i.e. technology), and this might contribute to the frequently noted (but not scientifically measured) tendency for British scientific invention to be exploited elsewhere.

The education and training of workers, managers and research staff is another area of major investment with a long term, and for the individual firm, uncertain return. An improvement in the general level of skill and expertise would seem, *a priori*, to be one of the most certain ways of increasing industrial efficiency, but training is normally very expensive, both in direct costs and in lost working hours, and the firm which incurs the costs will not necessarily reap the benefits. Firms which do not have training schemes may use part of the money they save to offer higher salaries or wages to people trained by other firms and thus gain all the advantages at a considerable saving to themselves. Such 'poaching' has existed for as long as there have been skilled workers to poach, and while the morality of the practice might be dubious, it is not illegal. (A particular problem exists with staff who know the firm's technical or commercial secrets and may take them off to a competitor when they move themselves. There can be no absolute safeguard against this in a free society.) Firms may secure their most highly trained and experienced staff by contracts, but if these were extended to all trained workers, it would involve the firms in commitments which they might not wish to undertake (for example, no redundancy without a 'golden handshake' for everybody) and they may not be considered in the public interest by the Courts.

If every firm pursued a policy of poaching rather than training, the result would be mutually destructive. Some industries have taken the initiative in trying to deal with this problem collectively by setting up industry-wide training schemes, but these have been voluntary, unless some form of coercion could be applied through other kinds of restrictive practice. It is difficult to devise laws which would be sufficiently flexible and specific to allow the government to *force* firms to undertake adequate training and education, so that again a combination of exhortation and subsidy has evolved. The government takes a *per capita* levy from all employers, and this is paid into a fund, supplemented by public funds, from which firms can claim assistance for approved training schemes or educational courses for their employees.

The government makes its biggest contribution in this field in general education. A substantial proportion of the money spent on secondary education, Technical Colleges, Colleges of Art and Design, Polytechnics and Universities accrues directly to industry in the form of a supply of skilled labour. University and College Business Schools are a new (as far as Britain is concerned) development in this field, involved the spending of public funds in providing graduates tailored as closely as possible to industry's needs, although there may be some conflict of opinion as to what

243

these needs are. The London and Manchester University Business Schools were partly financed by voluntary contributions from industry, and this gives private industry a stronger voice in the policies of these bodies than might be the case if they were financed entirely by the government.

Another technique open to the government is to use its powers as a monopsonist, or near monopsonist, in order to impose standards of performance on its suppliers. The government is the principal purchaser of military aircraft, medical supplies and large-scale civil engineering works, and indirectly through the nationalized industries of electricity generating and transmission equipment (including atomic energy), telecommunication equipment, mining machinery, civil aircraft and many other major items. The role of 'responsible monopsonist' is a difficult one to fill satisfactorily. A monopsonist can always drive a hard bargain, although it will not be in his interests eventually to ruin his suppliers. In the private sector, the motor manufacturers and large-scale retailers will usually succeed in obtaining lower prices from their suppliers than smaller firms will, but this is not just because they can insist on this, or even because they will investigate, advise on and even control their suppliers' production methods; it also arises because they are able to order in long runs, with adequate notice of changes in specification, so that the smaller supplying firms are able to gear up to a large scale of production. The government is in the position to do the same, and in so doing possibly produces a *general* increase in the efficiency of its suppliers which would benefit other customers as well.

Unfortunately, the government is obliged to work to a very broad definition of the public interest, and this may inhibit the full use of its potential power in this field. The purchases of government departments are subject to short-term budgetary restraints, and in the past this has tended to encourage a short view and a lack of continuity in the orders given to private industry. This was particularly noticeable in the case of the early motorway contracts, where large amounts of specialized equipment were required, but where the contracts were given out in a piecemeal fashion. No contractor can feel justified in making a big investment in the latest high-capacity techniques if the current contract is for two years only and there is great uncertainty about the next one. If he did make the investment, the price he charges would have to recover the cost of this long-lived equipment in a very short time. Either way, motorways cost more than they might have done. The responsible Ministry now operates to a long-term plan extending over ten years, and this offers a reasonable guarantee to the main contractors that there will be a continuous flow of work, and in return, the Ministry is able to exercise a much more detailed control of costs.

In defence purchases, the national interest has traditionally been identified with the highest attainable efficiency in the weapons, with long-run cost a secondary consideration. This leads to constant changes in specification (largely as a result of the large research expenditure in this field) and very short production runs, with consequential increases in costs. The aircraft industry has produced the most spectacular examples of initial cost estimates which multiplied tenfold or even more before the project was completed, but the tradition extends a long way back into history with Admiralty shipbuilding contracts. The problem here is political rather than economic—how to evaluate the risk to national security from not having the very best weapons that science can provide, and how to persuade military leaders to think in terms of economic costs. The Americans made rapid progress in this problem by appointing a senior business executive (Mr McNamara of the Ford Motor Corporation), as Secretary of Defence, and he instituted systems of 'cost-effectiveness'. In broad terms, this consists of setting a definite standard of performance for a weapon, and then finding the cheapest way of achieving this, and generally this meant producing long runs of perhaps not quite the best weapons which *could* be made. The products of the high technology industries are subject not only to the usual economies of large scale, but also to a learning process. Average costs may confidently be expected to fall as a function of time as well as scale, as managers and workers learn the tricks of each job and a host of small improvements in technique are instituted. Frequent changes in specification, even small ones, such as a monopsonist is able to insist upon, will lose these economies.

The government may also be inhibited from using one of the most effective weapons at its disposal by its concern for the Balance of Payments. The government as a monopsonist may be met by various forms of monopoly behaviour from its suppliers, producing effectively bilateral monopoly. It is difficult to make

I

general predictions about the outcome of bilateral monopoly situations, but if one of the parties is restricted in its freedom of action, it loses most of its advantages *vis-à-vis* the other. The suppliers can try to reduce their dependence on the government by developing other markets, especially overseas, but the government may not feel equally free to call upon foreign firms to undercut the domestic suppliers. If it does, it may be accused of undermining foreign confidence in the home industry, of leaving the country dependent on foreign producers for essential (especially military) supplies, of sacrificing British jobs, and of course of jeopardizing the Balance of Payments. As a result, there is an import content in government purchases which is probably below the optimum for a non-self-contained economy, and although foreign purchases are made (e.g. American Phantom fighters, Boeing civil airliners and Italian antibiotics) each major decision of this kind is a political risk.

Finally, even when the government has the will to impose stringent controls on the performance of its suppliers, it may not have the necessary means to do so. If all contracts were to be thoroughly analysed, standards set and performance maintained, the government would need more specialists in cost accounting and production engineering than it could hope to employ in a period when such skills are in short supply. All governments are sensitive to criticisms of excessive bureaucracy, so that even if it could be shown that such people could save their salaries many times over, their numbers would tend to lag behind the true requirements. Resources thus have to be concentrated on the very large contracts, with spot checks on others. The Public Accounts Committee of the House of Commons also conducts (largely *post-hoc*) investigations into supply contracts, and this Committee was largely responsible for bringing to light cases of overcharging in aircraft and missile contracts which have helped to give much greater political priority to this question.

Although economic incentives have constituted the main government approach to industrial performance, there remains the ultimate weapon of government—the law—to be brought into the picture. It is easier to use the law to control how industries behave than what they achieve since this form of control is essentially negative. However, the change in emphasis of economic policy in the 1960s involved among other things an attempt to intervene in the borderland between conduct and performance in the form of the Prices and Incomes Policy. It is reasonable to distinguish between the price structure in an industry, which is part of its conduct, and the general level of prices it charges, which is part of its economic performance, and the same applies to its wages and other cost items. The National Board for Prices and Incomes (PIB) was set up in 1966 (see also Chapter 6) as part of the Prices and Incomes Policy, with a similar composition to NEDC, to investigate particular wage agreements and price changes. It may recommend, for example, that a price increase should not be permitted, and the government may then make an order to this effect. The PIB would generally justify its recommendation by reference to the policies or structure of the firms concerned, and if the price increase were judged to be purely inflationary, the industry would have to take action to reduce its costs in order to maintain its profits. In a sense, the PIB is providing a form of free consultancy service, with limited powers of enforcement in the background. The Board has to spread its efforts between wages and prices, with wages naturally attracting most attention, and it is simply too small to be able to cover more than a small fraction of industry in any short period of time, and then only those parts which draw attention to themselves by ill-timed price increases. Again, one must conclude that the main purpose is educational, with the Board publicizing obvious weaknesses in some industries, hoping that others will take note.

To sum up, in spite of all the variety of approaches which have been tried, if an industry is determined to be inefficient there is little that the government can do about it. Most of the devices, such as subsidizing investment and research, paying for consultants, and, above all, increasing the total stock of knowledge, will only work in companies which are internally motivated towards greater efficiency. Cost efficiency methods in government purchases will weed out the most inefficient companies from this market, but there is no guarantee that the effects will spill-over into private markets, even though there is a likelihood that they will. All this amounts to saying that in a mixed economy, the government cannot take all the responsibility, and the associated credit or blame, for the economy's performance. It is more a question of politics than economics where the limits of responsibility should be drawn.

8.4 Government and industrial structure

Private industry represents, among other things, a large collection of private property rights, and it is a feature of capitalist societies (of which the mixed economy is a variant) that an individual has the right to dispose of his own property as he sees fit, subject to some limitation on his right to harm other people's interests in so doing. Government intervention in the structure of industry, affecting the size distribution of firms or establishments or their geographical distribution, clearly approaches this sensitive central issue very closely. The most fundamental change in structure occurs when ownership is entirely removed from private hands, and the government then has the power to reorganize the industry as it wishes. This is the policy of nationalization, which was examined at length in Chapter 6. Short of nationalization, a government clearly has problems in imposing its wishes for a change in structure on an industry determined to resist, although it has been frequently suggested that the *threat* of nationalization, representing the ultimate power of government, is one of the factors making private industry more amenable to 'suggestions'.

However, this over-dramatizes the process by which a government may influence an industry's structure. In theory, if a reorganization is justified in welfare terms, it should produce sufficient benefits to compensate all the parties involved and leave a surplus. This is the basis of most business deals, and the basis for the *ad hoc* industrial reconstruction of the pre- and post-war period, for the policy of the Industrial Reorganisation Corporation (IRC) and indeed for nationalization itself, since the compensation terms tended to value very generously the assumed earning power of the industries concerned. As with performance, a government may find it easy to deal with firms which are genuine long-run profit maximizers—it is simply a question of offering everybody concerned a good share of the benefits. An industry consisting of such firms is, however, less likely on the whole to require an external stimulus to reorganization than one which is set in traditional ways and not intent on seizing opportunities. So there appears to be a dilemma—the government either forces industry to make changes or does not interfere at all.

In fact, the situation is never so simple. Oligopoly, monopolistic competition, and, above all, various forms of collusive behaviour, may introduce a great deal of rigidity into an industry's structure.

Even when the individual firms wish to break out of it, the competitive risks may outweigh the potential individual benefits unless all the important firms, at least, move simultaneously. For example, if one oligopolist approaches another concerning a merger, it takes a great risk in revealing its problems and tactics to the other and may be in a vulnerable position if the approach is unsuccessful. Similarly, restructuring within a framework of price and market sharing arrangements will reduce the possible benefits to the firm with lower costs, unless it can get into such a position that it can overthrow the whole arrangement. Where there is collusion, the firms involved may choose to use their powers to keep out disturbing influences, such as new technology, rather than adapt the industry's structure to them.

The most general approach adopted by governments to this problem is to attempt to dismantle the collusive arrangements which produce the rigidity (this is fully examined in Chapter 6). British and American experience both suggest that limitation of collusive practices leads to the creation of larger firms. This may exchange one form of monopoly for another, but at least it offers the prospects of lower costs through scale economies. Even so, there is a major gap in policy to deal with oligopoly, where a number of large, but not necessarily optimally large, firms are frozen into a rigid structure by the threat of mutual destruction, and the more difficult the market conditions, the more frozen the posture. This is where an 'honest broker' may bring all of the parties together simultaneously, for mutual benefit. The most rigid structure will break down eventually, but the process may be long drawn out and subject to many accidental influences, so that if a reconstruction is generally beneficial, a great deal may be lost by waiting for it to happen.

Early examples of government attempts at industrial reorganization were confined to industries which were suffering from historical or cyclical decline, and which were unable to adjust their structures to the rapidly changing market situation. Coal, steel and railways were the three largest industries affected between the wars, and in each case the industry was subsequently nationalized, largely on the grounds that the reconstruction had not succeeded (see Chapter 7). In the case of coal and steel, the government's intention was clearly that the industries should reorganize into large units, but the approach was indirect, and via the industries conduct. They were encouraged to establish cartel-type arrangements to steady the market, and then expected to use this breathing space to carry through more fundamental changes. This strategy failed in the case of coal, but might have worked for steel if there had been time before the Second World War dominated the picture. The railway's reorganization was controlled in great detail by the government, and although it did not save the industry from further difficulties, these could have been worse if the industry had not had larger scale organization grafted onto it. The shipbuilding industry was given financial assistance in buying out obsolete capacity, but this affected only the fringes of the problem. It did not lead to a great increase in scale or modernization in the remaining yards.

Such examples did not encourage high hopes that government-aided industrial reconstruction could fundamentally affect the efficiency of industry as a whole, although it must be remembered that these attempts were made on industries which were already in difficulties and this is rarely the best time to introduce rational long-term changes. There is an obvious distinction between reorganizing an industry in order to let it survive in a contracted market, and reorganizing it so that it may take better advantage of opportunities for growth. It is into the latter field that the Industrial Reorganization Corporation (IRC) (see Chapter 6) has moved, and where the government, acting through IRC, is most closely in competition with private institutions, such as merchant banks, with the same aim in view.

The IRC is the outstanding example of a government body which was set up not to frustrate or divert market forces but to lubricate and accelerate them. It could best be described as the government's merchant bank, since it is free to use all of the devices and techniques of the capital market to achieve its aims. Its main purpose is to identify important industries which are badly organized (alternatively, its sponsoring Ministry may select the industries to be investigated), usually because the firms are too small for effective international competition, or because the division of products between firms is inefficient, with too many diversified firms with an interest in a product which could be more cheaply produced by one or two specialists. In such cases, IRC will bring the firms together and encourage them to negotiate a better arrangement, helping the deal along with advice and additional finance if necessary. The main difference between IRC and a private merchant bank is that the latter normally acts as an agent, so that the initiative for a change has to come from within the industry whereas IRC will usually make the first move. However, as its reputation as a powerful and efficient entrepreneur has grown, it has come to be seen as a useful ally by firms which want to make changes in their industry without making their own direct approach to competitors. The 'catalytic' function of IRC is generally all that is required—if an industry is ripe for change, then the process has simply to be started and the interested parties can usually sort things out to their own satisfaction and that of IRC. There have been cases (notably scientific instruments and bearings) where the direction of change did not satisfy IRC, since either the firms would remain too small or be absorbed into a conglomerate company which might fail to supply the right kind of management skill to it, and IRC has managed to block such developments (and impose its own ideas) by the use of its financial strength and capital market expertise, without resort to the law. The government has occasionally used IRC as its agent in the City to produce results which the market would not necessarily have approved. It was used, for example, as a means of retaining a nominal British shareholding in the Rootes Motor Company when it was purchased by the American Chrysler Corporation, this being a political gesture rather than an economic decision.

The IRC is an interesting example of how quickly an 'interventionist' body can be accepted, provided that it works through the market system and not across or against it. When it was first established in 1966, with available capital of £150 million, it was strongly suspected of being a means of 'backdoor nationalization', enabling the government to gain effective ownership and control of more private industries. For example, British press comment on IRC often made comparisons with what was thought to be its Italian counterpart. The latter (IRI) was a state holding company which inherited a vast miscellany of state interests in private companies and industries, most of which had been acquired accidentally when the banks were nationalized by the pre-war Fascist government.[12] However, IRC's intention is to turn over its capital as quickly as possible and this is incompatible with the idea of a holding company.

There is a danger that in following a policy which is acceptable, or even welcome, to the financial community, IRC will find itself at odds with other more 'social' policies, and in particular with monopoly policy. The mergers in the electrical engineering and

251

computer industries are quite incompatible with any model of a highly competitive domestic industry, but on the other hand, the urgent reason for these mergers was the increasing severity of foreign competition, which meant that a fragmented industry could only have survived with high protection, and would have been unable to compete abroad. There is also a problem of redundant labour following a reorganization, particularly where this occurs in a Development Area, for example, the IRC sponsored merger of English Electric and General Electric produced much labour redundancy in Liverpool. These redundancies were probably inevitable and could have been worse if the industry collapsed completely in the face of foreign competition, but there is some doubt whether IRC uses its obvious strength to the full in representing such social interests. Since all negotiations are highly confidential (as a necessary part of the policy of encouraging the trust of companies and banks) it is impossible to judge this from the outside.

There have been a number of instances of *ad hoc* industrial reorganization during the post-war period. Some of these have been of the 'traditional' kind, i.e. helping a depressed industry to meet a contracting or more severely competitive market. The Cotton Industry was helped with public funds to scrap obsolete or redundant capital equipment[13] but this measure was too negative in its effects, and did not increase the competitiveness of the remaining capacity to any great extent. The shipbuilding industry had a sum of £37 million made available to assist in reorganization,[14] but most of this was spent on the Clyde, and a large proportion did not remain in the industry in the form of new equipment, but was paid in compensation to the owners of the companies merged into the large groups. The industry subsequently became much more prosperous, but this coincided with a world-wide boom in the industry and it is difficult to judge whether the reorganization contributed significantly. The other main pattern has been the government's use of its powers as a monopsonist to force through changes in the structure of the supplying industries. The aircraft industry was reduced to two groups in 1961, the main exception being Handley-Page which chose to remain outside, but by 1969 found that it lacked the capital to survive in the airframe industry and meet its own development costs, and was absorbed by an American company. Nuclear power contractors were similarly forced into two groups.

although there was some question as to whether this should have ideally been just one, given the scale of the industry's international competitors. The government has also urged Local Authorities to combine together and use their combined bargaining power to force housebuilding contractors to work to a larger scale with 'industrial' building methods.

The pace of intervention in industrial structure thus seems to be accelerating, and if economic theory is correct in postulating a relationship between structure and eventual performance, the larger scale to which this intervention inevitably leads should generate lower production and distribution costs eventually, although there is always a significant lapse of time between the cause and effect. The structural changes leading to greater concentration and larger scale have been aimed almost exclusively at greater technical efficiency, and they are not always easy to reconcile with other policy objectives. There is a clear risk of inconsistency between the measures just described and those aimed at modifying the regional distribution of industry where technical efficiency was a secondary consideration. These are considered in the next section.

8.5 Regional policy

An industrialist wishing to extend his premises or open a new plant has to cope with a large accumulation of regulations and incentives operated by central and local government, intended to channel developments into certain areas of the country and certain zones within these areas. These controls have been inspired by two largely separate considerations. One is the deterioration in the quality of the physical environment caused by decaying towns and the dwindling countryside, and the other is the lack of geographical balance in industrial development, leading to excessive economic pressure in the Midlands and south-east of England, and under-utilization of economic resources elsewhere. The first has led to the growth of physical planning, implying highly detailed physical controls, and the second to regional economic planning, relying mostly on financial incentives. These two lines of policy have usually reinforced each other, but occasionally one may have to give way to the other. For example, the incoming motor industry established itself mainly in the Merseyside 'green-belt', the loss of this amenity being set off against the new employment created. Similarly, the authorization of potash mining on the Yorkshire Moors is justified by the additional employment in a difficult small pocket of unemployment.

Environmental planning is effected by a combination of persuasion and compulsion. All the larger local authorities have their planning departments, which can refuse permission for particular developments and have powers of compulsory purchase as a positive weapon. There are wide variations in different authorities' approach to their planning function, so that a manufacturer refused development permission by one authority may find it granted by another. If a firm is able to 'shop around' between authorities it reduces the risk of arbitrary and unfair treatment, but there is in any case a procedure for appealing against planning decisions, either to a Public Enquiry, or to the central government. Some parts of the country are effectively barred to industrial development, these being at the extremes of congested city centres in the prosperous regions, or thinly populated areas of natural beauty.

Local authorities with severe economic problems would normally be in a weak position to enforce a rigorous physical planning policy, since a developer's threat to go elsewhere could usually win concessions in such circumstances. However, in 1947 the Board of Trade was given the power to grant or withhold Industrial Development Certificates for all developments over 5,000 square feet (later reduced to 3,000 square feet in the Midlands and the South-East), and although the IDC has been mainly an instrument of regional economic planning, it has nevertheless strengthened the position of the local authorities in the Development Areas by limiting a developer's freedom to shop around.

The IDC is a discretionary instrument, and the effectiveness of the system has thus varied over time according to the vigour with which it has been applied. The machinery ran down in the 1950s, and partly in consequence there was a sharp increase in the proportion of all new developments taking place in the London Area. By the end of the decade, it was clear that the regional problem was not disappearing, as had been hoped, but that the regional disparities in employment and income were widening again quite rapidly, and severe restrictions were placed on the issue of further IDCs in the London Area. However, one of the main effects (common to all discriminatory devices) was to call forth great ingenuity in legally avoiding the controls—for example by a succession of small 'improvements', not requiring a certificate, instead of a single large development. Since 1965, the limit for Central London has been reduced to 1,000 square feet, but since the demand for accommodation is not directly affected, one of the main consequences of restriction of supply is to drive up the price (i.e. the rents) and this puts an increasing premium on ways of avoiding the regulations. Development permission becomes immensely valuable in such circumstances, and some would argue that this puts an entirely unfair burden on the public servants involved.

The IDC has been used to alter the regional distribution of industry by making developments difficult or impossible in over-crowded areas, but easy in the problem regions. Its effectiveness in this respect thus depends on industry's impetus towards expansion. If this is strong, then firms will settle for the chance to expand where they can, but if not, then firms may decide to postpone or abandon their developments if they cannot be exactly where they would wish. Opponents of the policy claim that this has been a common event, but it is impossible to measure such a negative effect, so that it remains a matter of opinion only.

Control over the supply of sites for development has been supplemented, especially in the case of manufacturing industry, by incentives intended to affect the demand. One of the first responses to the severe unemployment of the 1930s was the Special Areas Act of 1934, which designated the depressed coalfield industrial belts as Special Areas and permitted the appointment of two Special Commissioners to direct the efforts to help them. The main effort went into assisting migration out of the depressed areas, and the amount of capital available for direct assistance in creating new jobs was tiny compared with what post-war experience has shown to be necessary to make any real difference to such areas. However, migration was not a success, since not even in the prosperous regions was there an un-satisfied demand for unskilled labour or for the kind of skills created in heavy industry. The effort was increased following further legislation in 1936 and 1937, which permitted financial assistance to private industry, the building of Trading Estates and factories and rate and tax rebates. However, the scale of the problem was hardly affected by these measures. In 1939, there were still 57,000 unemployed in South Wales alone, and only

255

3,000 jobs had been provided in factories attracted to that area by these policies.

The war brought full employment and strategic dispersal of industry and military bases, conscription and direction of labour. The regional problem disappeared for a time, then reappeared when the war ended, but on a greatly modified scale. The economic background had changed to inflationary full employment, and the percentage rates of unemployment in the depressed areas were similar to those of the prosperous areas pre-war but nevertheless the recurrence of the pattern of a highly prosperous Midlands and South-East and relatively depressed periphery suggested that further action was required. The 1945 Distribution of Industry Act extended the pre-war legislation of cheap loans, advance factories and rent rebates, but with markedly greater effect. However, this was less a reflection of the efficiency of these measures than of the special circumstances of the time. There was an acute shortage of industrial capacity to meet peace-time demands and new products, and slight government pressure was thus enough to produce results. Half of the developments in the 1945–47 period took place in the Development Areas, but the proportion gradually tapered off thereafter, until in the middle fifties these areas were receiving new developments roughly proportionate to their share of the insured population.

At the same time, the gap between the Development Areas and the rest, in terms of unemployment and industrial growth, progressively narrowed, but this was mostly due to the recovery in demand for coal, steel and ships. By 1957, unemployment in the Development Areas was only one-and-a-half times that in the rest of the country, but then a serious attempt at disinflation in the country as a whole led to a mild recession, and the Development Areas showed themselves extremely vulnerable to deflationary unemployment. Meanwhile, the pressure to direct new industry to the old areas had been relaxed, and given a relatively free choice, light industry showed its former preference for the new industrial areas.

Although regional problems had become a major political issue again during the recession of the late fifties, previous experience had shown that it is most difficult to effect any redeployment of population or industry when industry itself is depressed. Movement of both is easiest when jobs are readily available (i.e. there is a shortage of labour) in the prosperous areas, but this is the time when the problem is least pressing, so that a government may easily be misled into ignoring it. Moreover, most job creation involves investment, and this is a time consuming process. It may therefore take several years for a change in policy to produce effects.

In the late fifties, the motor-vehicle industry was susceptible to pressure. A series of new models was due and increasing demand was putting increasing pressure on productive capacity. The industry badly needed more space, and could therefore be influenced to find it in the Development Areas. Regional policy thus made its greatest coup in sending Ford, Vauxhall and Standard Triumph to Merseyside, Rootes to Scotland and Rover to Wales with a number of smaller developments spread over all Development Areas. It is still not clear exactly how this was achieved, but there was obviously a great deal of direct negotiation between the government and the industry and not simply a series of responses to general controls and incentives.

At about this time, the IDC policy was revitalized and regional policy given a clearer set of general criteria. The Local Employment Act 1960 tried to define the areas in need of assistance principally in terms of the rate of unemployment, a rate of four per cent being the critical dividing line. The new Development Districts were smaller and more scattered than the old Development Areas, and experience showed that they were mostly too small to constitute balanced economic regions. The sharp dividing line could cause quick changes from one status to another and back again for one of these regions. Merseyside was originally scheduled as a Development Area, de-scheduled when it was thought that the motor industry had solved its problems, and then quickly re-scheduled. This is entirely contrary to all the lessons of the past that quick results cannot usually be expected in industrial policies.

The financial assistance under this act was discretionary, with an attempt made to favour labour intensive industries, but although this would economize on public funds, it would not necessarily ensure that the industries with the best growth prospects were attracted. In 1963, further standardization was introduced in the form of a standard rate of grant for all manufacturing development in the Development Districts of ten per cent of the cost of plant and twenty-five per cent of the cost of new buildings. In addition, firms were allowed to select their own period for

257

writing off their plant against their tax liability, giving them in effect an interest-free loan from the Inland Revenue.

In 1964, responsibility for regional policy passed to the Department of Economic Affairs in order to incorporate it more fully in other aspects of economic planning. One of the first steps was a reversion to the larger Development Areas, which could cover areas with problems of population decline and slow industrial growth as well as unemployment, but which should also contain smaller zones which because of good transport or other features would prove naturally attractive to industry (e.g. Newton Aycliffe in Durham and Skelmersdale in Lancashire). Efforts could thus be concentrated on the growth points, and the benefits should spill over into the surrounding problem areas. This is reasonable, given the greater degree of local mobility associated with private car ownership. The method of payment was changed in 1966 when the investment allowances were changed to investment grants (see Section 8.5). Firms in the Development Areas received grants of forty per cent on new industrial plant against twenty per cent on plant elsewhere (as a short-term measure to stimulate investment these grants were fixed at forty-five per cent and twenty-five per cent respectively for 1967 and 1968).

The levels of incentive were now very high, and the capital grants were estimated to be equivalent to 2·5 per cent of an average firm's total costs.[15] The main danger of such a system of subsidizing capital is that it may prove particularly attractive to capital intensive industry, which may offer the best growth prospects but will provide relatively little employment for a given outlay of capital in the short-run. There is some evidence that the capital intensive industries may not even offer the best prospects for the growth of employment. They have tended to get more capital intensive faster than the labour intensive industries became less labour intensive (although this could not continue indefinitely of course). Partly to offset this bias, manufacturers in Development Areas were given a subsidy for their labour through the Regional Employment Premium and Selective Employment Tax Premium (the REP/SET premia currently stand at £1·88 per week for adult males, and half of this for women and boys). This is estimated to reduce total costs for the average firm by a further 2·5–3 per cent.[16]

In addition, there is a battery of further measures of assistance —free retraining schemes, subsidized movement of key workers, grants for clearance of derelict land, preferential treatment in bank lending, favourable treatment in the award of government contracts and additional expenditures on the infrastructure, such as roads, electric power, etc. Extraordinarily generous treatment is given to firms moving to the Special Development Areas (usually areas of colliery closures) including up to five years free factory accommodation.

The total cost of government aid to the Development Areas was estimated to be £260 million for 1968-69.[17] IDC approvals for the Development Areas in 1968 promised 72,000 jobs, and a crude calculation would suggest that each new job in a Development Area cost over £3,000 in public money. However, it is important to distinguish between the financial cost of regional policy and the cost in real resources. Much of the expenditure consists of transfer payments, particularly in paying for investments which would have to take place somewhere, so that the cost in real terms is much more uncertain.[18]

It would be strange if the high levels of government assistance, coupled with a vigorous use of IDC controls elsewhere had not produced marked effects. The share of IDC approvals (measured in terms of estimated employment) accruing to the Development Areas in the period 1965–67 was fifty-three per cent (these areas containing about twenty per cent of the insured population) against twenty-two per cent in 1956–58. By 1968, Trading Estates provided 58·5 million square feet of factory space and 260,000 jobs. The unemployment gap was closing again, with the average rate of unemployment in the Development Areas 4·1 per cent against 2·3 per cent elsewhere, whereas previously it had been more than twice as high.

In the light of the extreme disparities between the levels of government assistance to industry in the Development Areas and elsewhere, it is surprising that any firm which was not very strongly committed to some other location could think of undertaking any expansion outside the Development Areas. American firms have shown themselves very sensitive to these incentives, and provide a disproportionately large amount of employment in Scotland and Northern Ireland (which has a set of incentives at least as great as Great Britain's and considerable freedom to negotiate special terms). Against this must be placed the very small proportion of industry which actually moves in any year from one region to another (see Chapter 4) and the high cost of movement for established businesses, particularly where they have been located in an interdependent industrial complex. Nevertheless, when allowance is made for the objective factors which might deter firms from settling in the Development Areas, a residue remains which can only be explained in subjective terms—a distrust of general prospects for industry in these areas, suspicion of the militancy of a labour force drawn from old industries and the unattractiveness of a decaying environment.

At the time when this elaborate structure of incentives was still being built, there were good grounds for suspecting that the attraction of the Development Areas would draw industry away from some of the immediately surrounding areas, which had problems of their own. In these areas towns tended to be relatively small, with badly run down social capital. They had not generally suffered from high unemployment, but they had experienced heavy outward migration and slow industrial growth or actual decline, and they presented a picture of chronic industrial stagnation. The name coined for such regions was the 'Grey Areas', of which the Lancashire Cotton Belt was the archetype, although parts of West Yorkshire, the North and West Midlands and Cornwall also qualified for this description.

Although the main problem of the Grey Areas was one of inadequate social capital, and the solution mainly one of urban renewal, their situation could deteriorate still further if new industry were entirely diverted from them. The Hunt Committee which was set up in 1967 to examine this problem could find little evidence of large scale diversion of industrial development from the Grey to the Development Areas, but nevertheless recommended that the North-West, Yorkshire and Humberside should be given an intermediate level of assistance, mostly in the form of building and clearance grants. It was also recommended that Merseyside should lose its Development Area status, i.e. that some resources should be switched from the task of reducing unemployment in Merseyside (which was beginning to show signs of moving towards the national average) into improving the physical environment of the rest of Lancashire. The last suggestion was rejected by the government, which obviously gave unemployment priority over all other social considerations. The principle of Intermediate Areas was accepted but applied in a more fragmented fashion than the Committee had recommended.

In forming a regional policy, a government is faced with a

major problem in deciding exactly what it is they are trying to achieve. Is there some pattern of population and industrial distribution which is 'better' in some sense than the one which is evolving in response to market forces? If so, in what sense is it better? Such questions involve a detailed assessment of the future and a clear scale of values and involves a commitment to a time-scale far longer than that which any democratic government can plan for itself. Is it feasible then to commit the whole country to a particular pattern, say twenty years hence, when there may be a new government with a different scale of values in two or three years time? It is unlikely that there will ever be a simple answer to the problem of reconciling parliamentary democracy, long-term planning, private gains and social benefits, but rather a series of experiments with different combinations.

One such experiment is the setting up of Regional Planning Councils, broadly representative of the main interests in each of the Planning Regions. These are intended to help to shape the economic plans of the regions by bringing a wide cross section of views to bear on the problems and proposals. There is some doubt about how effective, and indeed how representative, such voluntary bodies can be, although as in the case of NEDC they can have an important function in publicizing the issues. There has been a steady increase in pressure for a genuine devolution of political power to regional level, giving such Planning Councils more than just an advisory role, but this is unlikely as long as the chaotic division of local authorities into an almost random collection of large, medium and small bodies persists. The Redcliffe-Maud Commission[19] has made recommendations for standardizing local authority divisions which could introduce larger authorities with genuine economic planning powers. One of the main consequences of this would be to make a comprehensive national policy on the future distribution of industry and population much more urgent, since a lot of autonomous authorities competing for a share of the dwindling employment in manufacturing industry might simply 'freeze' the existing pattern.

8.6 Conclusion
This chapter has summarized very briefly some of the main points of contact between industry and government. Although it is neither detailed nor exhaustive, it will nevertheless give some idea of how the government may affect every aspect of an industry, so

that government policy becomes the biggest single factor affecting most of a firm's decisions. There are many who feel that this process has gone too far—that the business environment is now so artificial that there is no real way of knowing what is economically efficient and what is not, and that firms have been diverted from their prime function of making things to acting as agents for a variety of public policies. Others feel that it is still too easy for private interests to override the general public interest and the 'market' concept of efficiency is too narrow to be an adequate guide in any circumstances.

It is tempting to postulate that there must be some critical level of intervention, beyond which the whole economic system changes its form, but in fact the mixed economy has shown itself highly adaptable, provided that it is not overwhelmed by a mass of new interventionist legislation in a short period of time. However, there must be practical limits even though these are not sharply defined. The main limitation, as shown by post-war rationing, and more recently with wage restraint, is the extent to which the electorate is prepared to identify itself with, or to oppose, interventionist policies. If there is general non-co-operation, the policies will not work. Firms may fail to co-operate simply by a passive refusal to respond to incentives or to accept the economic and social priorities, such as rapid growth, that the government wishes them to adopt, although this may lead simply to more but different kinds of intervention.

An important new element is the increasing importance of the 'international business', now estimated to account for twenty-two per cent of British output. These are firms which form part of a business operating in other countries as well as the UK. The Ford Motor Company and Unilever Ltd. are typical examples. Such businesses can very effectively withdraw co-operation by transferring the affected activities to some other country. Concern is now being expressed that very large international companies (particularly in oil and mining), some of them with a trade turnover as large as the National Income of a small industrial state, have such a strong position in relation to any single government that international action may be necessary to bring them under some sort of public control. It is likely that the European Common Market will produce a legal code for a 'European' company which may limit the powers of a company to 'play off' one national government against another, but such developments will take time, and there will be obvious problems in achieving an agreed approach between all the different countries involved. Meanwhile the international companies spread rapidly and must influence national policy making.

There are also limitations from the government's side. The more comprehensive the legislation, the more difficult it is to ensure that the various parts are consistent with each other, and this is particularly true where the policies are divided between economic and social objectives. Even if a government is capable of setting a total objective and a definite scale of priorities, governments may change every few years, involving industry in a re-adjustment to new policies each time. Furthermore each new policy may involve the government in collecting new information from industry, and new policies may have to be implemented with inadequate data, since it had never seemed necessary to collect it previously. The collection of data relevant to government policies is in fact one of the main sources of conflict between industry and government. Firms have to employ staff solely in order to complete returns for the government, and these are sometimes of doubtful relevance to the interests of the firm or the government. Thus, one of the most important methods open to a government of ensuring that its industrial policies are relevant to its aims, while generating the minimum of resentment, is to make the greatest possible use of standardization, simplification and sampling methods in the collection of statistical information.

1 Bain, J. S., *Industrial Organization* (New York, Wiley, 1959); and Caves, R. E., *American Industry: Structure, Conduct, Performance* (Englewood Cliffs, N.J., Prentice-Hall, 1964).

2 Galbraith, J. K., *The New Industrial State* (London, Hamish Hamilton, 1967).

3 Mishan, E. J., *The Costs of Economic Growth* (London, Staples Press, 1967).

4 Hire Purchase Acts, 1938 and 1965.

5 The Council on Prices, Productivity and Incomes was set up in 1957 under the chairmanship of Lord Cohen.

6 *Conditions Favourable to Faster Growth*; and *Growth of the U.K. Economy to 1966* (both London, HMSO, 1963).

7 *The National Plan*, Cmnd. 2764 (London, HMSO, 1965).

8 See, for example, Polanyi, G., 'Critique of the National Plan,' *Planning in Britain* (London, Institute of Economic Affairs, 1967). This gives a very comprehensive list of the problems that would be encountered if anyone ever attempted detailed target setting in a market economy.

263

9 *Second Report on Science Policy*, Cmnd. 3420 (London, HMSO, 1967).

10 *Statistics of Science and Technology* (London, HMSO, 1968).

11 *Second Report of Committee on Science Policy.* On one basis of calculation Britain spends a higher proportion of its national income on research and development. See Caves, R. E. (ed.), *Britain's Economic Prospects*, p. 449 (London, Allen & Unwin, 1968).

12 Einaudi, *Nationalization in France and Italy* (New York, Cornell University Press, 1955).

13 Cotton Spinning Act 1948; and Cotton Industry Act 1959.

14 Shipbuilding Industry Act 1967. This assistance was administered by a Shipbuilding Industry Board. The scheme provided for extensive regrouping into regional units with greater specialization of shipbuilding yards.

15 *Committee on the Intermediate Areas* (Hunt Committee), Cmnd. 3998, para. 123 (London, HMSO, 1969).

16 *Ibid.*, para. 123.

17 *Ibid.*, Appendix 1, sets out the measures of assistance and estimated costs.

18 *Ibid.*, Brown, A. J.'s 'Note of Dissent'.

19 *Royal Commission on Local Government in England and Wales*, Cmnd. 4040 (London, HMSO, 1969).

CHAPTER 9

Industrial Efficiency

9.1 Introduction

An economic system is reckoned to be operating at maximum efficiency if available productive resources are used in such ways as to produce now, and in the future, the highest possible standard of living. But the standard of living is not simply a matter of achieving maximum output of economic goods and services per head. Man does not live by bread alone. The economist is well aware that some material goods and services which support our standard of living do not command a price and are therefore outside his purview. Also he has to assume for the most part that men are permitted to make a free choice between work and leisure. The production of more goods and services by forced labour would not, in the view of most people, result in a higher standard of living.

The economist accepts these limitations on the relevance of what he has to say about maximizing efficiency in the broadest sense. The industrial economist however has to accept further limitations. Obviously we are not likely to maximize economic efficiency if all available resources are not employed in some use or another, or if the achievement of higher output today is at the cost of a lower output tomorrow. Also, although it would be a difficult proposition to prove, it would be generally agreed that a reasonably even distribution of the national product is necessary to the achievement of maximum satisfaction. But the realization of these objectives of full employment, maximum rates of stable growth, and optimal distribution is mainly dependent upon the formulation and execution of appropriate monetary and

265

fiscal policies with which we are not concerned (increasing concern with the rate of economic growth has been directly associated with detailed Government intervention in industry, see Chapter 8).

We are much more concerned with allocative efficiency. This is achieved if resources of labour and capital are so distributed between firms and industries as to produce the largest aggregate and best combination of commodities which will satisfy the wants of consumers to the maximum extent possible. Welfare economists attempt to lay down rules about this. The validity of these rules has been much argued about but consideration of these controversies would take us far beyond the scope of this book. The important thing from our point of view is that we have no means of applying these rules or of checking up on whether they are being conformed to. We are committed to a very much more partial and pedestrian approach. This yields some doubtful clues about unsatisfactory industrial performance, its causes and possible remedial action. But by and large we have no answer to the question whether, to what extent, and why British industry is inefficient.

Theory suggests that if firms survive in a competitive environment they are efficient. Also that the most efficient firms will earn above average profits and will be seen to enlarge their share of the market. But we have already seen that monopoly elements are very persuasive in our industrial economy. Far from reflecting efficiency, survival may reflect restriction of competition and abnormal profits may reflect the exploitation of market power.

We have also previously noted how monopoly may be expected to promote inefficiency—principally by promoting misallocation of resources. Monopolies may produce too little and, by the same token, sell at too high a price and make abnormal profits. Moreover they may waste resources by using too many resources to produce those outputs. We have some crude measures of monopoly (e.g. concentration ratios) and will be interested to see later in this chapter if monopoly can be associated with unsatisfactory performance. On the whole we shall be surprised if any strong association exists because these measures ignore so many features of monopoly and competition which exist in particular situations, because monopoly power may not be accompanied by short-run profit maximization, and because a degree of monopoly power may be a necessary condition for producing the output which consumers demand with minimum use of productive resources.

We shall not have very much that is useful to say about whether resources are ideally distributed between different industries— whether we are producing too much food and too few vehicles. We can hope to say a little more about whether these outputs are produced with minimum use of resources. This will include consideration of whether firms are of the right size having regard to economies of scale and whether capital resources are embodied in forms which adequately reflect the existing state of technical knowledge.

9.2 Productivity and international comparisons

Our first approach to measurement of industrial performance is to regard efficiency as a relation of output to input. If current inputs can be made to produce larger outputs or if current outputs can be produced with fewer inputs then efficiency is improved. We shall not however be able to relate input to output in a way which will give us a notional target of one hundred per cent efficiency at which to aim. It is possible however to compare in this respect the performance of firms in the same industry or the performance of the same industry in different countries. A firm or an industry is deemed to be inefficient in so far as it is unable to match the performance of other firms or industries.

Inputs are generally classified as being labour and capital. Labour input can be measured and aggregated by counting heads. But some workers may be part-time and the number of hours work given by others will vary over any period so we often prefer to measure labour in man-hours. Also workers will differ in the skills which they possess, in the extent of their application to the job in hand, and in their loyalty to management and their employers. It is obviously impossible to assess these differences with any accuracy. We could assume that these differences are reflected in wages and salaries and 'weight' labour units accordingly. But differences in wages and salaries will reflect the relative scarcity of particular skills and qualities and this procedure will tend to iron out differences in performance which we are trying to measure. If one firm achieves a higher output per man-hour than another by using fewer but more highly skilled men it is difficult to say whether or not it is more efficient. (One investigation suggests that ten per cent of the difference in productivity between some US and British manufacturing industries can be removed by correcting for the higher proportion of female labour employed in Great Britain.) But probably no great harm is done by ignoring non-homogeneity of labour except where inspection of the data suggests it is of particular significance. Man-hours of labour employed give us a reasonably accurate measure of labour input in physical terms.

Capital introduces more serious complications. It mainly comprises fixed capital in the shape of more or less specialized buildings, vehicles, and machinery. Obviously it cannot be aggregated in physical terms (such as tons of steel embodied in it) and even if it could be so measured we could not add it to man-hours of labour to arrive at total input. Some rather unsatisfactory attempts have been made to assess capital input in physical terms, e.g. horse power in use and fuel and power input. It may be doubted whether either of these measures adequately reflects capital in use and in any case can tell us nothing about the age and quality of equipment.

So we have to measure capital in money terms. Strictly speaking the value of a piece of capital equipment once it is made and put into use is dependent on the net return which it is thought to be capable of earning over the rest of its life. If it is not expected to earn a profit over and above the cost of working and maintaining then it is practically worthless except as scrap. Expected profit is in any case very uncertain since we have no means of knowing the future market prospects of the commodity it helps to produce nor at what point in time it will be displaced by a machine of superior design. Obviously it will be quite impossible to value capital on a market value basis except in those rare cases where the assets have recently been sold.

For the purpose of assessing capital inputs therefore, we have to value capital on some basis related to its purchase price and measure from this its contribution to output in terms of the extent to which it is worn out in producing that output (depreciation). But many problems remain. In times of rising prices is the original cost of the asset to be updated to represent what it would cost to replace the asset today? What deductions are we to make where an asset has been in use for some years and is now partially worn out? This obviously must depend on some view as to the probable life of the asset. Accounting practices in the matter of revaluation of capital and treatment of depreciation will vary a great deal but when we are involved in comparing the performance of different firms we have little alternative but to base our calculations on the book value of the assets as shown in the balance sheet.

For comparisons at industry level we have other sources of information. Barna[1] has estimated the replacement cost of fixed assets in 1955 in British manufacturing industry on the basis of fire insurance values. The national income statisticians have derived estimates of gross and net capital stock for broad sectors of the economy from the annual gross capital formation figures by using a perpetual inventory method.[2] The difference between gross and net capital stock is capital consumption, i.e. the extent to which capital has been used up over the period in question. This is the money measure of the use of capital input but unfortunately we only have figures for gross capital stock for the main orders of manufacturing industry. In order to obtain these estimates arbitrary assumptions have to be made about the lives of capital assets. There is some evidence that the lives of capital assets have been under-estimated, i.e. the amount of capital in actual use is greater than the official estimates suggest. But these figures can be used to indicate the relative amounts of capital used to produce given outputs.

We shall return to the problem of combining estimates of the use of labour and capital to produce given outputs. Assuming for the moment that these estimates could be made in physical objective terms and can be added together, they have to be related to physical units of output. Here again we encounter grave difficulties because products described by a common name are not comparable. It makes no sort of sense to measure the relative efficiency of two car firms in terms of factor input per car if one firm is producing very luxurious cars and the other is producing small popular two-door saloons. No orders of industry and very few minimum list headings cover only a reasonably homogeneous product. This means that if we want to compare firms or industries on the basis of input per unit of physical output we have to confine ourselves to narrow comparisons of firms producing nearly identical products or to international comparisons of industries carefully defined to cover a reasonably homogeneous product such as cement, margarine, or cigarettes.

It would appear then, that the scope for any objective evaluation of industrial performance by relating input to output is

269

rather limited. It appears inevitable that we should have to aggregate either or both in money terms and this, as we have seen, introduces some elements of market evaluation which are hardly relevant to an assessment of performance. If we add labour and capital input in money terms and relate it to physical units of output we are in fact assessing efficiency in terms of relative costs of production. Such an approach has much to commend it but there are serious conceptual problems involved and such figures are not available on a uniform accounting basis. If we relate the money costs of inputs to value of output we are measuring efficiency in terms of the difference (i.e. profits) and this introduces additional difficulties of a kind already discussed. But the use of money measures does permit of very broad-based comparisons of performance.

Where a money measure of output is required the value of gross output is hardly appropriate since this will be influenced by the value of raw materials, power, etc., bought in from other firms. It is more usual to take the value of net output for purposes of performance comparisons, i.e. the value of gross output minus the cost of purchases from other firms. Net output measures the 'value added' by the firm and is equal to the factor incomes paid out, including profits. Figures for net output on an industry basis are published in the reports on the Census of Production which is taken every few years.

It is clear from what has been already said that meaningful comparisons of performance as a physical input-output relationship are most easily designed between firms in the same industry. It is generally possible to compare firms which are producing nearly identical products and perhaps using nearly identical technical methods of production. Even where this is not possible engineering studies of hypothetical plants can be used to establish comparisons with existing plants. In this way some of the variables affecting performance can be standardized and the effect of others on performance can be measured.[3] For example where capital equipment, scale of operation, and products are similar, any differences in labour productivity are likely to be due to differences in make-up of the labour force, in skills, in attitudes to work, in factory lay-out and so on.

But inter-firm comparisons are not likely to yield conclusions applicable to broad sectors of the economy. For this purpose we have to make enquiries on an industry basis. This immediately raises the question of establishing a basis of comparison. Perhaps the most fruitful procedure is to compare a range of industries in one country with similar industries in another. We can of course compare *movements* of output per man-hour (OPH) and wage costs per unit (WCU) in different countries. These figures show, over the past decade, for manufacturing industry as a whole in USA, Japan, West Germany, France, Italy and the UK that OPH has been rising most slowly in the UK (except for USA). Except for West Germany, WCU have been rising most quickly in the UK. But this tells us little about absolute standards of performance. Because the USA is commonly regarded as a pacesetter in manufacturing industry several studies have also been made of comparative performance in US and British manufacturing industry.[4]

These are called productivity comparisons because for the most part they measure performance in terms of physical output per man-hour, although occasionally, output is measured in terms of value of net output. Because of the difficulty of measuring combined inputs of labour and capital, output is related to one input only. The results do not therefore measure efficiency in any meaningful way. If output per man-hour is much higher in a US industry than in the corresponding British industry this may be because the US industry employs more capital per head. If, however, it can be shown that similar proportions of US and British manufacturing industry are engaged in the manufacture of fixed capital for domestic use then comparisons of (labour) productivity in manufacturing industry as a whole are of much greater significance.

These enquiries covered only a selection of manufacturing industries for which reasonable comparability could be established and relevant statistics obtained. The Rostas enquiry covered between forty and fifty per cent of manufacturing industry in both countries and was based on 1935–37 data. The Frankel enquiry covered sixteen to eighteen per cent of manufacturing industry in both countries and was based on 1947–48 data. The Paige and Bombach enquiry compares net output and productivity in all sectors of the economy for 1950 and makes detailed comparisons between selected manufacturing industries covering about fifty per cent of the manufacturing sector with some estimates for 1954 and 1957. We cannot go further into the detail of these investigations here but they all suggest that labour productivity

271

in manufacturing is between two and three times higher in the US than in Great Britain. It does not follow of course that the US can necessarily under-cut British manufactured goods in the market. The rate of exchange between the pound and the dollar is mainly influenced by prices of goods which enter into international trade. Relative wage rates (converted at the ruling rate of exchange) may be such as to reduce or eliminate the productivity advantage of the US in terms of selling prices.

Nor does it follow that there will be a corresponding difference of standards of living in the two countries. It is true that if output per head is measured over all sectors we are measuring the net product available per head of the working population. But the size of the non-working population is higher in the US than in Great Britain and the relative size of the manufacturing sector (which has higher productivity than some other sectors) is greater in Great Britain. So both these factors tend to redress the balance somewhat in favour of Great Britain.

The structure of manufacturing in the two countries (i.e. the extent to which either has put proportionately more resources into highly productive industries) can affect the comparison, e.g. one country may show high productivity in one industry which is important to it, though it is little represented in the other country; as between US and Great Britain this is of little significance. Also we need to remember that the standard of living depends on the output of consumption goods. If one country has a much greater stock of capital per worker then a higher proportion of current output has to be devoted to maintaining and replacing the capital. But productivity may be higher in the capital producing trades. The US does not appear to have a higher proportion of the working population in manufacturing engaged in the production of capital goods for domestic use.

But when all these qualifications have been made most informed observers would agree that physical output per unit of labour is greater in US manufacturing industry than in Great Britain and that this has influenced the achievement of a higher standard of living in the US. There is in other words a more effective transformation of input into output in US manufacturing industries. In this sense most US manufacturing industry is more efficient than its British counterpart. This suggests that we should try to establish some statistical relationship between differences in productivity and other variables. It should be noted that in particular cases specific factors may sufficiently explain differences in output per man, e.g. in coal mining they may be explained by relative thickness of seams, relative absence of faults and so on. Also the US is more generously endowed than the UK with power and industrial raw materials. These differences in productivity whilst affecting the overall efficiency advantage of the US economy should not much affect productivity comparisons for most manufacturing industry.

The trouble is that the factors which seem likely to cause differences in productivity are themselves inter-related and clear cause-effect relationships are impossible to establish. One would expect for example that productivity would be higher where capital per head was higher and this in turn would be associated with large sizes of firms (measured by output) and larger markets.

Measuring capital in terms of horse power per head and fuel input per head, both Rostas and Frankel found that for manufacturing industry as a whole, the difference in US and UK capital per head almost exactly matched the difference in output per head. But neither was able to establish any close correlation for individual industries. Frankel concluded that less than nineteen per cent of the variation in productivity ratios in particular trades is explained by variation of capital per head. These physical measures of capital however are extremely crude and take little account of difference in the age and quality of equipment.

Measuring the size of markets is also difficult. It may be equated to domestic consumption, domestic consumption plus exports or domestic production plus exports (i.e. total production). For most purposes the latter is taken. On this basis a close relationship has been established between relative advantage in productivity in various US and UK industries and relative size of markets—particularly if industries restricted to local markets are eliminated. (These conclusions by Rostas and Frankel have been generally confirmed by Paige and Bombach who estimate a correlation of 0·8 between productivity and total production in forty-four US and UK manufacturing industries.) But it may be doubted whether this takes us very far. In most industries the UK market would be adequate to support a number of plants of optimum size. It seems likely that Great Britain tries to support more variation of product relative to market size (thus limiting the benefits of standardization) though this is partly forced upon her by the requirements of export markets. Nevertheless, the total size of the UK market could probably support greater standardization and higher productivity.

What may be more significant than the size of markets may be the rates at which markets (outputs) are growing. When output is growing profits are likely to be rising, there is greater scope for innovation and fuller utilization of plant, the average age of capital falls and there is likely to be much less resistance to change by employers and trade unions. This may be an important part of the explanation of the emergence of productivity differences between US and the UK and may also explain the increasing advantage which some European countries appear to have over Great Britain. But the extent to which growth stimulates productivity and increasing productivity stimulates growth is not easy to ascertain. We shall return to this.

The relationship of differences of size of plants and differences in productivity is much affected by the measurement of size. In terms of employment US plants are not much different in size from their British counterparts. But in terms of capital or output the typical US plant, industry for industry, is much bigger. Output appears to be the most appropriate measure and on this basis the correlation with productivity differences is weak. It is negligible or negative when size is measured by capital or employment.

The attempt to relate these variables to differences in productivity has not therefore yielded very much by way of explaining what would appear to be relatively inferior British industrial performance. This perhaps is not to be expected since British productivity per man is now lower than that of most industrialized European countries in many important manufacturing industries and is rising less quickly.[5] These countries do not typically have larger plants or larger markets than the UK.

Attempts to relate differences in US and UK productivity to structural differences are equally unilluminating. There is little evidence that degrees of concentration have been significantly increasing in the UK (except perhaps over the last decade) or that concentration is higher in the UK than in the USA. In any case as we have already seen, degrees of concentration are poor indicators of either the existence or the exercise of monopoly power. There is much scattered evidence of inefficiency induced by monopoly situations in Monopolies Commission reports but no evidence that this is less so in the US in spite of their more vigorous anti-monopoly policies. Nor is there much evidence that the relative superiority of US industrial performance (as measured by productivity) has been diminished by the British onslaught on cartels after 1956 (see Chapter 6).

So we are increasingly pressed back to qualitative appraisals of one kind and another to explain relatively low British productivity compared with the US. Rostas for example has called attention to the possible importance of organizational factors (differences of managerial skills, factory lay-out, and planning the flow of work) and the willingness and ability of workers to work hard as explanations of higher US productivity. Frankel stresses the more flexible attitudes to work in a new country like the US and the comparative lack of institutional obstacles to managerial efficiency. In general terms, most explanations of Britain's inferior industrial performance stress inadequacies of organization, attitudes and practices both on the managerial and the trade union sides of industry.[6] But any kind of objective appraisal is very difficult to make in these fields. Dunning[7] demonstrates the superior profit performance of subsidiaries of US companies operating in the UK over their UK market rivals. But one wonders if overheads common to parent and subsidiary have been properly allocated between them. In particular do US subsidiaries in the UK benefit from the knowledge and experience, and research and development expenditures of the parent? Nevertheless this sort of conclusion is very much in line with the results of some statistical enquiries which show that very little of recorded increases in output are attributable to simple increases in factor inputs but appear to be due to organizational factors, technical progress and other human and institutional factors which cannot easily be quantified.[8]

The speed of innovation and the quality of capital equipment is probably of great importance. Research and development (R & D) expenditure (as a percentage of sales) is about twice as high in the US as in the UK and is much more concentrated in growing industries with sophisticated technologies.[9] But this is not easily squared with the higher productivity of German industry where R & D expenditure per head is lower than in the UK. But after the devastation of war and defeat one would expect that a higher proportion of Germany's fixed capital in manufacturing industry would be of recent date and design.

9.3 Recent British experience

The advantage of comparison between the performances of US and UK manufacturing industry was that the US sets a high standard of performance and also that since the same industries were being compared in both countries some use could be made of physical indicators of performance such as physical output per head.

We now turn to some comparisons of recent performance of British industries. The object here is to see if, in some sense, some industries are doing better than others and, if so, whether we are transferring resources quickly enough from the more efficient to the less efficient.

Table 9.1 (p. 278) summarizes some indicators of comparative performance for the SIC orders which cover British manufacturing industry. It would however be a mistake to attach very much importance to the actual figures. Orders are in most cases very wide groupings and we cannot expect to deduce very much from figures which average out the performance of a number of quite dissimilar industrial activities. Also some of the figures relate to different time periods and can in any case only be regarded as very crude estimates of such magnitudes as capital stock or profits as a percentage of capital employed. Nothing has been included on concentration because, for reasons previously given, concentration ratios by industrial order cannot be regarded as even approximate measures of monopoly power (see Chapter 2, p. 48).

One sense in which one industry may be deemed to be doing better than another is when a given combination of factor inputs in one is yielding more output in value terms than another. In the long run we would expect a transfer of resources from less productive to more productive uses and this would produce a long-run tendency to equalization of returns. But at any particular point in time non-equality of returns should indicate sources of 'inefficiency' and the direction in which we need to move in order to improve 'efficiency'. It would not have the same significance as differences in productivity between firms in the same industry or between the same industries in different countries.

There have been several attempts to compare the rate of growth of output with the rate of growth of combined input for different industries. Reddaway and Smith[10] have done this in effect by weighting the physical increase in labour by wages in the base period and increased capital (in value terms) by a notional fifteen per cent expected normal return on capital. This gives a value of increased input which when deducted from the increase in the value of net output will measure progress, i.e. that part of output increase which is not attributable to increased doses of capital and labour input but to improvements in the quality of these factors and of the skill with which they are organized and combined for use in production. It is assumed in other words that the prices of labour and capital in the base period reflects their respective productivities and therefore the amount of extra product which they would generate throughout the period of 'progress' did not take place.

A somewhat similar technique is used by Mathews[11] for the period 1948–62. In this case the growth of factor input is valued by weighting the increase in labour and capital by their respective shares in the national income in the base year. This is the growth in output which may be directly attributable to increase in factor input. The difference between this and the actual growth in output is called the 'residual' and may be compared with Reddaway's 'Progress'. It is noteworthy that these and similar investigations attribute the bulk of increased output to 'progress' rather than simple increase in factor inputs. (See Section 9.2.)

The results of both enquiries were broadly comparable. The rates of growth of output per unit of input measured by 'progress' or 'residual' were highest for engineering, vehicles, timber and furniture, paper and printing (plus chemicals in the case of the Reddaway enquiry). The lowest rates were for bricks, pottery, etc. clothing and other metals.

This of course does not throw light on amounts of output per unit of combined factor input. We have stated only that the rate of growth of output per unit of input was growing faster in some industries than others. Mathews calculates output per unit of combined factor input for the different industries for the base year 1948. Of the high performance industries listed above, engineering, chemicals and printing and paper had a higher than average 'take-off point'.

The detail of some of these calculations raises methodological issues which cannot be dealt with here. But it would appear that some industry groups were more efficient than others in the sense that we were deriving a higher product return from them for each additional dose of combined factor input.

Table 9.1 shows that engineering, chemicals, and paper have

Table 9. 1 *Some Figures bearing on Recent Performance of British Manufacturing Industry*

INDUSTRY	Order no. SIC 1958	Employment in thousands June 1968	Capital stock per head (£) 1960	Growth of employment 1959-68 per cent per annum	Growth of capital stock 1954-60 per cent per annum	Output growth 1958-67 per cent per annum	Value of output per unit of input 1948	Growth of output per unit of input 1948-62 per cent per annum	Gross profits as percentage of gross assets in quoted companies 1966	Research and development (R. & D.) expenditure 1966-67 on £ per head
		(1)	(2)	(3)	(4)	(5)	(6)	(7)	(8)	(9)
Food, drink and tobacco	III	816	1,814	+0·44	3·1	+2·7	1·15	−0·3	13·6	21
Chemicals and allied	IV	511	3,667	−0·1	7·9	+7·9	1·95	1·7	12·4	164
Metal manufacture	V	582	2,487	+0·1	6·9	+2·0	1·14	0·9	9·0	33
Engineering and electrical goods	VI	2,294	997	+2·2	4·2	+5·9	1·19	2·3	13·9	100
Shipbuilding and marine engineering	VII	192	654	−3·1	6·5	−2·9	1·02	0·2	3·7	17
Vehicles	VIII	809	1,319	−0·66	4·3	+2·4	0·92	3·4	12·6	255
Metal goods not elsewhere specified	IX	559	1,031	+1·1	3·8	+1·1	1·19	0·4	14·2	17
Textiles	X	697	1,947	−1·9	0·4	+1·5	1·11	2·1	12·2	18
Leather, leather goods and fur	XI	56 }	492	−1·2 }	0·9	−1·2	N.A.	N.A.	12·0 }	3
Clothing and footwear	XII	485 }		−1·2 }					11·4 }	
Bricks, pottery and glass	XIII	347	1,238	+0·77	5·6	+6·1	1·15	1·1	14·7	29
Timber, furniture etc.	XIV	304	737	+1·0	3·5	+2·7	1·12	2·3	12·1	
Paper, printing and publishing	XV	629	1,596	+1·1	4·0	+5·0	1·07	2·9	11·9 }	8
Other manufacturing	XVI	338	1,157	+2·4	5·8	+6·1	1·30	1·5	12·7	25
All manufacturing	III to XVI	8,619	1,466	+0·44	4·2	+3·6	1·15	1·7	12·4	69

shown the highest rates of output growth over the past ten years. Timber and vehicles on the other hand have shown slightly below average growth of output. It is very tempting to conclude from this that rapid growth of output is closely associated with increased efficiency in an industry. There are obvious reasons for thinking that this may be so. When total output rises, equipment and labour can be used more intensively (even at times of very full employment a high proportion of firms report that they are working at under-capacity), the need for additional inputs of capital to sustain the growth of output means that the average age

---

NOTES TO TABLE 9.1

Column 1	Employees in Employment. *Ministry of Labour Gazette*, Table 103 (January 1969).
Column 2	At 1954 prices. Capital stock (from Pyatt, *Capital Output and Employment* (London, Chapman & Hall, 1964), Table G, p. 27) divided by number of employees in 1960 as shown in *Abstract of Statistics*, Table 134 (1962).
Column 3	Calculated from the series in column 1. The figures are affected by changes in definition and classification in 1964 but not to any significant extent.
Column 4	Derived from Pyatt, *op. cit.*, Table G, p. 27.
Column 5	Derived from Index of Industrial Production: *Annual Abstract of Statistics*, Table 152 (1968).
Columns 6 and 7	Derived from R. C. O. Mathews, *Some Aspects of Post-War Growth in the British Economy* (Cambridge, Department of Applied Economics, 1965). Iron and Steel has been equated to order V, Electrical Engineering to Order VI, and Non-electrical Engineering to Order VII. Growth of output per unit of input (column 7) is derived by relating the increase in output to increase in factor inputs. The combined factor input is derived by weighting labour and capital according to their shares in total income in a base year. Column 6 gives a measure of output per unit of combined factor input in a base year (1948), the measure of combined input being derived by turning capital into equivalent man-years by multiplying it by the ratio of the wage rate to the average rate of profit on capital.
Column 8	*Statistics on Incomes, Prices and Employment and Production*, No. 24, Table C.3b.
Column 9	Cost of R. & D. carried out within or financed by industry. Derived from *Abstract of Statistics*, Table 155 (1968). 'Vehicles' includes heavy aerospace research expenditure. In addition to totals shown the Government finances research expenditure of about £200 million of which about half is defence expenditure.

N.A. = not available.

of capital employed will fall more rapidly, and research, development and innovation are likely to be stimulated by an expanding total market. Table 9.1 shows much higher R & D expenditures per head in these high growth industries. But it would be easy to exaggerate the significance of the association and to confuse cause and effect. Where the return to factors is high it is to be expected that more resources will switch to these sectors and promote a rapid growth in total output. Whether efficiency promotes output growth through lower costs and prices or whether growth promotes efficiency through more specialization, full capacity working and more modern capital equipment it is very difficult to say. In either event it would appear to be necessary that demand conditions should be such as to permit absorption of greater outputs.

So far we have been talking about output returns to combined factor inputs. It is also interesting to note the extent to which the different factors have contributed to output growth. According to Nicholson[12] the annual average rate of increase in the capital stock in British manufacturing industry 1948–64 (excluding textiles but including construction, mining and public utilities) has been about the same as the annual rate of increase in output (i.e. increase in capital productivity has been about zero). The rate of increase in employment has been much lower than the rate of increase in output or to put it in another way, the productivity of labour has increased. It follows that the ratio of capital to labour has been increasing.

It also follows that rates of output growth and rates of increase in labour productivity move closely in step since the output growth has been achieved with relatively slight increase in the labour force. The increase in output per unit of factor input has also moved closely in step with increase in labour productivity. But it is difficult to read much significance into these relationships.

If, however, the productivity of capital is low then this is likely to be reflected in the returns to capital and therefore in the rate of capital accumulation. There is indeed some evidence that this has been happening[13] and that the rate of capital formation has had to be sustained by 'forced saving' through taxation and company profits withheld from distribution. But if the labour supply remains more or less static then future growth of output comes to depend a great deal on increase in the capital stock per man. If one may generalize over the whole field of manufacturing industry it would appear that growth is necessary to sustain a high level of efficiency (and vice versa) and that rapid growth may depend on increased supply of *both* factors. The more rapid growth of some European economies and of Japan compared with the United Kingdom has frequently been explained by the more rapid increase in the labour supply in those countries.

But we are more concerned here with the experience of particular industries. We have seen that certain high-growth industries have also shown a high rate of increase of output per unit of input. The Nicholson data previously referred to suggests that for these industries (except chemicals) the rate of capital growth was below average and the rate of employment growth was above average, i.e. the increase in the capital-labour ratio has been below average. (This does not appear so clearly from Table 9.1, which attempts to bring together the most up-to-date figures available for each column and as a result they refer to different time periods. Vehicles have been a slow-growing sector since 1962 and employment has decreased.) The result is that rates of increase in capital productivity in these industries have been well above average. The reverse seems to be true of slow-growth, weak-performance industries such as food, drink and tobacco, metal manufacture, and shipbuilding though 'metal goods not elsewhere specified' is something of an exception. In those industries, except the last named, the pattern seems to be of rates of increase of employment below average, rate of increase of capital above average, rising capital-labour ratios and falling rates of capital productivity.

Study of recent experience of British industries therefore yields a rather hazy suggestion that rapid growth of output produces higher returns per unit of input by a more intensive use of existing capital rather than by a rapid build up of the capital stock and capital labour-ratios. This is likely to support a higher return on capital and so provide a base for further expansion.

This is supported by one study of public companies in four manufacturing industries which finds a fairly high positive correlation between growth and rates of return on capital.[14] The measurement of profits raises formidable difficulties and differences of accounting practice make it difficult to establish such correlation with any degree of certainty. But since growth implies increased market demand it would seem likely that the profit—sales ratio would be rising. If, as we have suggested above, the sales—net assets ratio is rising as assets are more intensively used, then the profits—net assets ratio (return on capital employed) must also be rising. Whether labour resources have been moved sufficiently quickly from weak to strong performance sectors is something which it is impossible to establish.[15] Labour has been moving out of declining or slow-growing industries like shipbuilding, leather, textiles and clothing but it may be doubted whether re-deployment has been as large or as rapid as might be desirable in the interests of efficiency, in view of the importance which seems to attach to increasing labour supply in growth industries.[16] But some non-manufacturing sectors like agriculture and mining have been losing labour on a fairly large scale and this must have contributed something to increased efficiency in the more successful manufacturing industries. But it is important not to identify too closely industries which are declining and those which are losing labour. The chemicals group of industries for example have grown very rapidly in terms of output during the past decade whilst marginally reducing their labour force.

There is very little evidence relating structural features with industrial performance. There is no significant association of increased concentration with growth of output and productivity and at least one authority has suggested that increased rate of growth is most commonly associated with falling concentration.[17] There has been very little study of the association of monopoly and restrictive practices with performance though Weiss[18] does find some association between concentration and abnormally high profits.[19] It seems that there is no satisfactory way of testing the prevalence of monopoly and relating this to the performance of industrial groups. The prediction derived from theory that monopoly leads to allocative inefficiency remains unsubstantiated at the level of industry. It is however possible to do more by close enquiry at the level of the firm. To this we now turn.

9.4 The efficiency of firms

It is not possible of course to distinguish clearly between the firm and the industry. The experience of industries which we have reviewed in the previous section represents the collective experience of the firms which compose it. But the distinction has its uses. For example, statistics bearing on some aspects of performance, are only available at firm level particularly those relating to costs, profits and capital employed. Close input/output comparisons in physical terms are most easily made between firms in the same industry (see Section 9.2).

It may be doubted however whether published rates of return on capital employed will measure the incidence of monopoly and the mis-allocation of resources predicted by theory. We have already referred to the difficulties of measuring capital employed and the variability of accounting conventions. In any case monopoly profits are easily concealed by inflating costs and high short-run profits are not incompatible with competition and efficiency. Some efforts have been made to relate profitability and size at the level of the firm and it can be argued that size is distantly related to concentration and monopoly. The more recent enquiries have suggested, if anything, an inverse correlation between size and profitability.

Our limited knowledge of price fixing procedures by firms in manufacturing industry does not help very much. The very small sample of monopolies of scale and cartels examined by the Monopolies Commission and Restrictive Practices Court suggest that monopolistic pricing procedures are very crude and not closely related to the costs of the particular goods in question. They often appear to be designed to yield a comfortable return even to the high-cost firms.[20] On the other hand they are sensitive to elements of competition which are rarely completely suppressed and it would appear that prices are rarely deliberately pushed to the point of maximum profit (see Chapter 6, p. 149). Studies of price-fixing procedures not associated with monopoly enquiries[21] suggest that prices are generally fixed by the addition of some conventional margin to estimated average variable costs at some output representing normal capacity working of the plant. The margin may be varied in the face of market pressures but in normal circumstances the manufacturer will keep to his margin and seek to enlarge his profit by expanding output rather than by raising prices. On the whole there seems little evidence to suggest that firms are as much interested in short-run profit maximization as theory suggests. Where there is so much ignorance of demand conditions and uncertainty about the future it is hardly surprising that price fixing in practice is somewhat at odds with the refinements of price theory. Moreover, the pricing procedures of firms in competition do not seem to be formally so very different from those selling under monopoly conditions except that in the former case the conventional margin may be put under stronger pressure.

It would therefore appear that prices charged and profits earned by firms are not likely to yield any useful clues about the sort of misallocation predicted by monopoly theory, i.e. restriction of supply and high prices. But perhaps the main source of inefficiency to be apprehended are of a rather different kind. In circumstances of competition one would expect, and efficiency would require, a steady transfer of productive resources from high-cost to low-cost firms as the latter steadily expand their share of the market—provided that they have both the will and the means to grow. The persistent tendency for production to be concentrated in the most efficient firms will be checked in the long run by the inability of the most efficient to keep their lead and by the struggle of the less efficient to survive by making successful innovations.

An attempt to check up empirically on this transfer mechanism and innovation process has been made by Downie.[22] His material was derived from a random sample of forty firms from each of sixteen trades and covered net and gross output per head and average annual earnings of employees in 1935 and 1948. The results of his analysis do not therefore reflect recent experience of manufacturing firms.

He discovered substantial dispersion of efficiencies between firms, a result which squares with evidence from other sources. The reports of the Monopolies Commission often revealed wide differences between costs of production per unit of output of firms producing similar products. (The inter-firm comparisons reported by Mr. L. C. Tippett, and referred to in Section 9.2, showed a two-to-one spread of operative hours per unit of output. See also note 20.) It is true that these comparisons are somewhat suspect because of product differences and difficulties of allocating overheads to particular products in multi-product firms. Also it is sometimes not difficult to understand how the high cost firms survive. They may for example be operating antiquated equipment on which depreciation is still being charged or which there is no intention to replace. Such firms may be content to sell at a price showing some return above average variable cost though appearing to sell at a loss. Also low-cost firms may not be able to expand without incurring steeply rising costs and high-cost firms may be favourably located in industries where costs of transport to the market are heavy. Measures of efficiency however skilfully devised may not reflect the competition strength of firms.

Downie discovered that wide differences in efficiency persist over time. Firms which had the highest productivity in 1935 grew faster than others but they were not typically amongst the most efficient firms in 1948. This provides some empirical verification for the operation of both the transfer mechanism and the innovation process. But perhaps the most significant finding was that industries with long tails of high-cost firms were frequently those with high concentration ratios or restrictive agreements. But there was only weak confirmation of the theory that the expansion of low-cost firms (transfer mechanism) was most impeded in such monopoly trades.

There is therefore some evidence that competition normally promotes more efficient allocation by transfer of resources to low-cost firms by stimulation of low-cost firms to improve their position. But without knowing more than we do about the occurrence of monopoly and its effects on manufacturing industry as a whole we are left in some doubt about the extent to which efficiency could be improved by its elimination.

A related line of enquiry is to ascertain the extent to which firms operate at a scale of output which minimize average costs. As we noted in Chapter 3 it is not easy to check up on economies of scale. (See Chapter 5 where the concept of economies of scale is discussed and some reference is made to the general results of enquiries into their occurrence in manufacturing industry.) What we require to know is the reaction of average costs to increasing output, given existing factor prices and the state of technology. If we trace the average cost of the same firm at different levels of output it will be impossible to isolate the changes which are solely due to scale of output. The same difficulty arises if we study average costs of all existing firms of different sizes—the lower average costs of large firms (if any) may be due to factors other than size and it does not follow that small firms could duplicate their experience if they became larger; for example, small firms may be engaged in the production of specialities in short runs. If output is not homogeneous it is difficult to measure it in physical terms and accurate comparable figures of average cost are almost impossible to obtain mainly because of difficulties of imputing capital costs. Some investigations therefore measure size in terms of employment and performance in terms of output per head or profits, but these are seriously deficient measures of economies of scale for reasons previously considered. Some investigations relate to establishments and therefore relate mainly to technological economies. Others relate to firms where we would expect economies of organization, finance, and marketing to be significant.[23]

It is therefore difficult to assess the evidence. But it would generally support the conclusion that in most manufacturing plants average costs will diminish with increasing output up to medium size of plants and in a significant number of cases up to the largest scale of plant in operation. It needs to be emphasized that little can be known about average cost at scales of output above that of the largest in operation but it may be suspected in some cases that when the expansion does take place further economies will be realized. Moreover, since optimum plants can be duplicated, it would appear that further economies may be available to multi-plant firms though it has been suggested that these are not generally significant.[24]

Market limitations and imperfections may prevent firms reaching the size which would minimize unit costs. Nevertheless the presence of firms operating at sub-optimal levels of output does afford some slight indication of wasteful use of resources in spite of our reservations about the nature of some of the evidence and the presumption that there is not necessarily a unique optimum output for all firms in a trade.

A recent enquiry[25] into economies of scale in five UK manufacturing industries avoids some of the difficulties mentioned above by use of engineering studies. From our present point of view the most interesting result was that the optimum size of plant was less than seven per cent of total output in three industries and was seventeen per cent and fifty per cent respectively in the other two. Bain[26] in a similar study of thirty US industries concluded that in seventeen of these the optimum output was less than ten per cent of total output and that, typically, the fall in average costs was not very sharp as the designed capacity of optimum sized plants was reached. If any conclusions can be drawn from this very partial evidence they would appear to be that some economy of resources would probably be obtained by reducing the number and increasing the size of some firms and also that the size of some very large firms can hardly be justified in terms of economies of scale.

There is not much doubt that the typical size of plant contributing the greater part of the output of trades is steadily being enlarged under the impact of technological change. We also know that size of plants has a significant bearing on the size of firms. Unless the size of markets increases to the same degree it would follow that concentration ratios will also rise and the impediments to new entry will increase. This as we have seen could counter-act any benefits accruing from economies of scale but there is insufficient evidence to enable us to conclude that it would do so. Equally there is insufficient evidence to enable us to support the views of those like Schumpeter and Galbraith who have stressed the benefits of very large firms (see Chapter 5, p. 122).

Our search for factors affecting efficiency and measurement of effects has not done much except to highlight the difficulties involved. Ability to survive and grow in an atmosphere of competition is perhaps the best indication we can get of industrial efficiency though we have to recognize that in some circumstances it may happen that increased efficiency may weaken the forces of competition. Also we are left with the feeling that industrial efficiency is only partially conditioned by the supply and quality of factors and their allocation between firms and industries. Much will depend on the management skill with which they are organized, and this is likely to be most effective where the law is hostile to monopoly, where economic policy promotes a high rate of growth, and where premiums are placed on hard work, inventiveness and risk taking.

1 *Journal of the Royal Statistical Society* (*J.R.S.S.*), Part 2 (1957).

2 *J.R.S.S.* (Series A), Part 2 (1955); and Part 3 (1964).

3 There are many examples of inter-firm comparisons. One interesting pioneer study in the field is reported by Tippett, L. C., *J.R.S.S.*, Part 2 (1947). See also *J.R.S.S.*, Part 3, p. 256 (1953).

4 Rostas, L., *Comparative Productivity in British and American Industry* (Cambridge, University Press, 1948); Frankel, M., *British and American Manufacturing Productivity* (Illinois, University Press, 1957); Paige, D. and Bombach, G., *A Comparison of National Output and Productivity in the U.K. and the U.S.A.* (Paris, OEEC, 1959). See also article by Hays, S., in *Progress*, No. 4

(1966). It is interesting that no close study has been made of comparative British and German industrial performance. In some respects conditions are more comparable between these two countries than between Britain and the USA.

5 Hays, S., *Progress*, No. 4 (1966); and *The Economist* (1 October 1966).

6 Caves, R. E. (ed.) *Britain's Economic Prospects*, Chapters 7 and 8 (London, Allen & Unwin, 1968).

7 Dunning, *Business Ratios*, No. 1 (1966).

8 Aukrust, 'Investment and Economic Growth,' *Productivity Measurement Review*, No. 16 (February 1959); Heath, J. B., 'British-Canadian Industrial Productivity,' *Economic Journal* (December 1957); Dennison, E. F., *Why Growth Rates Differ* (Washington, Brookings Institution, 1967).

9 Caves, R. E., *op. cit.*, Chapter 10.

10 Reddaway and Smith, 'Progress in British Manufacturing Industries 1948–59,' *Economic Journal* (March 1960).

11 Mathews, *Some Aspects of Post-war Growth in the British Economy*, Reprint No. 240 (Cambridge, Department of Applied Economics, 1965).

12 Nicholson, *Yorkshire Bulletin of Economic Studies* (November 1966).

13 Sargent, J. R., 'Recent Growth Experience in the Economy of the United Kingdom,' *Economic Journal* (March 1968).

14 Whittington and Singh, *Growth Profitability and Valuation* (Cambridge, University Press, 1968).

15 Caves, R. E., *op. cit.*, p. 264, expresses the opinion that, if anything, re-allocation towards the faster-growing industries seems to have been faster in the UK than in the USA.

16 George, 'Changes in British Industrial Concentration,' *Journal of Industrial Economics* (July 1967), cites examples of industries in which output has been declining and employment increasing.

17 *Ibid.*, but compare the article by Weiss cited in note 18.

18 Weiss, 'Concentration Ratios and Industrial Performance,' *Journal of Industrial Economics* (July 1963).

19 Whittington and Singh, *op. cit.*; and Samuelson and Smyth, 'Profits, Variability of Profits and Firm Size,' *Economica* (May 1968) do not find any relative association of profitability and size of firm.

20 An interesting recent example will be found in *Cotton and Allied Textiles* (Manchester, The Textile Council, 1969). Costs were found to vary by forty to forty-five per cent between better and worse firms in specific sectors of the industry. It was suggested that high-cost firms survive because many firms operate machinery long since written off, because some family concerns attach significance to non-commercial considerations and because the human and physical assets involved are not readily transferable to other sectors where they could earn a higher return. See Chapter 6 and paragraphs 579 and 580.

21 Andrew, P. W. S., *Manufacturing Business* (London, Macmillan, 1949); Barback, *Pricing of Manufactures* (London, Macmillan, 1964); and Fog, *Industrial Pricing Policies* (Amsterdam, 1960).

22 Downie, J., *The Competitive Process* (London, Duckworth, 1958).

23 Needham, *op. cit.*, p. 40 *et seq.* The author discusses other methods of estimating cost conditions, namely, engineering studies and survivor tests.

24 Bain, *Barriers to New Competition* (Cambridge, Mass., Harvard University Press, 1956).

25 Pratten, C. and Dean, R. M., *The Economies of Large-scale Production in British Industry* (Cambridge, University Press, 1968).

26 *Op. cit.*

Recommended Reading

General

ALLEN, G. C., *Structure of Industry in Britain,* 2nd ed. (London, Longmans, 1966).

BAIN, J. S., *Industrial Organisation* (New York, John Wiley, 1959). (An excellent book but written against the background of United States Industry.)

EDWARDS, R. S., and TOWNSEND, H., *Business Enterprise* (London, Macmillan, 1958).

NEEDHAM, D., *Economic Analysis and Industrial Structure* (New York, Holt, Rinehart and Winston, 1969).

SALTER, W. E. G., *Productivity and Technical Change,* 2nd ed. (Cambridge University Press, 1969).

Chapter 1

GOLDSTEIN, H. T., and CONKLIN, M. R., Chapter in *Business Concentration and Price Policy* (Princeton University Press, 1955).

Chapter 2

EVELY, R., and LITTLE, T. M. D., *Concentration in British Industry* (Cambridge University Press, 1960).

PREST, A. R. (Ed.), *The U.K. Economy* (London, Weidenfeld and Nicolson, 1969).

Chapter 3

NEWBOULD, G. D., *Finance of Industry* (London, Harrap, 1970).

PAISH, F. W., *Business Finance,* 4th Ed. (London, Pitman, 1968).

ROSE, H. B., *Economic Background to Investment* (Cambridge University Press, 1960).

Chapter 4

HOOVER, E. M., *The Location of Economic Activity* (New York, McGraw-Hill, 1948).

ISARD, W., *Location and Space Economy* (London, Chapman and Hall, 1956).

LUTTRELL, W., *Factory Costs and Industrial Movement* (London, NIESR, 1962).

Chapter 5

COOK, P. L., and COHEN, R., *The Effect of Mergers* (London, Allen and Unwin, 1958).

PENROSE, E. T., *The Theory of the Growth of the Firm* (Oxford, Blackwell, 1959).

PRATTEN, C., and DEAN, R. M., *Economies of Large-scale Production* (Cambridge University Press, 1965).

TOWNSEND, H., *Scale Innovation Merger and Monopoly* (Oxford, Pergamon, 1968).

Chapter 6

ALLEN, G. C., *Monopoly and Restrictive Practices* (London, Allen and Unwin, 1968).

HUNTER, A. (Ed.), *Monopoly and Competition* (*Penguin Selected Readings*) (Harmondsworth, Penguin Books, 1969).

HUNTER, A., *Competition and the Law* (London, Allen and Unwin, 1966).

ROWLEY, C. K., *Monopolies Commission* (London, Allen and Unwin, 1966).

STEVENS, R. B., and YAMEY, B. S., *The Restrictive Practices Court* (London, Weidenfeld and Nicolson, 1965).

SUTHERLAND, A., *Monopolies Commission in Action* (London, Cambridge University Press, 1969).

Chapter 7

HANSON, A. H. (Ed.), *Nationalization* (London, Allen and Unwin, 1963).

PRYKE, R. W. S., *Nationalization in Practice* (London, McGibbon and Kee, 1970).

RAMANADHAM, V. V., *Public Enterprise in Britain* (London, Cass, 1959).

ROBSON, W. A., *Nationalized Industry and Public Ownership*, (London, Allen and Unwin, 1965).

Recommended Reading

SHEPHERD, W. G., *Economic Performance under Public Ownership* (New York, Yale University Press, 1965).

TURVEY, R. (Ed.), *Public Enterprise* (Harmondsworth, Penguins, 1968).

Reports of Select Committee on Nationalized Industries. HMSO.

Chapter 8

BOUDEVILLE, J. R., *Problems of Regional Economic Planning* (Edinburgh University Press, 1966).

CAVES, R. (Ed.), *Britain's Industrial Prospects* (London, Allen and Unwin, 1968).

FLORENCE, P. S., *Industry and the State* (London, Hutchinson, 1957).

HARROD, R., *The British Economy* (London, McGraw Hill, 1963).

McCRONE, G., *Regional Policy in Britain* (London, Allen and Unwin, 1969).

SHONFIELD, A., *Modern Capitalism* (Oxford University Press, 1965).

Chapter 9

ALLEN, G. C., *British Industries and their Organization.*

CAVES, R. (Ed.), *Britain's Economic Prospects*, Chapters 7 and 10 (London, Allen and Unwin, 1968).

FRANKEL, M., *British and American Manufacturing Productivity* (Illinois, University Press, 1957).

Authors cited

Index

H ... r
p ... g
H ... k
fo ... .,
al ... d
un ... e
sh ... s
no ... o
co ... h
oth ... d

seemed connected almost against his will to some dreadful mystery. Helen wondered if love was enough to see her through.

0129592915